Escape the Improvement Trap

Five Ingredients Missing in Most Improvement Recipes

michael@cumberland chicago com

630-789-

Escape the Improvement Trap

Five Ingredients Missing in Most Improvement Recipes

Michael Bremer ◆ Brian McKibben

CRC Press
Taylor & Francis Group
Boca Raton   London   New York

CRC Press is an imprint of the
Taylor & Francis Group, an **informa** business

Productivity Press
Taylor & Francis Group
270 Madison Avenue
New York, NY 10016

Printed in the United States of America on acid-free paper
10 9 8 7 6 5 4 3 2 1

International Standard Book Number: 978-1-4398-1796-4 (Paperback)

Library of Congress Cataloging-in-Publication Data

Bremer, Michael, 1948-
  Escape the improvement trap : five ingredients missing in most improvement recipes / Michael Bremer, Brian McKibben.
      p. cm.
    Includes index.
    ISBN 978-1-4398-1796-4 (hbk. : alk. paper)
    1. Organizational effectiveness. 2. Reengineering (Management) 3. Organizational change. 4. Performance. I. McKibben, Brian. II. Title.

HD58.9.B735 2011
658.4'06--dc22   2010029744

Visit the Taylor & Francis Web site at
http://www.taylorandfrancis.com

and the Productivity Press Web site at
http://www.productivitypress.com

Dedication

Hopefully in everyone's life they have an opportunity to be impacted positively by people as they try to find their way. When I was young there were four people who were important to my development: Mary Bremer, my mother; Beverly and Sydney Loeb, an aunt and uncle who were constantly there to guide me when I was lost, and to share much enjoyment and laughter over the years. My grandmother, Ida Moore, who taught me the importance of working hard and staying focused on the task at hand. Finally, sometimes in life one is very fortunate. I am one of those lucky people to have been blessed with a spouse, Lynn Sieben, whom I love dearly. She constantly encourages me to pursue my dreams and to make a difference with my life. She truly completes me in many ways. This book is dedicated to the people who have made a major difference in my life.

Michael Bremer

Financial manipulation happens at electronic speed in the Wall Street casino, but real value creation still always happens at human speed. This book is dedicated to that latter group of loyal business team members everywhere who work tirelessly to make their organizations more effective and competitive. I hope they use this work to create more real value and get ahead of the financial gamesmen on Wall Street.

Brian McKibben

Contents

7 **Ingredient 4: Process Thinking**
Maximize Cross-Functional Process Performance
and Foster Deeper Process Understanding, Innovation, and
Execution of the Best Work Practices...................................... 161

List of Exhibits

Acknowledgments

Wow! I can't believe we finished. When you first start writing a book, it is almost overwhelming. Obviously, you would not start down this pathway if you did not have some story or message that you wished to share. But when you begin to write, you realize the challenge of organizing your thoughts, trying to sound at least semi-intelligent and, most importantly, meeting the challenge of writing something that the reader will find meaningful.

While we are responsible for the words in this book, we never could have done it without some special assistance. There are very many people we need to thank.

When you ask people if they are willing to review what you write, many people say yes. But this is mostly done out of politeness. It is a major hassle to review someone else's writing, to then compose your own thoughts, and then provide the writer with feedback. All of the people we asked to help were already very busy.

Fortunately for you, the reader, a number of people came forward and were immensely helpful in challenging our thought process, our logic, and our sometimes fuzzy writing. Words do not adequately express the depth of our appreciation; we are very indebted and thankful to all of these individuals:

- Jack McQuellon, from Caterpillar, for being one of the first reviewers, and for the insights he continued to share throughout this endeavor. Jack helped to focus the early writing on the world of performance improvement. Books have been written about each of our ingredients; we had only a solo chapter to devote to each topic. Jack urged us to stay focused on the "sweet" spot.
- Susan Herring, retired economist extraordinaire, who was not directly familiar with the world of Lean and Six Sigma, who challenged the use of jargon and forced us to clarify the messages we were trying to

express. Susan was our fastest feedback responder and helped us to clarify many of the points we were trying to make.

- Mark Preston from Acuity Brands stepped up to help when we were lost in the metrics chapter. He provided some of the material we used in that chapter and was very helpful in organizing our thought process throughout the book.
- Art Smalley, independent consultant and author, who shed some background and light on our Toyota story, although the final wording used is totally our responsibility.
- Bill Kennedy, independent private equity venture capitalist, who was very helpful in discussing his perspectives on the 80/20 Rule. He pointed out that we did not have seven ingredients (which was where we started), and that five of them were more important at a leadership level.
- Dan McDonnell from General Electric was always insightful and challenging. He shared a number of stories and experiences, some of which we were able to incorporate.

There were many other people who reviewed bits and bytes of the book. Their feedback and encouragement were also helpful at key points along the way. This group includes Ron Harper, CEO of Cogent Power; Jean Bruno, independent consultant and human resources guru; Joe Rizzo, from the Jacksonville Lean Consortium; and Scott Smith, president of High Performance Solutions (HPS). Each of these people gave us detailed comments on at least one chapter. Many others also shared useful insights: Bob Hafey, Sherrie Ford, Patty Hatter, Steve Spear, Ross Robson, Lisa Antoniotti, Sheila Carroll, Karl Odegaard, Bill Waddell, Doug Maki, Bruce Sieben, Barry Wood, Ellen Sieminski, Steve Liberatore, Tom Chamberlain, Bill Voigt, Richard Evans, Dave Hogg, Todd Lizotte, Bob Kerr, Jack Ward, John Chaput, Jerry Bricker, David Cochran, Ralph Keller, Brian Bush, George Koenigsaecker, Luke Faulstick, and Joe Fisher.

This learned group of people tried to keep us on the straight and narrow. I believe we usually listened to their wise counsel. But in the end, these words are ours and we bear total responsibility for them.

We also need to thank our spouses. Lynn Sieben has been my partner and best friend for more than 30 years. I could not have a better lifetime partner. The same thing is true from a business perspective with my co-author Brian McKibben, and the support he's had from Joanne McKibben through many years of developments in the background behind our writings.

Finally we need to thank Ruth Mills, the editor provided by Productivity Press. She plowed through it all and gave us feedback on clarity, getting to the point more quickly, and staying on the message. Her feedback was very helpful.

Once again, the words are ours, and we hope they will help you move your improvement activities to a more mature level of effectiveness.

Key People at Independence Enterprise, Inc.

(Listed in the order in which they are mentioned)

Andy Fletcher, Chief Executive Officer (CEO)

Will Rasmussen, member of the Board of Directors

Jack Morel, Chief Operating Officer (COO)

Lynn Shaunnessey, Chief Financial Officer (CFO)

Kate Beck, Vice President of Human Resources

Basem Hafey, a consultant on performance improvement working with Independence Enterprise

Ralph Voigt, coordinator of Independence's improvement initiative

Mark Ekberg, Vice President of Sales

Nora Schmidt, Vice President of Research and Development (R&D)

Dana Herring, an engineer

Sheila Carroll, Senior Vice President of one of Independence's largest customers

Margaret Allavoine, Sales Manager

Bill Kennedy, Finance Department

Introduction

We can save you $50 if you read only this first page. We don't wish to alien-
ate you, but don't bother buying this book if you don't already have a strong
desire to find a more effective way to continuously improve business performance. Nothing in this book will convince you that you need to change.
There have been many books written and many statistics published that talk
about the magnitude of improvement that is possible, yet most organizations
fail to improve their competitive position after adopting an improvement
initiative.

For example, General Motors had a 25-year relationship with Toyota
through its NUMMI joint venture, yet no one would confuse GM's performance today with Toyota's. NUMMI was the "New United Motor
Manufacturing Company" that was jointly run by Toyota and General Motors
for more than 25 years in Fremont, California. It's pretty obvious which
company is the better example of excellence. NUMMI changed from being
one of GM's worst-quality plants to one of its best-quality plants. If 25 years
of observing NUMMI did not do it for GM, then reading one book will not
do it for you. So save your money! It has to start with committed leadership.
And, as W. Edwards Deming once said, "You don't have to change. Survival
is not mandatory." It's your choice.

On the other hand, if you are frustrated with the ineffectiveness of
most organizational performance-improvement initiatives and their inability to truly transform an organization, this book may be able to offer you
some value. You would think that 30 years of organizations implementing improvement programs (since the days of Total Quality Management
[TQM] in the early 1980s) and not having a whole lot to show for it would
cause people to try to do things differently! You also might think that
after 50 years of implementing automation systems, with all of the problems that crop up after implementation, companies would fix *the process*

first. But from our perspective, the same pattern gets repeated over and over again. People make the same basic mistakes in slightly different ways.

If we could offer the world a packaged solution, we would do it. Even better, if we had *the* answer, we would share it. But there is no single answer; the world is too complicated. What is needed is a deeper level of thought, understanding, and action. This deeper level of insight cannot be taught, and you cannot go to a workshop or even read a book and get *the answer*. You gain these insights primarily through experience, and through the guidance of a knowledgeable resource to challenge your thought process.

How This Book Is Organized

Each chapter begins with a situation at Independence Enterprise (a fictional company, but every experience shared at Independence is from a real situation). The next section within the chapter begins to outline some basic principles for that particular ingredient. The principles are not a recipe. They are intended to push your thinking about that ingredient. For example, how can you look at this in a more holistic way? We then come back to Independence Enterprise to share how that company has begun to deal with some of the issues for this ingredient. Finally, we close each chapter with suggested deployment actions to help you apply the principles covered in that chapter to your own organization.

We begin the book (Chapters 1 and 2) with a detailed description of why most companies are average in terms of their improvement maturity. Chapter 3 provides a more detailed summary description of five ingredients that are either missing or weakly applied in most business performance-improvement recipes. They're not new or probably even surprising, but they are critical to providing a solid foundation for improvement.

Entire books have been devoted to each one of the ingredients. We tried to stay focused on how each ingredient impacts an organization's level of maturity for performance improvement. Most organizations do not progress beyond an average level of effectiveness regarding their ability to improve, relative to other organizations in their respective industry. Most improvement initiatives are stuck at an immature level of development, in that they merely help the organization to survive—they do not transform the organization's competitive position.

Based on our experience, we have concluded that many organizations do not do these activities well. These five key ingredients are not hard-wired into most improvement initiatives. If you wish to accomplish more with your investments in performance improvement, you should include them in your recipe. They can differentiate your business from the competition and help to accomplish more meaningful change. The five ingredients that go missing or are significantly underutilized in most improvement initiatives include

- **Chapter 4, Customer Value:** Business improvement efforts must be carefully aligned with the product and service value that a business sells to its customers. It all starts and ends there. Improvement dollars need to be aligned with those output values to be justified and meaningful.
- **Chapter 5, Engage People:** Although this seems obvious, it's done in a mediocre way by most management teams, possibly due to a failure to understand the practical aspects of how it's done. No company will reach industry-leader status without passionately engaging its employees.
- **Chapter 6, Key Metrics:** Good metrics will drive spontaneous, companywide performance improvement. Wrong or bad metrics will take you down. Understanding the difference is critical.
- **Chapter 7, Process Thinking:** Everyone needs a mental model for thinking about how business processes work, how to find and eliminate waste in that work, and how to do it as a key part of daily activities.
- **Chapter 8, Executive Mindset:** This is a prerequisite for dealing with the other ingredients.

Our hypothesis regarding these five ingredients is based on the results of organizations ranging from Toyota, Danaher, Robert Wood Johnson Foundation, ThedaCare (a Wisconsin-based healthcare system), and Seattle Children's Hospital to smaller organizations, such as the Old Town School of Folk Music in Chicago, which do a very good job of improving; and organizations such as Motorola, GM, and Ford, which have pockets of excellence inside but are currently performing in a more mediocre fashion. The mediocre companies have adopted all of the tools, but they have not truly transformed their businesses to operate in the top 20% of their respective industries.

Several different assessment tools are offered for your use. We close the book in Chapter 9 with a more formal assessment instrument and process for looking at how effectively the five missing ingredients are woven into your improvement activities.

Look at Your Organization's Ability to Improve Relative to Your Industry

Looking at your ability to improve relative to other organizations in your industry is a critical view. Using the automotive industry as an example, GM, Ford, Chrysler, and most European manufacturers watched Toyota, Honda, Nissan, and more recently Hyundai, improve at their expense for the last 30 years. As they watched, they tried to adopt the improvement tools used by the improvement leaders, but they failed to fully transform their competitive position and to achieve or maintain industry leader status. We could look at healthcare, cell phone manufacturing, and other industries and find similar stories.

More Critical Thinking Skills Need to Be Learned and Used

This book is intended to help you improve your critical thinking skills about business performance improvement. When you learn at Toyota, your boss does not tell you what to do. Instead, you are expected to figure it out. When you think you know, then you ask, "Is this right?" You, the learner, are then further coached by the boss asking questions to help you gain deeper understanding of the situation and to better see reality in a holistic way. When you have an organization full of people who can critically think at this level, people truly are that organization's most important resource.

   People we've met who have had the opportunity to be trained by a "true" Toyota Sensei describe a very common experience. The Sensei:

- Does not give an answer; the Sensei only asks questions
- Challenges your thinking to see if you understand the real problem
- Points out the fact (through questions) that your solution to the problem under consideration (and we always have one) is not right; it does not go deep enough
- Makes you go to the source and observe for yourself; you cannot depend on other's insights until you have seen it with your own eyes
- Asks if the people impacted by the problem have been consulted and whether their views have been taken into account
- Guides the problem solver in the use of the scientific method to more deeply understand the problem, so that once fully understood, the solution will reveal itself

- Shows respect to the person being guided (see the Fujio Cho quote below)
- Guides the problem solver into realizing that multiple solutions exist, and that maintaining a focus on multiple possibilities will reveal further insights

A true Toyota Sensei is constantly operating from this paradigm with the people being mentored.

Unfortunately, there is a very limited number of "true" Toyota Sensei. This is a person with more than 20 years of experience in the world of Toyota, with experiences on both the operations side and the executive leadership side. Many folks claiming this mantle today have visited the organization a few times and studied Toyota, or perhaps they worked there for 4 or 5 years. But they do not have the deep knowledge of a 20-year veteran. Occasionally, you will get someone with deep insights into the world of Toyota who is not a 20-year veteran. John Shook is one of those people. Steve Spear is another one of those individuals; see his article "Decoding the DNA of the Toyota Production System" (Steven Spear and H. Kent Bowen, September/October 1999, *Harvard Business Review*) and his recent book, *Chasing the Rabbit* (McGraw-Hill, 2009). We will draw on some of their insights in this book.

Many books have been written about *what* happens in a Toyota-like environment with Sensei guidance. And many people have commented on the frustration in trying to emulate *how* Toyota-like thinking flows through opportunity identification, measurement, analysis, improvement development, implementation, and sustainment. That process has been part of the Toyota culture for so long that there is little discernable infrastructure that other companies can copy to build a similar continuous improvement (CI) culture. It truly is part of their DNA.

Some CI infrastructure "cookbooks" exist, but they fall short of the holistic organizational view and deep understanding that a sensei develops, and most of them focus on adopting and using improvement tools. But the tools will not do it! Business CI efforts are doomed to mediocrity until organizational leaders, like a sensei, internalize an integrated organizational view of the business process model (Chapter 7) and develop deeper insights on how to provide adequate support systems to sustain well-designed business processes at high performance levels. It's that holistic organizational view that we're offering with this book. We felt this book was needed to describe the mental model behind a true sensei's string of "Why?" questions.

Why We Wrote This Book

We are veterans of observing and assisting organizations in the world of
performance improvement. You could not name a three-letter improvement
program (TQM, Business Process Reengineering [BPR], quality control circle
[QCC], quality of work life [QWL], Value Based Management [VBM], Lean Six
Sigma [LSS], etc.) or other terms like *reengineering, Lean,* or *Six Sigma* that
we have not done. We have helped clients with all of these methodologies
over the last 25 years. We will draw on the limited insights we have into the
world of Toyota and other organizations that are doing an outstanding job of
improving.

Michael Bremer initially learned about the world of business performance improvement as a very young man in the 1980s when he was given
responsibility for creating a companywide improvement effort for a Fortune
30 company, Beatrice Foods. He spent time with Dr. W. Edwards Deming
(process thinking), Dr. Joseph M. Juran (employee engagement, focus on
the vital few), and Phil Crosby (quality is free, cost of quality). The Beatrice
improvement initiative (called Strive for Excellence) was one of the improvement models looked at when the Malcolm Baldrige Quality Criteria was
originally developed. Michael was also privileged to be mentored by several
senior executives from other Fortune 100 companies who had significantly
more experience in the world of business performance improvement.

Brian McKibben practiced business process improvement from a technical viewpoint in engineering and operations management roles through
the 1970s and 1980s. He found that a difference between the industry leaders (with highly effective, essentially Lean Sigma business practices) and
the also-rans was often just a matter of big-picture thinking supported by
detailed process-engineering follow-through. And major business turnarounds can be done practically over night, if the whole business team
knows, understands, and moves in the same direction.

Brian's epiphany about *the people side* of continuous business performance improvement came from work with other Cumberland Group partners (Q+ Process: Team-Based Approach for Continuous Improvement in
Products, Services, Operating Processes and Working Relationships) in the
late 1980s and 1990s. Brian realized that what he thought were *technical* accomplishments have often been made possible by almost accidental
provision for the support systems needed to sustain *the people side* of new
or improved business processes. The business process model (Chapter 7,
Exhibit 7.3) was created from the realization that customer requirements,

value-adding processes, and support systems (for the operating team) must be addressed in context (holistic business-process view; not accidental, piecemeal, or lacking key ingredients) for major business improvements to be meaningful, successful, and sustainable.

When Michael co-authored his second book *Six Sigma Financial Tracking and Reporting* (2006), he began to gain new insights about why most performance improvement initiatives fail to transform an organization's competitive position. Over the next three years he continued to research and explore this conundrum. Finally, after the urging of his long-time business partner Brian, they decided to write this book. In a keynote presentation, Michael said, "When you do this type of work, sometimes you literally see people grow before your eyes, as they gain a greater degree of control and influence over their life at work. It is an intoxicating experience. If organizations can engage more people at this level, they truly would be a wonderful place to work." We hope this book will help move a few organizations closer to this ideal.

How This Book Can Help You

Most leaders do not understand—or perhaps do not believe—the tremendous magnitude of performance improvement that is possible. We are not talking about 10% or even 40%. Organizations that have experienced a true Lean transformation have performance improvements of 200% and 400%. You cannot possibly do this operating the way you currently operate or the way you lead today. You need to experience a personal transformation to begin to appreciate the phenomenal level of improvement that is possible. North American companies do not have a cost problem relative to global competition if they focus on real customer value. John Shook succinctly captures the real problem in the title of a book he co-authored, *Learning to See* (2003). Those are such great words, and they hold so true. We need to vastly improve our capability to better understand value to key customers and to see the magnitude of improvement that is possible! Then, we need to unleash the incredible power of transformation of which the people who work inside your organization are capable.

The actions above that a Toyota Sensei performs nest very well with our belief in leadership's role in creating an environment of daily improvement and developing people's ability to do their best work. A book is not a sensei, but we have laid out our view of the basic principles for each topic we discuss. The material in each chapter is intended to help you gain greater insights on that topic. We close each chapter with deployment actions you can take to implement the basic principles. It is impossible for you to address every action item at the end of all the chapters. You need to consider your situation, hopefully have a dialog with other key players in your business, and then prioritize the actions you plan to take over the next 12 to 24 months.

We encourage you to find a sensei who can assist you in your personal growth. That person might come from inside your organization, from your board, or from the outside. The objective view of a third party who is not directly involved in the issues you face can be very helpful to foster new thinking and to consider new possibilities. It takes 3 to 5 years to fully transform a business, learning along the way, and adjusting as you go.

Enjoy your journey!

Chapter 1

The New Normal
Just Because Your Organization Is Better than It Used to Be Doesn't Mean You Have a Competitive Advantage

Progress lies not in enhancing what is, but in advancing toward what will be.

—Kahlil Gibran

INTRODUCING INDEPENDENCE ENTERPRISE, INC.

CEO Andy Fletcher was just returning from a quarterly board meeting. He was feeling somewhat frustrated with one of the board members, Will Rasmussen. Will kept prodding Andy about the business performance improvement initiative under- way at Independence. Andy explained that the Lean Sigma improvement process had saved the organization millions of dollars during the current year, but Will kept saying, "Show me the money!" He wanted to know specifically where the money was in the profit and loss statement (P&L), because the net earnings for the corpo- ration had not shown a significant change since the Lean Sigma initiative started. Andy committed to give a detailed report on the effectiveness of their improvement activities at the next board meeting.

With that testy but seemingly innocuous exchange, the Independence manage- ment team began a journey of renewal and transformation that surprised every- one involved. When Andy Fletcher returned to his office, he called Jack Morel, Chief Operating Officer, and Lynn Shaunnessey, Chief Financial Officer. He asked them to help determine the effectiveness of Independence's improvement activi- ties. So they agreed to meet over the next four weeks to do an assessment. Lynn said she had recently been to a half-day workshop where some guy discussed the effectiveness of improvement programs and some type of an improvement maturity model. She thought it was interesting, but probably did not apply to them, so she had filed the information. Given this conversation, she decided to go back and look at the information again.

This book describes why organizations may have reported significant savings from their formal business performance improvement initiatives, but their competitive position did not change and they did not create more value for shareholders. We will periodically return to the Independence Enterprise story to illustrate key points in the book. The Independence Enterprise story is drawn from real situations: real people faced these challenges and gained the insights we share.

The Reality of the New Business Environment

Since the end of World War II, the competitive landscape has been largely defined by U.S., European, and Japanese companies, but this is rapidly changing. The business realities of the past will not be the business reality of tomorrow. The global transformation sweeping manufacturing is now striking healthcare, financial services, and other sectors. In order for North American and European companies to survive and prosper in the face of these sweeping changes, a radical transformation in their approaches to implementing improvements and creating value is needed. China and India are rapidly climbing up the value chain, and new economic players, such as Brazil and their neighbors in South America, are emerging.

This all adds up to the inescapable conclusion that, as competitive as the last few decades have seemed, the next 20 years will be even more so, and it will take a higher level of management thinking to succeed. As the old saying goes, "you ain't seen nothin' yet!"

Gaining competitive advantage is the ultimate goal of improvement. There are many powerful business tools known by their acronyms (Toyota Production System [TPS], Total Quality Management [TQM], value-based management [VBM], time-based management [TBM], quality control circle [QCC], statistical process control [SPC], and so on) and others known by their keywords (Lean, Six Sigma, and reengineering). Implementation of these methodologies rarely results in competitive advantage—and you can test this statement by doing this one simple exercise:

- Write your organization's name at the top of a sheet of paper.
- Next, make a list of the types of activities your organization has underway that are designed to improve business performance.
- Now, erase the name of your organization, and write the name of your toughest competitor at the top of the page.

Is it likely that your competition is going about business performance improvement in a very similar fashion to your own company? We're guessing the answer is *yes*.

So at the end of the day, everyone is better, but no one has gained a competitive advantage. Your competitors have access to the same books and seminars as you; they are equally capable of recognizing the need for improvement; and they are probably following the same cookie-cutter approach to implementation that you are: training, forming project teams, and doing follow-up measurements. As a result, *most improvement efforts accomplish little more than keeping up with the competition.*

There is a subtle but meaningful difference in the way highly effective improvement practices are implemented. We begin to define these differences in Chapter 2. Organizations with highly effective improvement practices follow a different rule set than *average* organizations. To further evaluate your organization's improvement effectiveness, take the "Assess Your Organization's Improvement Level" test near the end of this chapter, in Exhibit 1.5.

We've written this book for people who have been struggling to make improvement happen in their organizations and are frustrated with results that are less than expected. We define the term *improve* fairly broadly: for example, a new business strategy is a specific improvement hypothesis by the leadership team that decides to adopt it.

We do not focus on improvement tools (Lean, Six Sigma, etc.) because we assume you, the reader, have some degree of familiarity with the world of performance improvement and many of the common tools. Rather, we look at the things leaders *fail* to do—the weak actions or the lack of actions that jeopardize performance improvement efforts. We will share specific steps you can take to get more leverage from your investments in improvement tools, so you can move toward a sustainable industry leadership position.

As a key starting point, we outline five ingredients that are weak or missing in most improvement recipes (and we describe these five ingredients in detail in Chapters 4 through 8).

In many ways, this is a very simple book whose goals are to show your organization how to:

■ Find better ways for your people to work together
■ Operate with a high degree of ethics and integrity
■ Add more value to your key customers
■ Improve your organization's performance in a more meaningful, sustainable way that will result in more effective outcomes.

The Performance Improvement Dream

Take a look at the performance improvement initiatives implemented around the world over the last 20 years, which are shown in Table 1.1. The popular improvement methodologies have a "hook," very much like a Top 10 hit song. They have a lyric that people find appealing, or there is something about the beat of that particular methodology that resonates.

Don't these hooks sound enticing? Who could possibly resist the temptation to have their organization seamlessly marching to these themes?

When senior executives introduce a major organizational improvement initiative, they typically say something like the following: "We are going to adopt this great new way of operating in order to:

■ Reduce costs
■ Improve competitiveness

Table 1.1 Popular Improvement Initiatives of the Past 20 Years and What Attracted People to Each

Initiative	The Hook
Total Quality Management (TQM)	Understand your customer's requirements
Reengineering	Design your process like an engineer
Time-Based Management	Get work done faster
Lean Manufacturing	Eliminate the "waste"
Six Sigma	Data-driven decision making and reduction in variation

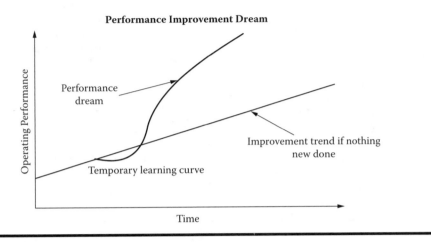

Exhibit 1.1 Performance improvement dream.

- Improve earnings per share
- Improve customer satisfaction
- Address a major organizational issue
- Improve employee–management relationships

And the list goes on.

Those senior executives have a dream of how much better their organization can become, and their expectations might be illustrated as shown in Exhibit 1.1.

The message is clear and familiar. A major performance improvement initiative involving the entire organization is expected to achieve great things!

The Reality of Most Improvement Initiatives

But, over time, reality sets in, and actual results typically fall far short of lofty expectations, resulting in a lot of pain and disappointment. Refer to the Typical Trend of Improvement after Initiatives line in Exhibit 1.2. It does not matter whether it's Lean, Six Sigma, or the initiatives of years past, such as TQM, cost of quality, or time-based management. The results have been consistent over the last 20 years: 3 to 5 years after companies begin these initiatives, *leadership rates the initiatives as a failure more than 70% of the time,* according to studies over the years by McKinsey, Bain, and others.

Is it true that the initiative is a failure? Leaders probably feel this way because they see that customer relationships, financial performance,

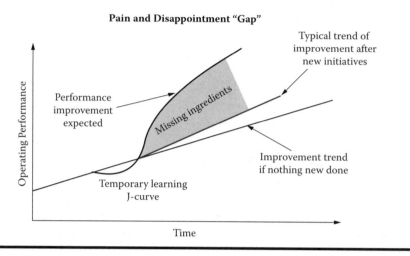

Exhibit 1.2   Pain and disappointment gap.

and employee engagement did not significantly change. But when you look at the facts, the organization usually *has* improved. Unfortunately, *those improvements did not lead to competitive advantage.* For example, the U.S. automotive industry changed a great deal over the past 35 years, but this change did not generate competitive advantage for most companies.

Improvement Results and the Car You Drive

Which newly made car would you rather buy to drive 50 miles back and forth to work every day?

- ■ *First choice:* a high-end model 1971 car made using 1971 design, processes, parts, and procedures.
- ■ *Second choice:* a car that was made by any manufacturer yesterday.

Most people say, "I would buy the car made yesterday" because the quality, reliability, and energy efficiency differences are obvious.

So there have been major improvements in automobile manufacturing, as well as in healthcare and most other industries, even though making an automobile and providing healthcare are much more complex today than they were 40 years ago.

But relative to competition and relative to the voice of the customer, most automotive manufacturers *have not improved their competitive positions:* they're still *average* (and the same story is true in just about any other industry). They did not accomplish the great leap forward in front of everyone that they were anticipating. This has been a recurring phenomenon over the last 30 years, as organizations adopted one improvement methodology after another.

So it's obvious that most companies have made huge strides in product and operations effectiveness. But at the end of the day, most organizations still remain average relative to their competition and relative to industry leaders' status, in spite of their significant accomplishments and ambitious business improvement initiatives.

So how did these grand plans fall so short of expectations?

Improvement Results within an Industry

It does not matter what industry you consider. You can look at all hospitals in North America, or all financial services organizations, or all automotive component part manufacturers. It's a mathematical fact that 50% of all organizations in any given industry are not performing as effectively as the other half. We simply need to decide which metric we want to use, and there will be an average level of performance.

The next key point is that most organizations are clustered tightly around the median: that is, 30% are slightly less effective than the median competitors, and 30% are slightly more effective than the median competitors. So over any 10-year time period, 60% of the companies in any given industry exhibit mostly average performance, just keeping pace with the pack.

Look at the graph in Exhibit 1.3. It's a major challenge to move from an average amount of improvement in performance (Level 3) to transforming an enterprise into something new (Level 4). An insidious improvement "trap" actually inhibits a Level 3 organization's ability to transform to Level 4 (which we explain further in Chapter 2). In reality, only a handful—less than 20% of an overall industry—break out of the pack and transform their enterprises.

These problems are not unique to today's popular improvement methodologies like Lean and Six Sigma. Similar shortfalls happened when organizations adopted TQM, reengineering, and other previously popular improvement methodologies.

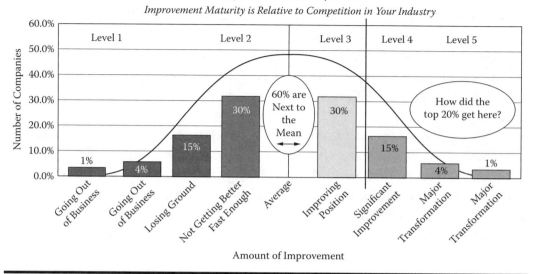

Exhibit 1.3   Improvement maturity curve.

Understanding the "reality" of how we compare to our competition is a key starting point. Most of us think we are better than our competitors. For example, an informal survey of companies attending the Annual Conference of the Association for Manufacturing Excellence revealed that 70% of respondents felt they were in the top 20% in terms of improvement effectiveness.* Obviously, 70% of the organizations cannot be in the top 20% of an industry! Yet if people operate from this misguided belief, it makes it more difficult to overcome unfounded complacency and take committed action to improve.

Progressing to a Level 4 or 5 requires changing leadership and employee behaviors that perhaps were positive ways to operate in the past, but are not the best behaviors to use for future success and the new competitive reality. Although the improvement tools are important, they are only a starting point. Just learning and using the tools will not move an organization into the top 20% of an industry. In contrast, here's what differentiates an organization in the top 20% of its industry:

■ The leadership of a top-20% organization does a better job of clearly defining the outcomes the organization must accomplish.

---

* Possibly only elite companies showed up at this conference, but their stories, struggles, and shared accomplishments seemed pretty normal. Ask the people you work with how good your company is. I'll (Michael Bremer) bet a beer no one says, "We are just average."

- The leadership of a top-20% organization applies *process thinking* to the performance improvement initiative itself.
- A top-20% organization does a much better job of *engaging people in* the organization to do more critical thinking.

Before you read on, think about how, or if, those three characteristics play out in your organization. Then, also think about how they play out in your personal span of control (department, work group, and so on). Your first reaction is probably that you do a pretty good job; we all want to believe we are doing a good job. Test this thought as you read further and use some of the simple assessments available in this book.

Five Levels of Improvement Maturity

The five levels of maturity for organizational performance improvement initiatives (which were shown at the top of the normal distribution curve in Exhibit 1.3) are graphed and labeled in Exhibit 1.4. The following sections describe each level in a bit more detail.

A Level 1 Organization Is a Disaster. There are so many problems in an organization at this level that no one has the time or interest in

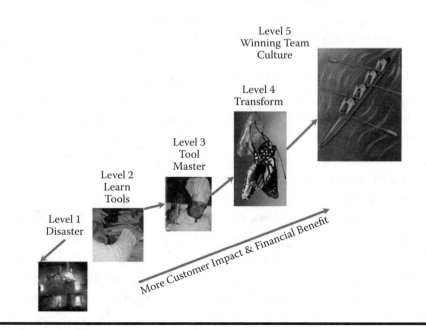

Exhibit 1.4   Five levels of improvement maturity.

attempting a performance improvement initiative. One can argue that they should, but typically this would not be perceived as the most important action currently needed. "Fires need to be extinguished first,'" would be the typical reaction.

This category includes organizations that are significantly underperforming their industry.

A Level 2 Organization Is Just Learning an Improvement Methodology or Tool Set. That methodology or toolset could be Lean, Six Sigma, supply-chain management, or others. The Level 2 organization might be working with a consulting organization or a *sensei* (i.e., a recognized guru). It is trying to prove that the tools work in its environment. Most of the training the Level 2 organization is doing involves teaching people about the tools.

Companies at this level (approximately 30% of the industry) are slightly losing ground to the rest of their industry.

A Level 3 Organization Knows the Improvement Tools Very Well. They have a number of employees who would be considered a master chef or tool master (e.g., Master Black Belt). Most of their improvement activities are centered around the Tool Masters. Those individuals may serve as project team leads or facilitators.

Companies at this level (approximately 30% of the industry) are slightly gaining ground on their overall industry.

But Level 3 organizations have a hard time getting in touch with reality relative to their competitors and to true customer needs. They are too inwardly focused. Level 3 organizations have implemented meaningful changes, and they are better than average. Unfortunately, leadership in a Level 3 often believes they're at a Level 4 because so much has improved in the way the organization operates. This disconnect from reality, relative to the outside world, becomes a major roadblock and decreases the probability of real transformation; it traps the organization in Level 3. We are all blinded (trapped) to a degree by the assumptions we make, beliefs we hold, and the limited number of data points we know about.

A Level 4 Organization Has Begun to Transform Its Business. Approximately 15% of the organizations in an industry are at Level 4. An organization in the top 20% of its industry can be a great place to work. Level 4 organizations have a pretty good knowledge of the basic improvement tool set, but more importantly, the *entire* organization—not just the tool masters—are driven to serve customers and stay ahead of the competition. Leaders in Level 2 and 3 organizations strive to serve customers better, but a Level 4 organization is much more effective at doing this. Level 4 organizations begin to create new businesses, entirely new value streams, and add value to their customers in meaningful, systemic new ways. This transition from Level 3 average to Level 4 and 5 greatness is a major challenge.

A Level 5 Organization Has a Culture Different from Any of the Other Four Levels. Level 5 organizations are also very rare (less than 5% of an overall industry). Organizations at this level tend to focus less on how good they *are* and more on how good they *are not.* Employee engagement in Level 5 organizations is more than twice as high as a Level 3. Leaders in a Level 5 organization are very much in touch with reality. People do not try to hide problems or resolve them quietly out of sight. Leaders are just as concerned about a near miss as they are an actual defect or error.

These organizations are very process and outcome focused: they are constantly striving to create the "perfect" process for their main business activities. Perfection is their primary goal and they measure their progress in terms of how far short of perfection they fall. A Level 5 organization is on the journey toward True North.

Organizations do not automatically progress through the five levels. A Level 2 organization can certainly mature from learning about the tools and become a Level 3 tool master. The important challenge is to move beyond Level 3 into the top 20% of the industry, and that is the primary focus of this book. Most organizations never progress beyond Level 3. The better job an organization does of being a tool master, the less likely it is to progress into the top 20%. That tool *strength*, when used to excess, actually becomes a *weakness* that prevents the organization from progressing to the next level: in other words, the company gets trapped in Level 3.

Quick Test: Assess Your Organization's Improvement Level

Here is a quick test to determine if your organization is a Level 3 or lower versus Level 4 or higher. Your first reaction may be to ignore this survey because it looks too simple to be meaningful, but the questions are serious, and it is a starting point for a reality test. Think about your organization. It's a struggle in most organizations to consistently do these three things well. Ask yourself the three questions in Exhibit 1.5. If your rating has less than two stars (*), then at best you are a Level 3.

A Level 5 company does all three consistently, including the very difficult third one.

Question	Rating[a]
Have you been able to dependably sustain and replicate elsewhere the gains from improvement projects?	
Have key overall business performance metrics (e.g., financials, new revenues, customer loyalty, strategic results) shown meaningful change as a result of improvement initiatives?	
Are your employee engagement survey scores more than two times your industry average?	

[a] Ratings:
  (–) Failing to do good job of this; more negative than positive.
  (+) Inconsistent; sometimes we do it well.
  (*) We consistently do this very well.

Exhibit 1.5   Quick test: Assess your organization's improvement level.

A more in-depth assessment is required to determine the specific level of improvement maturity. Ideally, this is looked at from a supply-chain perspective, your customers pulling from you and your suppliers. But first you need to do a better job in your own backyard.

INDEPENDENCE ENTERPRISE ASSESSES ITS IMPROVEMENT LEVEL

Lynn gave the Exhibit 1.5 quick test assessment to Andy and Jack. They looked at it and thought it was interesting, but they didn't see how it applied to them. Surely, they were a Level 4 organization, given all of the improvement projects they had implemented over the last several years. After all, costs were down, customer service levels were higher, and employees were typically enthusiastic about participating on improvement project teams.

But Andy said, "Let's try it." He asked Lynn and Jack to fill out the Quick Test—Improvement Maturity Assessment, giving consideration to the company as a whole. They would use the results of the assessment to begin their analysis. [Chapter 2 reveals the surprising results.]

So, Are Performance Improvement Initiatives Worthwhile?

The answer is, "It's a mixed bag." If you think about the mere fact that an initiative needs to be adopted in order to improve, that is a glaring confirmation that a major problem exists in the way the organization has gone about improvement in the past.

Then, when you look a little deeper at how most organizations measure their progress, what they typically show is a savings report. Unfortunately, cost savings alone will not improve the competitive position, increase customer satisfaction, or better engage employees. That myopic view—focused on cost reduction—tends to lead toward programmatic approaches to solving the problem by adopting X improvement methodology, instead of a more systemic approach that from the beginning works toward integrating the improvement process within the business culture and management processes. So right from the start, there is a governance problem.

Fortunately, there is a consolation to this depressing insight. What are your competitors most likely doing at roughly the same time? They are probably implementing an improvement initiative similar to yours. And the good thing is that your competitors are *also* doing a mediocre job of implementing it. So looking at the big picture—especially in comparison to the overall industry—not too much seems to have changed. Your organization is merely keeping pace, even though you have gotten better and your people have some reasons to feel positive about their accomplishments. Still, is there any wonder why people tend to rate these things as failures 3 to 5 years after they roll them out?

Most organizations in business, government, and in the nonprofit world have simply progressed from one improvement program to another, *with no major underlying changes in the fundamental way they operate.* If this pattern is going to change, we need to change the basic way we go about making improvement happen. A program will not do it (although a program can help you get started).

Leaders and every associate who works in an organization need to realize that improvement itself is a process. Top 20% organizations constantly seek *to improve the way they improve.* Leaders realize they have a primary responsibility to develop subordinates for success, and people are held accountable for high-performing work. But the first place to look for improvement is in the process. As mentioned, Level 4 and 5 organizations (the top 20%) are process maniacs. They are constantly trying to create the perfect process. And when the process is not perfect, they improve it—again and again. Level 5 companies (the top 5%) do that as a companywide, integrated, practiced, disciplined, overwhelmingly powerful, fast-moving, high-performance team.

Level 4 and 5 companies are both much different than their average competitors. Can you image what they would be like to work for? Can you imagine how much better your organization could be if it clearly communicated a Level 5 vision and constantly strived to achieve it? Sit back and think about it.

Summary

There is an expression we have used for many years that has held true over time: "Reasonable people, equally well informed, seldom disagree." This book is intended to help people and organizations become better informed so they can collaborate more effectively and agree on bold new steps to improve their businesses. It is for anyone who wishes to become more involved in improving the business processes she or he operates. We want you, the reader, to become more informed about reality, relative to the way your organization goes about improvement. It does not matter where you fit in the organizational hierarchy. Nor does it matter if you work in manufacturing, in services, or for a nonprofit organization.

Our hypothesis is that most organizational improvement initiatives fail to yield a significant change in an organization's position relative to its competitors, and that five key ingredients are weak or missing from most organizational improvement recipes. Chapter 2 summarizes these ingredients. We describe each ingredient separately for convenience purposes, but in reality, that list is the minimum that needs to happen in order for an organization to truly begin to transform its competitive position and to move into the top 20% of its industry.

Give some consideration to actions a private equity group (PEG) would take if it were to take over your business tomorrow.* First, the group would seek to deeply understand the potential of your business. It would ask questions like these:

- How much can your business grow?
- How could the PEG turn $1 of equity investment into $3 to $5 of value in a 3- to 5-year period?

Next, the group would try to understand customer demand and what drives it:

- Who are your valuable customers? Which customers are laggards that should be pared?
- How does your company compare to its competition?
- What do your customers really think about your company?

---

* Orit Gadiesh and Hugh MacArthur. *Lessons from Private Equity—Any Company Can Use.* Cambridge, MA: Harvard Business Press, 2008.

All these questions would be on the group's radar screen. It is critically important in addition to deciding what your company will do, to also decide what your company will *not* do. PEG leadership would make these decisions and deploy them.

A few critical initiatives would be launched to reduce costs, accelerate growth, and address key issues (normally, three to five issues, because more than that causes the company to begin to lose focus). After the value proposition was well understood and defined, the PEG team members would align metrics, make certain they have the right people in the right jobs, and focus on effective execution. The PEG team would address issues that inhibit executing the 3- to 5-year growth plan.

The private equity group approach outlined above closely parallels the actions an effective leadership team would take to address the five ingredients that are missing in most improvement recipes. In Chapter 8, "The Executive Mindset," we also map the five missing ingredients to the steps taken to accelerate growth at the Nissan Motor Company.

"We already do that!" is one of the reasons why it is so difficult to learn. Because the material is *familiar*, we think we *understand* it, so we fail to look for deeper, more profound meaning. One of our favorite quotes is from Satchel Paige, a phenomenal pitcher in the Negro Baseball League for many years. He once said, "It ain't what you know that gets you in trouble. It's what you *think* you know that just ain't so." We encourage your experimentation and hope to inspire a more holistic and realistic look at organizational performance excellence and improvement. We encourage you to challenge your beliefs. Dig deeper to look at *what you think you know* about your current improvement efforts and be open to the reality that *it might not be so.*

Then, take action and improve the way your organization goes about the business of improvement. The executive leaders at Toyota have probably never heard of Satchel Paige, but they rigorously practice keeping in touch with reality and constantly trying to more deeply understand "what they think they know that just ain't so."

Chapter 2

What Does It Mean to Escape the Improvement Trap?

Whenever you find yourself on the side of the majority, it is time to pause and reflect.

—Mark Twain

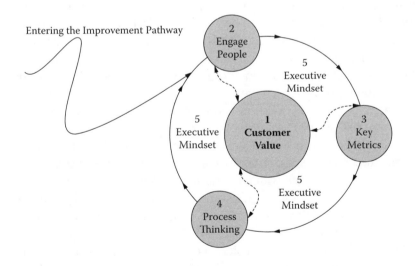

INDEPENDENCE ENTERPRISE INC. ASSESSES
ITS IMPROVEMENT LEVEL

Andy Fletcher looked at his watch and realized he had only 30 minutes before the meeting with Jack and Lynn, his COO and CFO. Andy had intended to spend more time getting ready for the meeting, but this week had been just crazy. One of the company's largest customers was threatening to pull its business and source it from China. And Sales and Operations were having another war over several issues. He made a phone call to set a meeting time with the key customer.

Next, Andy pulled up the assessment e-mail Lynn had sent after their last meeting, and he looked again at each of the questions:

Question	Rating
Have you been able to dependably sustain and replicate elsewhere the gains from improvement projects?	
Have key overall business performance metrics (e.g., financials, new revenues, customer loyalty, strategic results) shown meaningful change as a result of improvement initiatives?	
Are your employee engagement survey scores more than two times your industry average?	

Then he paused to consider the ratings:

(–) Failing to do a good job of this; more negative than positive.
(+) Inconsistent; sometimes we do it well.
(*) We consistently do this very well.

He was tempted to simply put an asterisk (*) for all three questions, but then he remembered the problems they had had with their last new product rollout—even though a project team had worked on this process for the past 2 years and had implemented many good changes. This last rollout did not go well, and apparently, there were still more issues to address. So for question 1, he entered a (+): Inconsistent; sometimes we do it well.

He looked at the second question and felt they could do better, but they were probably doing OK on this. So for question 2, he also entered a (+).

For question 3, he remembered a conversation with Kate Beck, the company's vice president of Human Resources, about their employee engagement scores. Kate said their scores were in alignment with the industry averages. So for question 3, he realized this was also a (+). He realized his company was inconsistent in all three areas.

Right after Andy completed his survey, Lynn and Jack came into his office. Andy asked them about the results of their surveys. Jack said, "This was a complete waste of time. I gave all of the questions a star (*) rating, because our business has significantly improved over the last 5 years. We are not the same company!"

Andy said he felt the same way, but they probably could do a little better, so he had rated everything with a plus (+).

They both then turned to look at Lynn. She turned a little red in the face. They were surprised because Lynn was usually such a calm character.

Lynn took a deep breath to regain her composure, and said, "Well, perhaps I approached this a little differently. My first reaction was also to rate each question

with a plus. But I decided to go talk to a few folks and gather some simple data.
I took our list of improvement projects from this year and pulled 10 at random.
I then went to talk to some of the people who worked on those teams. Remember
the changeover team that worked on the console control line?" Andy and Jack both
nodded.

"Well, the project team had reduced changeover time by 70% in its pilot test.
But today, we are doing the changeovers only 30% faster than last year. I also
looked at a project we did on faster cycle times to process requests for quotes. The
team's pilot results showed significant improvement, and everyone supported it. But
one year later, not all of the recommendations have been implemented. And again
we are not performing anywhere near the pilot test results. It was a similar story on
9 of the 10 projects, so I rated question 1 a minus.

"Next, I looked at our savings reports on the Independence Quality
Improvement Program. Over the last 3 years, we have reported more than $5 mil-
lion in savings, but our margins have not changed. Then I looked at sales to our
key customers. They are a little bit higher, but we are not doing particularly well
with them on our new products."

Andy glanced at Jack, who seemed to wince as Lynn mentioned new products.
Lynn then said, "So I gave question 2 a minus score.

"I was not sure about the engagement category: I found the term confusing,
and I really wasn't sure what the term engagement meant. So I went to talk with
Kate Beck in Human Resources. Kate told me that engagement is about passion—
that people really care. It means the employee has a very positive emotional
connection with the organization or perhaps their boss, and that connection
influences the person to exert greater discretionary effort to his or her work.

"Kate went on to explain to me that companies that perform surveys have a
variety of definitions, but these points are key:

- Trust & integrity: How well managers communicate and 'walk the talk.'
- Nature of the job: Is it mentally stimulating day-to-day?
- Line of sight between employee performance and company performance:
  Do employees understand how their work contributes to the company's
  performance?
- Career growth: Are there future opportunities for growth?
- Pride about the company: How much self-esteem does the employee feel by
  being associated with the company?
- Coworkers/team members: Do coworkers pick you up, or do they drag you
  down, in terms of their attitude about the organization?
- Employee development: Does the company make an effort to develop
  employees' skills?
- Relationship with one's manager: Does the employee value the relationship
  with his or her manager? Does the employee recognize the manager's sincere
  efforts to support the employee's own efforts to improve the portion of the
  business process for which she or he is responsible?

"Kate also told me that our own employee surveys include several questions that pertain to employee engagement. She said that 33% of our employees said they were highly or very highly engaged. The average in our industry is 29%, so we are slightly better than the overall average."

Lynn then said that when she heard those results from Kate, "I was amazed. Given the great people we have working in the company, how could our scores be so low? So I also rated the third question a minus."

Jack started to protest the low scores Lynn had given the company, but Andy said, "Wait a minute, Lynn may have something here. Perhaps this is why Will Rasmussen was giving me such a hard time after the last board meeting." Andy then turned to Jack and said, "Jack, I am not trying to find someone to blame for these problems. I'm trying to better understand what is going on. I think it's important for all of us to have a better understanding of reality. It seems like we often fall into the trap of talking about our business the way we want it to be, rather than the way it really is. You know what is happening with our latest new product rollout. Sales and Operations seem to be doing more finger pointing at one another, rather than spending time identifying the root causes of these issues."

Jack paused for a moment and looked at Andy and then Lynn. He then said, "Well, as I mentioned earlier, I really believed this was a complete waste of time. My desk is piled high with a host of problems, including several important issues with the new product. I know both of you are busy as well. I did not think I had time for this, but after this morning's conversation, perhaps I need to look at this in a different light. Sometimes it feels like we solve the same problems over and over again. Or people in one part of our business fix something, and at the same time, someone else is fixing it a different way. I used to have more time to develop some of the bright engineers in our group, but there is less and less time for doing that these days.

"We have implemented many positive improvements over the last several years, but somehow it doesn't feel all that much better. Lynn, remember that Improvement Maturity Model you shared with us? Do you have any information from that seminar on what it means to be average?"

Lynn said she was pretty sure she had something and would send it to them as soon as she returned to her office. Lynn had recently attended a one-day seminar by an external consultant on performance improvement, Basem Hafey. She sent Exhibit 2.1 and the following information, which she had received at Basem's presentation, Average Organizations and the Missing Ingredients.

What Does It Mean to Be Average?

The maturity levels shown in Exhibit 2.1 reference the effectiveness of improvement actions for an overall business. The curve is not focused on a specific methodology, such as Lean or Six Sigma. An organization can be highly effective at improving (Levels 4 and 5) and not use Lean, Six Sigma,

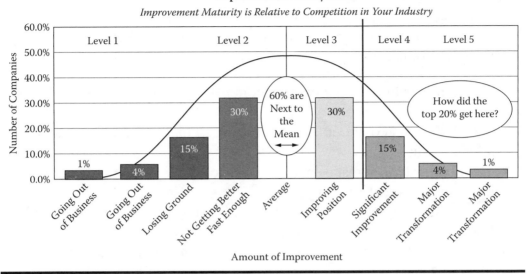

Exhibit 2.1   Improvement maturity curve.

or any other programmatic methodology. An organization can also have islands of excellence inside, but the overall business operates at a more modest level of effectiveness.

There are two levels of maturity for average performers:

- A Level 2 organization is slightly losing ground to their industry.
- A Level 3 organization is slightly gaining ground; it is better than the mean.

Let's take a closer look at each level.

Characteristics of Level 2 Organizations

Industry performers at this level are usually just learning an improvement methodology or they are going back to improvement basics. Here's a typical sequence of events:

1. Someone with clout in a Level 2 organization decides an improvement need exists, or an executive becomes enamored with a new methodology that he or she has discovered.
2. Then, a Champion of Improvement is appointed to lead the organization's initial efforts at learning and using the relevant tools.

3. Training events teach employees about the tools (e.g., 5S, Value Stream Mapping, Statistical Process Analysis, etc.).
4. Then the organization embarks on a journey to prove the tools work in their environment.

Also, the results in a Level 2 organization include a number of common traits:

■ People get excited about the opportunity to make some changes and address issues.
■ The organization wrestles with the difficulty of sustaining the gains from improvement projects.
■ Leadership wants it to work, but doesn't become personally engaged, hoping the folks it's been delegated to will follow through.
■ Therefore, the organization ends up with *isolated islands of improvement* that falter over time. Improvements people wish to make often bump up against functional lines of authority and die a slow death. But some improvements do stick, and the organization is getting better. Unfortunately, they are doing it at a slower pace than the rest of their industry, so they are slightly losing ground from a competitive perspective.

Characteristics of Level 3 Organizations

A Level 3 organization tends to focus on improvement *projects*, so most improvement primarily happens through project team activities. Because of the *tool* emphasis, the improvement activities are run by a select group of tool masters (e.g., Black Belts in Six-Sigma environments). Level 3 organizations are very likely to have a vice president or director of improvement who coordinates improvement activities. People inside such an organization are probably not aware of this, but the way they are going about improvement is a very normal approach, and very similar to how most of their competitors are going about it.

At Level 3, several people inside the business know the improvement tools very well and could also be considered tool masters. A few people on the leadership team are more engaged in the improvement activities than in Level 2 organizations. But the improvement structure exists *in parallel* to the line organization running the business, so the improvement process is not actually part of how the business is managed. There is also more of an operations focus. Sales and administrative activities are typically not as engaged in improvement as the operations portion of the business.

People feel very good about their accomplishments, but for the most part, the gains are still hard to fully sustain. Improvements tend to focus on functional departments directly linked to operations. Business performance metrics focus more on the functional silos rather than cross-functional process performance. Authority still primarily sits in functional silos. Therefore, Level 3 organizations largely try to *do a better job of what they already do* versus *creating new cross-functional business capabilities.*

Leadership in a Level 3 organization certainly wants the improvement initiative to succeed, but leaders are typically busy running the business, and they expect the improvement experts—that is, the parallel organization—to deliver project savings. In monthly or quarterly meetings, leaders review improvement projects as an independent subject, separate from conversations about how well the business is operating.

Examples of Level 3 Organizations

We are surrounded by Average. Motorola brought Six Sigma to General Electric, but when you look at Motorola's performance over the last 20 years, it is definitely average (at best) relative to Nokia and Samsung. Over the last 5 years (for the most part), Nokia and Samsung both show rising sales, cash flow, and net income. Motorola had a great run with their Razr*™ phone, and then the wheels fell off the cart once again. Its improvement organization has many black belts and master black belts, all trying to do the right thing. But the organization has not outperformed its competition.

In the automotive industry, General Motors, Ford, and Chrysler have pockets of excellence on the inside, but they are not at the top of the game in the automotive industry—even though they have been looking at the way Toyota and Honda operate for more than 20 years. And they have adopted all of the improvement tools, but none of the domestic U.S. or European auto manufacturers have transformed their businesses or radically improved their overall competitive positions. During that same time frame, Nissan and Hyundai have made major advances in their competitive positions.

---

*™ Trade mark of Motorola

What Is the Improvement Trap?

Surprisingly, there is a trap built into the way that most organizations structure their improvement activities that inhibits their ability to transform. Structurally, performance improvement initiatives tend to run in parallel to the *real* business. Experts lead the improvement initiative and they try to do the right thing, while leaders focus on the real business. The "trap" occurs when the improvement initiative becomes successful enough to take on a separate life of its own—instead of becoming part of the real business—that is, how we do business here every day.

On paper, the improvement initiative can look like a good return on investment, especially when savings is the key metric. But the initiative's *isolation*—based on the strength of its success—prevents it from exerting the promised enterprisewide leverage originally envisioned. As long as the initiative remains a strong parallel entity, its power traps an organization in the Level 3 average stage of the bell curve shown in Exhibit 2.1.

When leaders abdicate their improvement responsibility to a staff group, a new power structure is created in the organization. The staff organization will complain about the lack of leadership support, but they will take on more responsibility trying to find the "right" things to improve. It's a catch-22 predicament: while the staff leaders are trying to do the right thing, they remove responsibilities from the line organization. The improvement staff takes more responsibility for shepherding what should be improved, rather than line managers. And the line managers are busy with the real business, so they let the staff take that responsibility. That cycle continues, with the line organization never effectively assimilating daily improvement responsibilities. The strengths that got them that far, which are now used to excess, become a *weakness* that inhibits the organization's ability to transform. Therefore, the improvement initiative remains isolated, and the organization is effectively trapped at a Level 3.

Opportunities and Reality

Millions of dollars in savings might have been reported, but cost savings in a Level 3 organization is a pretend world. Based on the reported "savings," a Level 3 organization may appear to have improved, but the key business performance metrics (financial, market share, etc.) often do not show a significant change. A Level 3 organization is doing better than 50% of its respective industry, and people believe that process cost savings results reported from projects will be a seamless addition to the bottom line, but the reality is very different. Half of the savings reported are most likely "soft savings," where time or capacity was made available. And although no one says this, the feeling is that somehow these *soft* savings will automatically turn into *hard* dollar savings.

Unfortunately, soft dollars only turn into hard dollars when leadership proactively does something to make it happen (i.e., cut expenses or use the freed-up capacity to make and sell more products or services to the customers). By primarily focusing on cost savings, leadership is not taking a hard look at what needs to be done to grow the business and foster better relationships with customers. Those conversations probably do take place in the business, but they happen elsewhere, and not in conversations regarding the improvement initiative. This separates the organization's initiative from the real business. Unfortunately, you cannot "save" your way to greatness.

The great equalizer is that no competitor is perfect. We've yet to see an organization with leaders wearing capes, like Superman. As we write this book, both Toyota and Honda are experiencing major problems, along with the rest of the automotive industry. A number of leaders from Toyota and Toyota's first-tier suppliers sound very arrogant in presentations about how they operate. In many ways, it's very much like listening to leadership from the U.S. Big Three in the 1960s, "We are fantastic!" In Toyota's push to become number 1, it has stretched its resources to some degree. Relative to the rest of the competition, Toyota still stands tall at the top of the game in the automotive industry, but there is no guarantee it will stay there.

Opportunities exist to displace these leaders. Just look at the examples of excellence referenced in books like *In Search of Excellence* (Peters and Waterman, 1982), *Built to Last* (Collins and Porras, 1994), or *Good to Great* (Collins, 2001). Each of those books listed companies that were stellar examples of excellence at the time. Yet many of the organizations described in those books are experiencing major problems today, and some no longer exist. So there are no guarantees in the world. There are only opportunities.

Five Common Missing Ingredients

The improvement trap can be avoided by adding a few ingredients to the traditional improvement recipe. The list may surprise you in its simplicity. When you first look at the list of ingredients shown in Exhibit 2.2, your reaction might be, "Is that all there is? We already do that!"

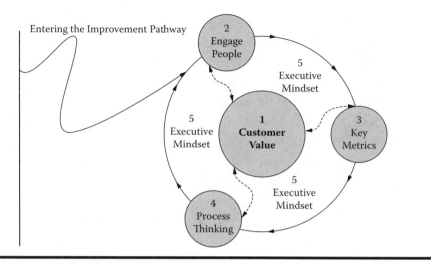

Exhibit 2.2   Improvement pathway.

This is partially true because there is nothing new on the list, and the differences are not easy to see on the surface. However, the critical thinking and detailed level of execution of these items in a Level 4 organization is subtly but meaningfully different from a Level 3.

Again, most organizations say, "This is motherhood and apple pie; of course we do that!" But Level 2 and 3 organizations do not do this *to the same depth* that it is effectively done in a Level 4 organization. Level 4 organizations realize more benefit from improvement activities because:

1. They have a meaningful, clear business value proposition and strategy that drives key improvement actions.
2. Their leaders create an engaging environment where people can do their best work; the environment fosters and facilitates collaborative learning, experimentation, and value creation.
3. They focus on the vital few, meaningful metrics for the current environment, and they avoid drowning in irrelevant details.
4. Their process improvement efforts maximize cross-functional process performance and foster deeper process understanding, innovation, and execution of the best work practices.
5. They have an *executive mindset* that focuses on customer value, people development, process performance, and business improvement outcomes, not solely on savings.

In Chapter 3 we discuss why these ingredients are so important. We will also lay out a roadmap that you can use for getting started. Each of the five ingredients on this list is more fully described in a chapter devoted to that topic (in Chapters 4 through 8). We wrap up the book with a more detailed assessment process you can use to determine the "gap" between where you are today (baseline) and where you want to go. With the assessment, you can prioritize your best current opportunities to bolster your business performance improvement initiative, and what issues you should address in the near term.

INDEPENDENCE ENTERPRISE LOOKS AT WHAT'S MISSING IN ITS IMPROVEMENT EFFORTS

Andy sent an e-mail to Lynn and Jack. He felt the characteristics of a Level 3 company pretty much described the improvement activities underway at Independence Enterprise. The equity value (stock price) of Independence had not changed much over the last three years, even though the company had implemented a significant number of improvements. Andy wanted to discuss to what extent the missing ingredients were indeed lacking in their improvement recipe. He also asked Jack to invite Ralph Voigt, the coordinator of Independence's improvement initiative, to their next meeting.

CHAPTER WRAP-UP: A CHECKLIST FOR YOU TO ASSESS *YOUR* ORGANIZATION—ARE YOU JUST AVERAGE?

1. Do the quick test shown in Chapter 1 (Exhibit 1.5) to assess your company's improvement level. Talk to people involved in your improvement initiative and improvement projects to get their views on realized success and sustainability. Get factual information to verify opinions.
2. Look at the engagement-related results from your employee surveys to determine your employees' real level of emotional commitment to your business.
3. You cannot *save* your way to greatness. Do you primarily monitor the success of your improvement activities by looking at savings reports?

4. At the end of the day, both for-profit and not-for-profit organizations need to look beyond cost savings from multiple perspectives, to learn if a business is really improving, so consider the following:
   a. Your business's results versus those of your key competitors (keep in mind that a competitive view will differ in a nonprofit environment)
   b. Your business results with your key customers
   c. Actual results with your employees (Are they becoming more engaged? Are high performers staying with your organization?)
   d. Financials are important (revenue growth, net earnings, etc.), even in a nonprofit world, because if there is no margin, there is no mission.
   e. Mission impact (however this is defined). Have improvement activities increased your effectiveness in accomplishing this?

If your improvement activities are not ultimately providing more funds (i.e., cash flow and profits) for fulfilling your vision, then how effective can they be? Avoid the temptation to focus on short-term cost reductions, which is where the vast majority of your competitors focus. Instead, improve key metrics by creating more value. Review the five missing ingredients (in Chapters 3 through 8), and see how improving one or more of them might make a meaningful improvement in your business performance improvement recipe.

Chapter 3

The Pathway to Becoming a Level 4 and Level 5 Organization

An Overview of the Five Key Ingredients to Improvement

First comes thought; then organization of that thought, into ideas and plans; and then, transformation of those plans into reality. The beginning is in your imagination.

—Napoleon Hill, American Author (1883–1970)

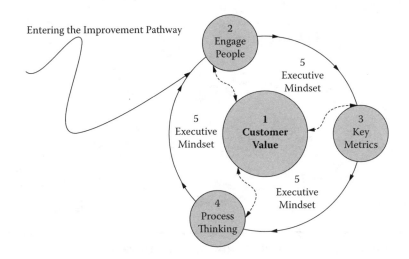

INDEPENDENCE ENTERPRISE, INC. CONSIDERS THE FIVE KEY INGREDIENTS TO IMPROVEMENT

The reading material that Lynn Shaunnessey, CFO, had shared piqued Andy's interest. Andy Fletcher decided to invite Basem Hafey to meet with the leadership team to discuss his research on average organizations and the ingredients missing in most improvement initiatives. Basem's discussion with the leadership team pretty much covered the summary information outlined in this chapter.

Following the Improvement Pathway

The outer wheel in Exhibit 3.1 describes a basic improvement process with one major difference. The outer wheel is intended to focus on how effectively your organization goes about the business of improvement. How well do you do it? Do you do a better job of improving than your competition? The inner wheel focuses on the five key missing ingredients, including the executive mindset. The executive mindset is shown in the white space between the ingredients, because that is the glue that holds everything together and creates space inside the organization for people to modify and fine-tune all five ingredients.

Improvement Maturity Pathway to Enterprise Excellence

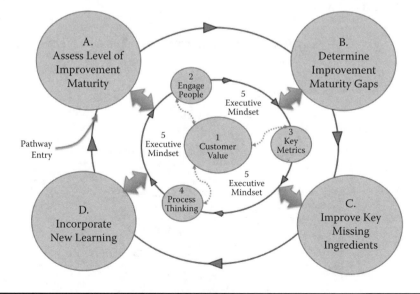

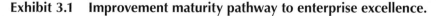

Exhibit 3.1   Improvement maturity pathway to enterprise excellence.

Realize that no matter how much we write, we can't give you the answers for your specific situation. The answers come from you taking time to figure out what is right and to determine the proper thing to do. Figuring out creates knowledge. The right thing to do usually involves trade-offs such as, "If we do this, we get more of X, and/or we get less of Y." That is why improvement is challenging and why it is so important to have a good understanding of the world beyond your immediate job responsibilities. This model serves as a template for critical thinking.

Let's take a slightly closer look at the ingredients to understand why they are so important. We will close the chapter with an overview of the outer improvement process wheel and the steps to take to get started.

Summary of the Five Ingredients Necessary to Break Out of the Improvement Trap

The ingredients have been discussed, debated, and vetted by a close group of our associates (with more than 300 years of accumulated experience), who have run organizations, have been responsible as individuals inside large organizations driving improvement, or have served as consultants or advisors, guiding leaders down an improvement pathway.

Based on our shared experiences, we have concluded that many organizations do not do these activities well. These ingredients are not hard-wired into most improvement initiatives. If you wish to accomplish more with your investments in performance improvement, you should include them in your recipe. They can differentiate your business from the competition and help accomplish more meaningful change. If everyone starts to do these things, then obviously the competitive edge is lost, and other ingredients might need to be bolstered, added, or replaced in the improvement recipe.* However, we will be surprised if that ever happens. This is all about human commitment to the pursuit of perfection. Only the top 20% will ever work smart enough and hard enough—as an inspired team. This book is for leaders aspiring to this level of performance.

---

* Other ingredients in the support systems of the Business Process Model (in Chapter 7) can also become weak or missing, and jeopardize the competitive health of an enterprise. An executive mindset for improvement maturity (Ingredient #5) is an effective countermeasure for other missing ingredients that can spoil the stew.

Chapters 4 through 8 describe each ingredient in more detail. A summary of why each ingredient is so important to the improvement recipe is articulated in the following sections.

Ingredient 1: Make Sure Customer Value Drives Improvement

It sounds obvious, but many organizations do not have a crisp, clear value proposition. Do they understand that typically 20% of the customers represent 80% of profits? Does everyone on the leadership team know why those customers buy? And 50% of an organization's customers are typically 5% of profits.

But legacy activities inside a business inhibit taking action on this group. If my department spends 70% of its time serving what we later dub the Ugly 50, what will I do if a chunk of that work goes away? What will happen to my power base?

If the value proposition is not crystal clear for the top 20% and actions are not being taken to deal with the Ugly 50, then you could not possibly be improving the right stuff. If Ingredient 1 is not done very well, the whole will suffer—even if all the rest of the ingredients are done well. There is an endless list of things that can be improved, but the value proposition clarifies what is *most* important to the customers who pay the bills.

Ingredient 2: Engage People's Passion and Creative Energies

This also sounds obvious, but ask yourself this question: "If someone inside your organization feels the company direction is not correct, would that person be comfortable sharing that thought?" Would someone listen to that person's thoughts and would he or she discuss the concern in a nonthreatening or in a demeaning fashion? A few people will come forward and share their thoughts. But most people we have talked with over the last 20 years have said, "It is easier to keep my head low. I try to do a good job every day, but they don't want to know what I really think. And if I did say it, no one would care."

This has held true in professional positions, blue collar, service industries, and manufacturing. It does not matter if the person is right or not. The question is: Are your employees willing to ask about something they don't think is right? Or is life easier if they keep quiet?. If the employee has a good idea (and people close to the action often have meaningful insights), useful knowledge does not get shared. Even if the idea is a poor one—if they are reluctant to ask—the organization misses an opportunity to clarify reality for the employee. So either way the organization loses and the employee becomes disengaged. In your business, do your leaders truly have a deep respect for people (rather than just muttering the words)? And do they actively develop people's critical thinking skills and abilities so they can fully contribute to the business mission?

Ingredient 3: Establish Key Metrics

Many organizations are drowning in metrics. And if the value proposition is not crisply defined, then functional groups or departments will have entirely different interpretations of what *value* means. They will usually define it as something that is good for them and helps them to meet their metrics, even if it results in conflict across departmental lines of authority. A well-known saying is, "you get what you measure." If poorly designed business process metrics are misdirecting people's efforts, then you may get too much production of things that don't add value, and too little production of things that do. Conversely, good metrics are often a key springboard to improvement because they are part of making business processes visible for improvement work.

Ingredient 4: Develop Process Thinking/Understanding Capabilities

This ingredient may be a little more challenging to understand. Many books talk about the importance of *stretch goals*, but what about the capability of the process? The process does what the process is capable of doing. Ninety-five percent of all problems inside an organization are *process* problems, not *people* problems. Stretch goals for the business should include a focus on improving the capability of the core value-creation processes, although few leaders manage that way. Once the capability of the process is improved to consistently meet customer requirements, there is no need for a goal; the process will do it. Process managers just need to monitor a few key metrics to make certain the process capability does not change; and the organization constantly seeks better leading indicators to help ward off future problems. It is a different way of thinking, measuring, and working with people.

Ingredient 5: Establish the Executive Mindset

The executive mindset is the glue that holds these ingredients together and provides focus. If leadership is loose on any of the above items (and in most cases it is), your company will not rise to the top of your industry in a sustainable fashion. Anyone can have a brief moment of fame and luck, but staying there takes discipline that starts with an executive mindset that never loses sight of the whole recipe for enterprise success. While the five ingredients in this book are typically problematic, others (mentioned in Chapter 7 on process thinking) can also become weak or missing as well. However, the risk of that is far less with an executive mindset that keeps all the ingredients of Levels 4 and 5 improvement maturity in view and working well. From a leadership governance perspective, most improvement programs focus on dollars saved. A company can continue to cut costs until nothing is left. We are not saying that savings are not important. But *you cannot save your way to greatness.* Leadership needs to look beyond mere dollars saved when assessing the effectiveness of improvement activities.

A Top 20% Company Has a Very Good Handle on All Five Ingredients

Leaders in Level 4 and 5 companies manage the above ingredients to guide and drive improvement. The leadership team constantly hones its ability and the ability of its associates to better see waste. As Steven Spear, author of *Chasing the Rabbit* (2009; a Toyota Story), once said: "They focus on how short they fall from perfection, and less on how good they are." (personal conversation)

There are multiple improvement pathways, as shown in Exhibit 3.2. A Level 2 organization can fairly easily jump to a Level 3 pathway by learning the tools and using them. The jump to Levels 4 and 5, however, is more difficult. As discussed in Chapters 1 and 2, Level 3 organizations run their improvement activities in parallel to the real business, managing improvement as though it were a separate strategy that could be done on the side. They tend to focus on improvement projects and dollar savings.

In contrast, top 20% organizations integrate the five ingredients, which are missing in most improvement recipes. The upward slope on the pathway to Level 4 and 5 implies the organization is constantly increasing the effectiveness of those five ingredients.

It's not just our experience that tells us this is true. Interestingly, a study released in June 2009 described "Next-Generation Manufacturing in the

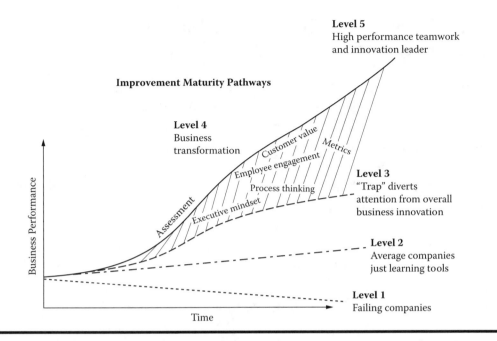

Exhibit 3.2   Improvement maturity pathways.

United States."* The findings of the study are somewhat alarming and closely parallel our list of missing ingredients:

- Gaps exist between strategies critical to success and implementation effectiveness.
- Customer-focused innovation is not done effectively.
- Employee engagement scores are low.
- Processes and improvement performance lags world-class competitive standards.
- Effective supply-chain partnerships offer a competitive advantage, but good ones are the exception, not the rule.
- Measurement systems are inadequately deployed.
- Green/Sustainability ranks low on attention, even though regulations are increasing.
- Global engagement is a low priority, even though emerging markets such as India and China offer high long-term growth potential.

---

* Available at the Small Manufacturers Web site, www.smallmanufacturers.org/picts/NGM-Overview-and-Findings.pdf

Which Came First at Toyota: The Tools or These Ingredients?

When people refer to Toyota and performance improvement, they usually talk about the Toyota Production System (TPS) and Taiichi Ohno's use of Lean tools because at a surface level, those are the easy things to see. It is more difficult to see the support systems underneath (the way things work or the way work gets done). Ohno focused on a very systematic way of making improvement happen. But he was limited to working in *manufacturing* because of his position in the company. So Toyota started with the systematic use of improvement tools.

Very few people talk about the transformation on the *management* side that took place under Eiji Toyoda's guidance after he became president of Toyota in 1967. Toyota's version of adapting the missing ingredients followed Eiji's rise into senior leadership positions. Eiji introduced an early form of Hoshin Planning (strategy deployment) in 1962 as part of Toyota's Total Quality Control activities. That was huge in terms of coordinating cross-functional activities. Although it may not be totally fair to entirely credit the management transformation to Eiji, he certainly was a major catalyst to move Toyota's cross-functional groups in this direction.

There are three different management themes that are part of Toyota's DNA. They have evolved over the years, but can be traced back to the original values expressed by Sakichi Toyoda when he founded the company. They are referenced in Exhibit 3.3 and they are explained below:

1. Respect for People. This was established by Toyota's founder Sakichi Toyoda, and when Kiichri Toyoda became president, he continued that philosophy.
2. The Toyota Production System (TPS) had its birth after Taiichi Ohno visited America in 1950. He took ideas learned from Ford, and wastes that they identified in the production process, and he began development of what we now call the TPS.
3. Toyota was still looking to be successful outside of Japan when Eiji Toyoda became president in 1967. He began to focus more strategically (executive mindset) on what Toyota needed to do as a business. And he began to drive more cross-functional cooperation across the enterprise. Eiji laid the foundation for the management part of TPS outside of operations.

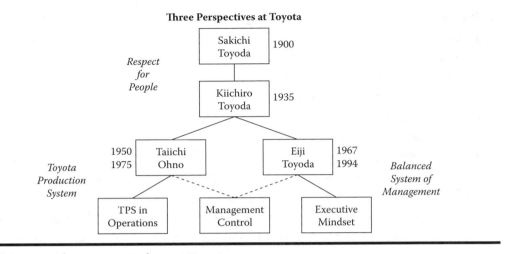

Exhibit 3.3   Three perspectives at Toyota.

Ohno's team had been plugging away with the Toyota Production System for more than 20 years. Eiji was the one who originally recruited Ohno to the engine machine shop in the early 1950s: Eiji was running the transmission shop in the 1950s, while Ohno ran the engine lines. Ohno worked under Eiji as both progressed up the ladder. Eiji was Ohno's protector in the company and was closely attuned to what was going on. During that time frame, the organization showed steady, incremental improvement in profitability during the 1960s.

By 1970, Toyota was very competitive, if you date that as 20 years of TPS work. By then, the company had pretty much eliminated the quality and productivity gap with the United States. Still, the vehicles were basic in design, and they were not exporting much in 1970. The explosion in growth followed the creation of this strong foundation.

The organization's competitive position substantively changed after Eiji Toyoda's management system (built around Human Resources, Purchasing, Design, Marketing, Sales, etc.) took hold. Taiichi Ohno was the manufacturing systems guy, Eiji Toyoda was the overall management systems guy leading the charge, and Shotaro Kamiya drove changes on the sales side. The steady operating profits came in the 1980s (a couple hundred million dollars to a couple billion per year).

Yet the really big operating profits for Toyota ($7–15 billion, etc.) did not really come until the 1990s, when Toyota established a new business model with its launch of the Lexus brand in the United States. It was a totally bold strategic move that built on the company's quality foundation. Lexus established a new level of outstanding automotive quality and excellent customer service in the industry. (The importance of creating new business models is further discussed in Chapter 4, on customer value.)

It is shocking how seldom people reference the bold strategic move made by Toyota when it launched Lexus. Just imagine telling your distributors, "Oh by the way, we are launching a new line, and we are creating a new distribution channel to sell it." That move transformed the entire automotive industry, and Toyota went there first. Toyota's strategic moves were copied by several Japanese companies, but none of the North American or European manufacturers followed this pathway.

One might argue that Shoichiro Toyoda (who was president from 1981 to the late 1990s) added a fourth perspective in the 1990s that focused on the environment and the global community and helped Toyota become more open to sharing knowledge with people and companies outside of the Toyota network. (More information is available on these aspects of Toyota in *Inside the Mind of Toyota,* by Satoshi Hino, published by Productivity Press, 2006.)

In the world today, Toyota may be experiencing some longer-term problems. It is much easier to be humble when you are not number 1! When you listen to Toyota senior executives over the last several years, there seems to be a degree of arrogance that was not there 10 years ago. We have heard several executives speak about the executive mindset, the warrior culture, and Toyota's superiority (in its approach) to the rest of the world. When people talk like that, it would seem that the humility or humbleness that characterized Toyota for so long has evaporated. Not by every executive, for sure, but if a critical mass begins to feel that way, it creates openings for others—which is cool! It's an opportunity, especially for the rest of the automotive industry, if Toyota competitors can radically change the way they operate. Akio Toyoda recently became CEO, partly to address these issues.

INDEPENDENCE ENTERPRISE DECIDES TO ANALYZE THE VALUE IT CREATES FOR CUSTOMERS

Andy was not sure if Independence needed to do a full assessment of the missing ingredients. He liked the ideas Basem shared, but Andy really thought Independence was doing a very good job in most of those areas. Andy and Jack asked Lynn, the CFO, to lead a small group of people in analyzing customer value and the implications of the points made by Basem Hafey in his recent session with the leadership team.

Lynn formed a cross-function group, putting some people on the team from each of the three major business units. One unit sold plastic component parts to medical device manufacturers. A second unit sold electronic controllers for software testing. The third unit sold controllers for maintenance people doing mechanical testing in the field. She also put people on the team with different functional responsibilities and levels of authority. In the end, she had team members from strategic planning, operations, sales, financial reporting, and information systems. The team members named it the Value Team. She shared the summarized notes from the leadership team's meeting with Basem. The team's primary responsibility was to make certain that Independence's improvement activities were effectively focused on increasing customer value.

Several of the team members were excited about this opportunity. They felt a number of issues existed with Independence's customer relationships. This was an opportunity to get more attention from leadership and to do a better job of understanding the "real" issues involved in achieving more robust business performance improvement efforts and results.

CHAPTER WRAP-UP: EXECUTION—FOLLOWING THE PATH

The five missing ingredients rose to the top of our list, and clearly, they must be driven by leadership. These ingredients provide a clear focus for the leadership team on how to improve the improvement process. The pathway to becoming a Level 4 or 5 organization is actually pretty simple, but it's not easy to do. If your organization were good at making improvement happen, you would not have needed to launch a major improvement initiative. If you launched an initiative, then you are admitting that you have not done a good enough job of improving in the past. It is pretty simplistic thinking to believe some improvement methodology like Lean or Six Sigma is going to fix this problem. Leadership has a major responsibility to help the organization get better at making improvement happen. And this requires some critical thinking; begin with these steps:

A. ***Assess your level of improvement maturity.*** Start with the quick test shown in Chapter 1 to assess your company's improvement level (Exhibit 1.5), which was used by Independence Enterprise at the beginning of Chapter 2. Make sure to do some gathering of data; don't just rely on your beliefs. Ask several people to do the assessment so you can begin a dialogue. (Chapter 9 gives more information about a detailed assessment to look at how effectively your organization goes about the business of improvement.)

B. ***Determine your improvement maturity gaps.*** How effectively does your organization go about the business of improvement? How well have you incorporated each of the ingredients that go missing in most improvement recipes? Prioritize your actions to improve the weak or missing ingredients. For example, you might use the strategy deployment process (outlined in Chapter 4 on customer value and in Chapter 8 on the executive mindset). Leadership needs to define the 3 to 5 things that are most important to accomplish over the next 3 to 5 years (but focus on *only 3 to 5 things that are most important*—and no more than 5!). Those activities need to cascade into the organization, so that improvement projects have better alignment and so that functional departments can seek common ground for cooperation. You need to determine which of these ingredients are missing or if they are weakly applied in your improvement recipe.

C. ***Improve the key missing ingredients!*** It does not count if you don't execute. Do it, test it, refine it! This is the normal part of any improvement program. But the preceding A and B steps are usually not well integrated. That is one of the reasons why most improvement initiatives only result in an average amount of improvement and the competitive position does not change. Focus on the missing ingredients and key priorities for the organization. That is where cross-functional improvement action begins (the way people work together). And adding a major dosage of process thinking (Chapter 7) will make process improvement efforts more effective in the near term and more fully sustainable over the long run. You can't do it all; you will need to decide on the current priorities for your situation.

D. ***Incorporate new learning.*** Realize that the outside world is a moving target, and that you need to continually get better at making improvement happen. Once you move, your best competitors will follow. New competition is cropping up all across the globe. That is why it is so important to have the value proposition crisply and accurately defined and kept up to date. Improvements need to focus on what is most important. For example, in 2009, the global economies changed so much that many value propositions needed to be redefined, and many new opportunities have been created. If process thinking is a key component of your actions, sustainability will still be a challenge, but it will be much less of a problem.

Organizational leaders have an opportunity to create a more meaningful workplace and a truly team-based work culture. That's a key differentiator of Level 5 industry leaders. It is a much different challenge than a simplistic focus on cost reduction. We hope the readers of this book rise to the challenge to transform their business for the twenty-first century. Given the changes in technology, the impact of business and consumption on the global environment, and the rapid pace of global competition, nothing short of major transformation will be sufficient. You cannot continue to do what you currently do, in a slightly better way, and be a successful enterprise 10 years from now.

Now let's take a closer look at the five key ingredients, starting with Ingredient 1: Customer Value, which is covered in detail in Chapter 4.

Chapter 4

Ingredient 1: Customer Value
Develop a Meaningful Business Value Proposition to Drive Improvement Actions

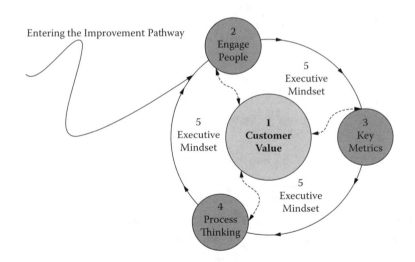

INDEPENDENCE ENTERPRISE ASSESSES ITS VALUE TO ITS CUSTOMERS

Independence Enterprise had a long history of success. Many of its products were market leaders. The engineers at Independence took great pride in their designs, and they had won many awards over the years. The leadership team felt the organization was very customer focused.

The organization had also started using strategy deployment two years ago. It had fifteen key objectives. CEO Andy Fletcher felt the company was doing pretty well in this area, other than a few new-product development issues.

Mark Ekberg, vice president of sales, met with Lynn's Value Team members, and he gave them his view of why customers purchased from Independence: "Customers buy from us because we have the highest quality in the industry and our service levels are great. If they have any problems, they can call us and we address the issues right away. Our surveys show high levels of customer satisfaction. And we have more features on our products than any other manufacturer, so it gives our customers lots of flexibility. They really value our products."

Several members of the Value Team thanked Mark for sharing his viewpoint. After Mark left the room, Nora Schmidt, vice president of research and development, asked, "Did everyone agree with Mark's assessment of quality? Do more features improve quality or do they simply increase costs?" No one had an answer.

Lynn Shaunnessey (CFO) said, "That is one part of the team's responsibilities. Does Independence define quality through the eyes of the customer?" Lynn went on to challenge the team to talk to customers and to involve members of the leadership team in some of their customer visits. She emphasized the importance of the team being open minded and not jumping to conclusions too quickly.

Principles to Consider Regarding How Your Organization Improves Value to Your Customers

What does *value* have to do with improvement? In one word, the answer is "everything!" If an organization does not get its products, services, and markets right, nothing else matters. If people inside an organization have a deep understanding of value from a customer perspective, then they can create *more* value.

On the other hand, if the value concept is misguided, then how can anything else that follows possibly be on target? Slightly paraphrasing Peter Drucker: "Value in a product or service is not what the supplier puts in. It is what the customer gets out and is willing to pay for. Customers desire to pay only for what is of use to them. Nothing else constitutes value."*

This is more important today than in the past. In many ways, the economic turbulence we are experiencing today may be more the norm than the period of economic superiority and growth we experienced over the last 100 years in North America and Europe, for the following reasons:

1. The increasing interconnectedness of global economies and financial systems has raised the stakes of any individual country's disruptions.

* Drucker, Peter, *Innovation and Entrepreneurship*, p. 206, Harper & Row, 1985.

2. A shift toward less financial regulation during the 1990s in the United States and Europe likely played a role, too.
3. The Internet has enabled ever closer and faster global links.
4. The emergence of a vast pool of savings in Southeast Asia following the 1996 Asian crisis, coupled with overly stimulative U.S. monetary and fiscal policy, also allowed bubbles to develop. Popping those bubbles increased turbulence substantially.
5. The emergence of vast new developing economies (particularly India and China) that can quickly implement new technologies and are keen on education also may have helped to undermine "Western nation" investment bias, which used to moderate global capital flows and interconnectedness.

Customer Value Should Drive Improvement

It sounds so obvious. However, although most organizations have an *approximate* understanding of value, many leadership teams do not appear to deeply understand *why* their customers buy from them. Nor is this knowledge readily available to share with employees who work throughout an organization. There is an unspoken assumption that "we all know." But value, just like quality, changes over time. Actions that differentiate an organization today will not provide differentiation tomorrow, as competitors close the gap. Therefore, it's important to have a deep and a correct understanding of the value your organization is providing to your customers.

Without those insights, organizations cannot possibly optimize their improvement activities. Such is the plight of Level 2 and 3 organizations, which are operating in the land of mediocrity. Leaders in Level 2 and 3 companies *talk* about customers and their importance. But the people who work in these types of enterprises often end up serving their *bosses* more than they focus on doing what is in the best interest of a *customer*.

In contrast, Level 4 and 5 organizations provide solutions to customer problems, take advantage of opportunities presented by customers, and satisfy customer desires. It is important to clearly understand what solutions your organization provides, and then use that knowledge to differentiate your products and/or services from competitive offerings.

Case Study: The Procter & Gamble Improvement Turnaround

Alan Lafley, retired CEO of Procter & Gamble, is often credited with turning around P&G. In several interviews over the years, he emphasized a common theme:*

> The first lever we pulled was getting the company refocused on its purpose and values. P&G's purpose has always been to create better brands and better products for a better everyday life for our consumer. We somehow lost that very simple sense of purpose and had to get it back by making sure that every employee understood it and lived it. We stressed this core value by communicating everywhere that P&G is not doing its job unless we win with the consumer, and the boss is not P&G, the boss is our consumer. As we reinforced this core value across the company, we then made what we called "How to Win" choices:
>
> - ■ Demonstrate a deep understanding of the consumer through brand leadership and an ability to drive innovation.
> - ■ Establish supply chain leadership through a deep connection with trading partners and customers.
> - ■ Really drive global learning and spread that knowledge across the company.

Paraphrasing Lafley for our purposes, your value creation processes must be known, and you must be correct on three perspectives:

1. Know what your real value engine is: Make sure you are not just looking at the end piece of the process.
2. Correctly assess your performance capabilities: What is your "reality"— for real—not the reality as you would like it to be.
3. And most important, you need to correctly identify what your customers truly value.

In an interview with the *McKinsey Quarterly*, Lafley talked about strategies:

> I started with P&G's values and said, "Here's what's not going to change. This is our purpose: to improve the everyday lives

---

* Tony Friscia,. "A Conversation with P&G CEO Alan Lafley," *AMR Research*, April 18, 2008.

of people around the world with P&G brands and products that deliver better performance, quality, and value. That's not going to change. The value system—integrity, trust, ownership, leadership, and a passion for service and winning: not going to change. The six guiding principles, respect for the individual, and so on: not going to change. OK, so here's the stuff that will change. Any business that doesn't have a strategy is going to develop one; any business that has a strategy that's not winning in the marketplace is either going to change its strategy or improve its execution." And so on. So I was very clear about what was safe and what wasn't.*

Lafley goes on to say:

Developing a strategy meant deciding which industries, geographies, core capabilities, and competencies to focus on. We also had to understand where growth was going to come from, having the right branded products and brand mix, and having the ability to drive into developing markets, which is where there was economic growth. As an example, we decided to shift the company's portfolio from two-thirds household products to one-half household and one-half personal, beauty, and healthcare.†

How Other Companies Have Heeded (or Ignored) the Importance of Providing Value to Their Customers

The deep thinking expressed by Alan Lafley is the kind of thinking that is needed to guide what to improve. It creates a natural hierarchy to determine improvement priorities. Your customers may not even be aware that a problem, opportunity, or desire exists until they see a powerful, compelling solution.

For example, just focusing on consumer electronics, consider such breakthrough high-quality products as Apple's iPod, Motorola's Razr, and RIM's Blackberry—all of these created new value in existing markets. Apple went on to completely redesign the iPod through several generations of new products. In fact, Apple continuously cannibalizes existing products, with

---

* Rajat Gupta and Jim Wendler, "Leading Change: An Interview with the CEO of P&G," *McKinsey Quarterly*, July 2005.
† Tony Friscia, "A Conversation With Procter & Gamble CEO A.G. Lafley" *AMR Research*, April 18, 2008.

each new generation bringing new entrants into the market. The iPod and Blackberry also had new business models and thus had a longer shelf life than the Razr.

The Razr product-development team was an amazing story of improvement inside Motorola by a skunkworks team, which happened against stiff initial resistance. Once the formal organization became involved and the product was successful, many people wanted to take credit for it. Unfortunately, Motorola rode a great product into the ground. Unlike Apple, Motorola simply made minor modifications to the Razr. Motorola's cell phone businesses have historically tried to avoid cannibalizing products with high margins, and the company has therefore repeatedly lost out to new entrants that changed the market. It does not matter how much you improve the operations or even reduce your costs, if your value proposition is not right.

Typically, people don't think about new product development from a business improvement perspective. In reality, it is one of the most important ways a business can improve to make inroads against the competition. New products are not just about the *product*. In addition, this is a major way for a company to improve *the way it operates*. Customer value, effective new product development practices, and the ability to seamlessly deliver high-quality products all play a role in success.

Over time, employees inside an average organization lose sight of what customers truly value. People become more internally focused when they don't have regular doses of customer exposure! Engineers are accused of overengineering, suppliers develop things they can make but that customers really do not value, and there may be some differentiation in a new product or service, but the marketplace does not see it as significant. When people who do not directly touch customers make decisions about what they believe adds value, new features creep into physical products.

Famous products that lacked sizzle include: Apple's Newton, New Coke, Sony's Beta Max, and decades ago, the classic Ford Edsel. Here is an excerpt from an actual postmortem assessment of a failed technology product:

> Due to an inaccurate assessment of customer needs … [t]he company suffered lost sales due to poor product design on the XX and YY. We incurred significant changeover costs, which deteriorated profit margins on two existing product brands. Even though both models had similar components, manufacturing improvements were not implemented due to the lack of cash flow.

Life is not good if the assessment of customer value is not reasonably accurate.

Customer Value Should Be Built into Product Design

If your value proposition is not clear and correct, it is especially devastating after the design phase of new products, because 70% to 80% of a product's cost is locked in by the time the design is finished. Removing costs after a new product has been launched is too late; in fact, it's the reverse of how things should be done. The entire subject of new product development points to the importance of obtaining a good understanding of customer value *up front,* and then locking the design. After the functional and technical specifications are finalized and design is begun, any change is extremely risky! The risk of quality shortfalls, cost overruns, and project delays grow exponentially as the new product development cycle progresses. Value propositions that lack clarity and accuracy cause turf wars inside a business and misguided attempts to improve.

Organizations that provide little customer value are condemned to a commodity supplier status, with little opportunity to differentiate their products and services. They will waste money, time, and resources constantly trying to convince customers to buy a product or service that misses clearly targeted customer needs. Or they will offer products or services that have very little differentiation from competitive offerings, and thus watch the products/services turn into commodity offerings, where price may be the only differentiator. The results are higher costs and lower margins.

Companies that get stuck making products or providing services that do not require much knowledge or expertise will lose business to new market entrants from Asia and elsewhere around the globe. If it is a commodity offering, it will appropriately go to the lowest-cost place in the world to make and distribute the offering. *Value means providing solutions to customer issues.* If companies fail to accurately get in alignment to provide value-adding solutions to their customers, they will cease to exist. This is not an outsourcing problem (a topic we discuss in Chapter 7). Instead, this is a leadership team problem and a lack of energy devoted to figuring out what needs to be done to survive. Organizations that consistently operate this way will remain average at best; they will never be a Level 4 or 5 company relative to their competitors.

A Strategy Is an Improvement Hypothesis

In its simplest sense, a strategy is a hypothesis that specific actions will yield a desirable result. One set of strategies should focus on what you *don't* want to do. For example:

■ What should the organization *stop doing* relative to the 80/20 Rule and the Rule of 16? (Both of these are discussed later in this chapter.)

However, the other, more fun part of strategy asks these questions:

■ What do we wish to do *new*?
■ And what do we wish to continue doing *even better*?

In their insightful book, *Competing for the Future* (1994), Gary Hamel and C. K. Prahalad* point out that there are two ways to increase net income:

1. Increase the numerator (revenue)
2. Decrease the denominator (cost)

North American and European companies have become experts at managing the denominator. Although sometimes this is necessary to survive, it is not a long-term growth strategy. Unfortunately, cost is an easy number to manipulate; just think about savings reports that most companies use to measure the progress of their improvement activities. How many organizations report millions of dollars in savings, but when you look at their profit and loss statement (P&L) and key business metrics, little has changed?

Many purported strategy statements don't even reflect a strategy. How is *"to be a low-cost producer"* a strategy? It is an end result perhaps, but it is not a strategy. Many times, when people say "strategic," they follow it up with *key objectives*, such as market share, profit improvement, revenues, asset base, and so on. Objectives, however, represent target levels of performance *results*.

In contrast, strategy should refer to these questions:

■ *Where* does leverage exist to grow?
■ *How* does the company plan to strengthen the organization's position with customers and against competitors?

---

* Gary Hamel and C. K. Prahalad, *Competing for the Future*, Harvard Business School Press, 1994.

If your strategy is not clearly defined, your organization loses a valuable communications and focusing tool. Once again, it's more difficult to know what to improve, and to know what is a priority. Lack of clarity will lead to more organizational infighting than alignment as people debate the intent. For example, if your organization seeks to become a low-cost producer, what is your strategy to accomplish that goal?

Traditional strategic planning looks at the four views shown in Exhibit 4.1. Take the questions shown in Exhibit 4.1, and consider them from an improvement perspective. They might be reworded as shown in Exhibit 4.2.

A Strategy is a Business Improvement Hypothesis

Exhibit 4.1   Traditional strategic planning questions.

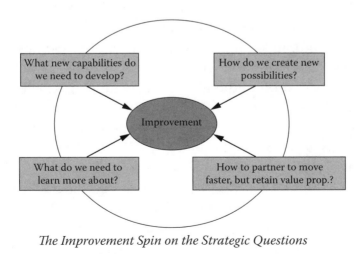

The Improvement Spin on the Strategic Questions

Exhibit 4.2   Four key strategic questions to drive improvement.

Apply Four Key Strategic Questions to Your Organization

The first place to apply those questions is to your organization's key customer group. How can your organization create more value for the customers that you have already deemed important? This is the first place you should look for business growth. This is where your salespeople should be spending their time, rather than looking for incremental sales opportunities or sales opportunities that just happen to fall on their doorstep.

The second major place to look for growth is described in a wonderful study by IBM entitled, "Expanding the Innovation Horizon."* It defines three types of innovation:

1. ***Business Model Innovation***—This is innovation in the structure and/or financial model of the business.
2. ***Operational Innovation***—This is innovation that improves the effectiveness and efficiency of core processes and functions (traditional improvement focus).
3. ***Products/Services/Markets Innovation***—This is innovation applied to products, services, or go-to-market activities (traditional new product development focus).

In terms of differentiating a company from its competition and developing a longer-term sustainable advantage, IBM's conclusions were that new business models provided better than a 5:1 operating margin growth, in excess of competitive peers over a 5-year period.

Real-World Examples. For examples of new business models, think of Lexus in the automotive industry and Apple's iTunes in the entertainment industry. In the future, redefining new markets and developing profitable business models to service them will be critical to future growth. How many poor people are there around the globe? A few million, a billion, more? New business models for serving that market look like the microlending started by Muhammad Yunus and his Grameen Bank and Opportunity International (headquartered in Oak Brook, IL).

New low-cost business models are being created daily in India, and although they will not all survive, the ones that do will challenge long-established successful corporations. Consider the indiOne Hotel in Bangalore, India, standing among a sea of hotels that charge more than $200 per night.

---

* IBM Global Services, Expanding the Innovation Horizon: The Global CEO Study 2006 on Innovation. http://www-07.ibm.com/sg/pdf/global_ceo_study.pdf

In contrast, the indiOne charges $20 per night, and it's modern: every room includes an attached bathroom, an LCD television, a wireless broadband connection, a small refrigerator, a coffeemaker, and a work area. The common areas include a pleasant cafeteria, an ATM, a business center, and a small gym. The hotel, which positions itself as the provider of "smart basics" for the intelligent traveler, is very profitable. Its gross margins were 65% in 2005, compared with 30% to 40% for typical luxury hotels. And the business model is scalable.*

Rethink Your Strategy Statements. Next, give some consideration to typical business strategy statement. For example, consider these, which were pulled from real published strategic statements:

- "Gain Market Share."
- "Seek new market segments for products."
- "Accelerate product launches by strengthening R&D."

If you're not sure about your reaction to the above list, you should know that ours is *"Yuck!"* They are extremely simplistic motherhood-and-apple-pie statements that apply to *any* business. They do not begin to compare to these:

- **Edward Jones (Financial Services Firm):** "Offer trusted and convenient face-to-face financial advice to conservative individual investors willing to delegate their financial decisions through a network of individual financial adviser offices."
- **Apple Computer (2001):** "Have our computers sit in the center where consumers can edit videos, transfer MP3 files to their listening devices, burn and mix CDs from MP3s all with a Mac digital hub."
- **A Midwest plastics manufacturer:** "Pursue custom-designed (engineered) high-tolerance plastic component parts for the medical devices industry."

These strategic statements are more specific and useful in terms of decision making inside an enterprise. David Collis and Michael Rukstad wrote an article entitled, "Can You Say What Your Strategy Is?" (*Harvard Business Review,* April 1, 2008). In the article, they ask whether leaders can clearly state their business strategy in thirty-five words or less. They also state that an important part of a strategic statement is its ability to clarify what makes

---

* C. K. Prahalad. "The Innovation Sandbox," *Strategy & Business* 44. Autumn 2006, http://www. strategy-business.com/article/06306?gko=caeb6

your company *distinctive* from a competitor's. The strategy should focus on the value proposition, and the organization's unique ability to deliver that customer value.

Each of the three strategy statements above (beginning with that of Edward Jones) begins to move in this direction. It takes a lot of discussion and debate to develop clear meaningful statements. The second set of strategy statements above help to define a *win* (as we discuss in more detail in Chapter 6, on key metrics). In contrast, the first group of strategy statements are general statements, they do not provide much focus, and as a result, they will not aid trade-off discussions that take place inside an enterprise.

If you're still not convinced, consider the following.

Make Sure You Have a Deep Understanding of Value

If senior leaders do not have a deep understanding of the value created by their business, they are likely to make short-term decisions that have negative repercussions for long-term survival. Over the last 20 years, many North American executives have made quite a few poor strategic decisions that had only a short-term focus. And the same is true in Europe. Just look at the drop-off rate of companies that were at one time listed in the Fortune 500, which have now disappeared, or companies that were simply mismanaged. Enron, Bear Stearns, Lehman Brothers, AIG, and Arthur Andersen ran into problems due to greed or a lack of ethics. Motorola, Pfizer, Boston Scientific, and GM all had the honor of being on the Ten Worst-Managed Companies in America list,* certainly partly due to leadership's inability to understand customer value for their businesses.

For example, beginning in 2008, financial services organizations have suffered from a lack of deep thinking about their sources of value creation. Senior leaders were comfortable with the high returns being provided by financial instruments they created, sold, and owned, when they were making money. But how many leadership teams understood exactly what was being traded and the associated risk? Given the business results in 2008 and 2009, many leaders clearly did not have a deep understanding of the real value equation. We could cite similar problems in healthcare, nonprofit

---

* 24/7 Wall St., "The 24/7 Ten Worst Managed Companies in America," June 18, 2008. Available at http://247wallst.com/2008/06/18/the-247-wall-st-4/.

foundations, and many other industries; few of us are immune to this need for deeper understanding.

Deep understanding also applies to functional departments and the organization's employees. If functional leaders cannot clearly see beyond their functions, they are very likely to make internally focused decisions that undermine the effectiveness of the overall process. And if employees do not understand the context of their work (i.e., the reason why they do it), it is more difficult for them to know why improvement is so important. If management and union leadership primarily focus on getting their piece of the pie, they lose sight of why the business exists, and cooperation becomes difficult. A deep understanding of the purpose of the business and the value creation processes are beneficial to all parties.

Gary Hamal, C. K. Prahalad, and McKinsey & Company have each written extensively over the last 20 years about the poor job most organizations do in setting business strategy.

We agree, and that is why customer value is missing Ingredient 1.

Strategic Thinking: GM & Saturn versus Toyota & Lexus

Now this story is total conjecture. But it is a fact that both GM and Toyota launched new car divisions. Let's use this little fable to look at strategic thinking (or the lack thereof) in two different companies.

Once upon a time, people inside the world of GM said, "We need to develop some new relationships with our customers. We are still number 1, but we have been losing share lately." If we dig down deeper, perhaps even these conversations took place:

"What if we did this with a luxury car?"

"Oh my goodness, you can't do that! It would upset the people in the Cadillac Division and our dealers."

"OK, well we don't do a very good job building small cars. Would we upset any of our dealers if we do this thing with small cars?"

"Probably not, and the dealers don't make much money on them anyway. So yes, let's try that. Let's launch a new small car division and a new dealer network. We can improve the way the dealers service customers at the same time."

A similar conversation may have taken place in Toyota. Their thinking might have evolved along these lines: "Let's go talk to some (potential customers) and do some data gathering. What exactly are those crazy baby boomers doing now? Interesting, they really seem to appreciate cars from

Europe. In our conversations, they said, 'The European cars handle better, look more cool, and are fun to drive.'" Toyota may even have even asked, "Would you be willing to pay a little more for this type of experience, in a really great car?"

With all due respect to the people at Saturn, which was definitely an improvement on GM's capability of building small cars, there is little to no margin on small cars. From a strategic perspective, it is hard to imagine a well-thought-out strategic conversation on this topic, but perhaps someone said, "We are going to become the small car expert and kick butt! We can efficiently manufacture these *low margin* vehicles. Maybe if we take 40% or 50% of the market, we will recoup our investment and show some profitability."

It would seem from looking at the facts, that even if GM did an outstanding job (and the Saturn team was pretty good), GM could not have possibly improved it fast enough to make a difference (in profitability) to their overall business.

Back to Toyota. From a strategic perspective, they might have said, "Wow, here is an opportunity to build *high margin* cars and seize a new opportunity with all those baby boomers who are buying European cars. How can we do that? I have an idea! Let's launch a new car division that establishes a new standard in terms of customer service! We will do it through a brand-new dealer network that must be trained in the sales strategy for this new product and the service levels that will be expected by this demanding group of customers. And oh by the way, when a customer drops off a car for service, let's give them a loaner for free."

Which strategy would you rather follow and which one lends itself to improvements that would have greater impact on a business?

Apply the 80/20 Rule: Which Customers Value What You Do?

All customers are not equally valuable. From a value perspective, it is important to understand why key customers buy from you, at a very granular level. Typically, 20% of an organization's customers represent 80% of its profits and revenues. This is commonly referred to as Pareto's Law, and it applies to a number of perspectives: 20% of the products made by a manufacturer typically generate 80% of profits; 80% of a foundation's grants might go to 20% of the institutional groups they fund, and so forth.

In the case of business-to-business sales, every person on the senior leadership team should be out in the field talking to the top 20% of your customers. Some organizations assign a key customer to each member of the leadership team. The reason for doing this is to stay grounded in reality, because we are typically not quite as good as we think we are. There is an endless list of things an organization can improve from an internal perspective; it's too easy to improve things that are not important. A broad-based understanding of the value proposition should drive improvement activities.

As a general rule of thumb, business volume with the organization's key customer set (the top 20%) should double every 3 to 5 years. If this is not happening, either the organization does not understand the value equation or it is falling short of deeply understanding the four key strategic questions related to improvement (shown in Exhibit 4.2).

An 80/20 Case Study

The senior leaders of a hospital in the eastern United States were pretty sure the 80/20 Rule did not apply to them. They were legally obligated to serve any patient that showed up on their doorstep, and because they were a nonprofit institution, the idea of profit versus mission was a constant topic of discussion.

Sister Margaret was a senior administrator in this organization. In a leadership team meeting, she said one of the principles of the Sisters of St. Frances was, "No margin, no mission!" Leadership knew the hospital made most of its money on cardiology and orthopedic services. With that thought in mind, and wanting to be better prepared for a changing competitive marketplace, the hospital's senior leaders decided to have a study done of their customer base. What they learned changed the way they managed the institution.

They decided to take a *demographic* look at their entire patient/customer base, giving consideration to age, married/single, gender, income level, and whether or not they had children in the household. Using that demographic information, the hospital leaders then divided their patients into more than 40 life-stage segments. Sure enough, 8 of the 40 life-stage segments (20%) provided 5 times the profitability of an average patient, and approximately

75% of all revenues in this segment. Most hospitals still largely serve a regional geographic market. After this analysis was done, the leaders realized they had less than a 10% penetration of their geographic territory for customers that potentially fit this demographic profile.

When the leaders realized their penetration was so low, it was obvious that some type of a communication should be sent to the targeted demographic group. They offered a free healthcare screening and several hundred people registered. When the health test was conducted, a significant number of younger patients were deemed to be at risk for cardiology problems.

When an organization makes a good strategic move, the unintended consequences (things you did not think about) tend to be more positive than negative. The hospital's leaders discovered new ways to look at their customers. They provided more preventative care for patients, in fulfillment of the hospital's mission, and they explored patient retention issues. The value equation shifted from looking at profit for one single visit to what the hospital needed to do to maintain a positive relationship with a patient over a period of years.

They also looked at some of their key processes from the physicians' perspective. It turned out that orthopedic surgeons were talking to 8 patients to get 1 surgery. The other 7 did not require that level of care. So they explored how the doctors could more effectively use their time. They changed the process so that patients were able to talk to a sports doctor first. Very often, the patients needed therapeutic services, not surgery. Implementing these process changes allowed the orthopedic surgeons to improve their interview-to-surgery ratio; they had to talk with only 4 patients to get 1 surgery, rather than 8. So the surgeons had more time to do their work in the operating room, rather than sitting in their office doing interviews.

These changes resulted in more profitable revenues for the hospital. The key customer profiles became the focus for a number of improvement activities, including marketing services, patient scheduling, and a new preventative care service. Once leadership and associates inside an institution have this knowledge, imagine how effectively they can focus their improvement activities. Improvement activities, focused on value to key customers, leads the way to a powerful transformation.

How 80/20 Thinking Can Help Multibusiness Organizations

Using 80/20 thinking in a multibusiness corporation is a very powerful concept. Many organizations have used it to look at products and services.

We are certainly not the first to suggest using it for customer analysis, but we probably do emphasize having a clear understanding of the value proposition for the top 20% a little more so than normally happens. The tool seems simple and relatively straightforward; unfortunately, that can be deceiving.

Many organizations are composed of multiple businesses. Within each of those businesses, there may be multiple value streams. A simple definition of a value stream is: it's a small business within a bigger business (i.e., a select group of customers will keep an internal group of employees and equipment busy, serving their needs on a full-time basis). Typically, the value stream will be a family of products/services with similar information flows, material, and work content. It could be limited to just operations, or it may actually become a complete small business to serve a specific customer group and include support services like sales, engineering, and finance.

Each business and each value stream has its own 80/20 Rule set. If an organization tries to apply the 80/20 Rule in terms of customer profitability to multiple businesses or value streams to come up with one key 20%, the resulting answer will probably be misleading. You can't cherry pick individual nuggets out of multiple businesses and simply add them together. Each business has to be looked at as a unit. In a multienterprise company, does the leadership team know where the company's value-creation pockets exist? They are most likely inside enterprises owned by the corporate parent. Do the value cells or value streams receive appropriate funding for future value generation?

An organization with only one or two large customers or a governmental unit would look at the 80/20 concept with a perspective that differs from what we just described, but the core concept is the same. Ask yourself these questions:

- What do you do that your customers care about?
- How can you do it better than anyone else?

Even in government, there is a trend toward outsourcing services. Cost is a factor. But more insights would be gained from taking a value-added perspective (looking at value through the customers' eyes). Simple cost reduction is the easy escape; figuring out how to add more value requires deeper thought and more active engagement of people inside the enterprise.

Understand the Rule of 16

The top 20% of an organization's customers are 16 times more profitable than the bottom 50%. The bottom 50% typically contributes 5% of profits versus 80% for the key customer group. In fact, an organization is losing money on some of the revenues from customers in the bottom group. A segment of the customers in the bottom 50% typically consumes much more than their fair share of organizational resources. They drain energy, and they suck up time that could have been spent on innovation and taking care of key customers. Selling to the balance of the bottom 50% is not a problem, if you have the capacity and they are not absorbing resources that should concentrate on the top 20%.

An organization should be increasing its prices to problematic customers in the bottom 50%. If they don't want to pay, let the competition service them and lose the money. But compensation systems and performance metrics often make it difficult for people to do the right thing with these customers. People are rewarded for making an incremental sale, rather than the *right* sale to the *right* customer. One reason people don't have time to innovate is that they are too busy fighting fires related to the 50% of customers who only generate a very small percentage of profits, yet they absorb a disproportionate amount of resources in terms of time and energy. It's not unusual, for example, for a company to decide to *temporarily* compensate sales people on gross sales instead of contribution margin to new customers in a strategic target market niche. The point is that it should be a deliberate, planned part of the strategy with solid reasons why the near-term strategy will contribute to long-term business success.

Understanding Customer Requirements

When listening to the voice of the customer, classify the data into categories. One popular method is Kano Analysis, named after the developer of this tool. Kano theorized that organizations, like people, have needs and wants. And these needs and wants can be segmented into a hierarchy. The hierarchy provides a logical pathway to meet and exceed customer needs on the most important requirements, as shown in Exhibit 4.3 (Kano Analysis for a hotel). Kano's categories include must-be's, primary satisfiers, and delighter requirements.

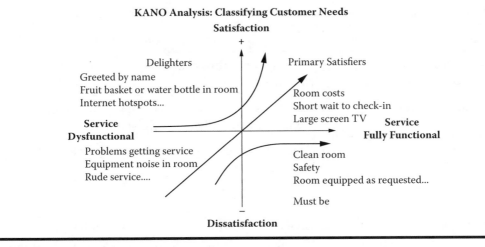

Exhibit 4.3   Kano analysis.

1. ***A must-be requirement*** can dissatisfy if it is unmet, but adding more of it will not further increase customer satisfaction. It is a basic requirement of customers; they will not do business without it. For example, in the hotel business, the customer's room is either clean or it isn't, and there isn't any halfway point.
2. ***A primary satisfier*** is one where the more these requirements are met, the more the customer is satisfied. But to some degree, there is a trade-off between the business and customer needs. A simple example: a $50 decrease in room cost may satisfy the customer more, but it will also take $50 away from profits. Leadership needs to orchestrate these trade-offs to get the right balance.
3. ***Lack of a delighter*** does not cause dissatisfaction, but it will delight clients if it is present. The delighters *add no value unless* the process meets the must-be's and the primary satisfiers first. For example, if a customer is given a smoking room in error, it will not matter if a fruit basket is present.

Table 4.1 shows some examples of each of Kano's categories.

Unfortunately, not all customer needs are delineated so clearly. Sometimes, customers are unhappy but have trouble articulating the reason for their unhappiness. This is often a problem with data from customer interviews done by third parties. A company may have a lot of data, but it may not be filtered correctly.

Table 4.1   Kano Analysis Categories with Examples for the Hotel Industry

Category	Example for Hotel Industry
Must-Be's	Clean room, proper room type available when you arrive, safety, etc.
Primary Satisfiers	Room cost, short wait to check in, room comfort, competent/friendly/attentive staff, etc.
Delighters	Greet by name, Internet hotspots, fruit basket, large-screen TV, etc.

Therefore, you should use proven, comprehensive methods to capture the voice of the customer (VOC). The customer's interests are almost always more complex than meets the eye; there are multiple dimensions and levels. VOC methods from Six Sigma are usable. Quality function deployment (QFD) and other tools can also help clarify priorities.

INDEPENDENCE ENTERPRISE APPLIES THE 80/20 RULE TO ITS CUSTOMERS

The Value Team members (whom Lynn chose at the end of Chapter 3) discussed the stories and concepts that their consultant Basem Hafey had conveyed to the leadership team. Basem Hafey shared the hospital case study and the 80/20 Rule story mentioned earlier in this chapter. Kate Beck, vice president of Human Resources, summed up what the hospital had learned: "To the extent the hospital leaders can align its improvement activities with key organizational strategic objectives, they are going to have a significantly more positive impact on their key performance targets. But first, they needed to clearly define those strategic objectives and better understand what value they had to offer."

Dana Herring, the youngest engineer in the room, was listening to the conversation. He was not sure why they had invited him to this meeting. Working for Independence was OK, but he much preferred playing with his blues band at night. The energy levels were so great when they were playing their music. He paused for a moment and then blurted out, "The hospital got in touch with their Mojo. They got their Mojo workin!*" The rest of the group turned and looked wide-eyed at Dana. "You know, how you get in touch with what is working. It's more about what is going on outside than inside. Like, how do your actions make other people feel? When we do our music, sometimes it's like magic. We just connect with the audience, and everyone feels it!" Dana turned a little red in the face and settled back into his chair.

---

* James Cotton played with Muddy Waters for twelve years, and in 1961, the band played The Newport Jazz Festival where Cotton played his now famous *Got My Mojo Working* harmonica solo.

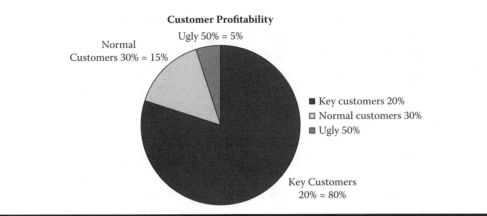

Customer Profitability

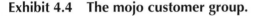

Exhibit 4.4   The mojo customer group.

Everyone was quiet for a moment, surprised that Dana had said something. Ralph Voigt (who was in charge of the improvement initiative) jumped into the quiet space and said, "Remember that 80/20 thing we did last year? We looked at our product line and the same ratio applied: 20% of our products constituted 80% of our sales. We looked at the balance of those products and finally got rid of more than 100 things that were taking up space and we hardly ever sold. Now we're talking about doing the same thing from a customer perspective."

Jack Morel, COO, was listening to the dialogue. He thought Ralph and Dana had a point, and he kind of liked Dana's Mojo line. Jack said, "Let's dub the key 20% of our customers that provide 80% of revenues and profits as our Mojo Group (see Exhibit 4.4). And we better be doing a good—no, a great job with them!"

INDEPENDENCE ENTERPRISE REASSESSES HOW WELL IT DELIVERS VALUE TO CUSTOMERS

The Value Team divided into three subteams to study their key product value streams (product families) to see if they could gain any insight about value from a customer's perspective. They were charged with discovering Independence's Mojo, by directly talking with people who used their products and to individuals responsible for making buying decisions.

Electronic Controllers Market. This study team spoke with a number of people in several customer organizations. CEO Andy Fletcher and Kate Beck in Human Resources went to speak with one of their largest customers, who was considering switching to an overseas supplier: Sheila Carroll, senior vice president.

Sheila conveyed what other customers were too polite to express. She said the only reason her company purchased from Independence was because the competition was even worse. Sheila said the quality is very good, but the sales people are arrogant, and they don't listen to what she needs. She talked about the overly complicated equipment they buy from Independence. Her company needed to run training classes to teach people how to use the equipment and to point out features they did not want their employees to use.

Sheila said, "I'm glad to see Independence out in the field getting customer feedback. Please let me know what changes you plan to make after you finish your analysis. We would like to maintain you as a supplier but as you know, we are actively looking for other sources." Kate promised to let Sheila know the results of their analysis.

The electronic controller market was not a big industry in terms of the number of players. There were about 30 potential customers around the globe, but the revenues were very large. Six players were the predominant force in the industry. Independence sold to only three of those organizations. And it would have been very traumatic to lose one of those customers.

The team learned that products took too long to roll out—no surprise. New products were too complicated, and many of the new product features went unused. Customers were not aware many of the features even existed, a big surprise and disappointment to the engineers on the team. The Value Team also felt Independence should target one additional key player in the industry.

Medical Component Parts Market. The plastics subteam had responsibility for the medical device component parts market. Independence sold to quite a few customers. Much of the business was low margin, and there were many competitors. Approximately 10% of the customer base yielded higher margins, and the success rate at closing the business when a sales call was made was pretty good. So the study team decided to pay attention to this segment. They labeled this segment Specialty Plastics.

Specialty Plastics customers turned out to be a fun group to interview. They very much liked the quality of component parts from Independence. It turned out they wanted to use Independence to do even more work, if the company had the capability to manufacture very high- (tight-) tolerance plastic parts. Each component part needed to be perfect relative to their specifications. They were willing to pay for the engineering, if they were confident their needs would be met.

After interviewing a number of customers in this segment, several team members were wondering why Independence competed in commodity components parts, when so much new opportunity seemed to exist with the Specialty Plastics group. The team did some customer analysis and decided the Rule of 16 definitely applied to their market: 50% of the customers Independence was servicing only contributed 5% of its profits. And many of these were difficult customers to service. They decided to label this group the Ugly 50, which are shown in Exhibit 4.4 as the 50% of customers who equal 5% of profits.

Maintenance Controllers Market. The third study team spoke with customers who purchased controllers for field maintenance work. This was not a fun set of customers to interview. Many of the companies in this customer group were close to dropping Independence as a supplier. They found the company arrogant and its products irrelevant.

The study team validated that Independence was at the leading edge of technology development for this field. But when they looked at the products that customers in this industry were buying, they learned that they represented 15-year-old technologies, and these were purchased mostly from Independence's competition. The older technology was simpler to understand, easier to install, and much easier for the maintenance staff inside the customers' organization to use and maintain. Independence was delivering a very sophisticated product, but it was not delivering solutions to the customers' problems.

The study team decided to take a brief look inside Independence to see if they could gain any insight about the marketplace disconnects. Inside Independence, there was no clear agreement across functional lines of authority on what a solution should be. It seemed like Independence was often its own worst enemy, as different functional groups lobbied for their view of the world during product development. Sales and engineering rarely agreed, and there was little direct customer input.

Margaret Allavoine, an Independence sales manager, was on this team. She said, "At first I was surprised at what we were discovering. But the more I listen to people inside Independence speak, the more I realize I have always known this was going on. I have just never been sure what to do about it. We get into these fights with Operations and even within Sales. We make decisions about what we believe our customers want, but we don't really talk to our customers about these ideas. And as time goes by, more and more features creep into our product, because someone thinks it's a good idea. Then, as the product design keeps changing, our schedules start to slip, and the costs keep going up. It's no wonder we keep floundering in this market."

EVALUATING POLICY DEPLOYMENT AT INDEPENDENCE

Lynn Shaunnessey's subteam also looked at the strategy deployment process inside Independence (this tool is further explained in Chapter 8, on the executive mindset). Independence had 15 key objectives, with improvement targets spread over the next 3 years. An excerpt from their Strategy Deployment Matrix is shown in Exhibit 4.5. Independence had recently adopted this strategic planning tool to maintain focus on a small number of key long-term objectives. Each breakthrough objective was directed at achieving a significant performance improvement.

Lynn shared a comment from Basem Hafey's meeting with the leadership team on Hoshin planning. He said, "It's a very powerful tool; organizations should use it to provide focus. But average organizations get trapped in the old paradigm, where the people on the top know best. And they try to command and control what is going on down below—believing that will make the organization successful. Level 4 and 5 organizations use this tool to provide focus. They make certain they know what is going on one level below their direct reports. It helps them to better see and understand the impact of decisions made by the leadership team. Organizations that had more than three to five Hoshin Goals lost focus."

The subteam looked at all fifteen of the breakthrough objectives in the matrix. None of them directly related to the customer-related issues that the three business subteams had discovered. The fifteen items were all reasonable tasks, but were they the most important? Were they really breakthrough targets? Bill Kennedy, from the Finance

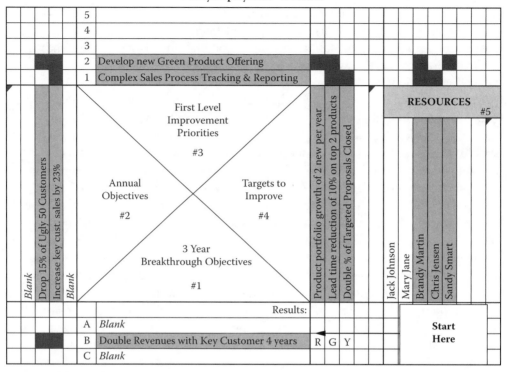

Exhibit 4.5   Policy deployment master worksheet.

Department, looked at the list. "Perhaps this begins to explain why we never have time to improve. We said we wanted focus, but I participate on three teams working these objectives. We rarely all show up to a meeting, and although our project sponsors seem to want this to work, they don't spend much time on it either. Issues are constantly arising with customers, and we get diverted to take care of those problems."

Nora Schmidt from R&D said, "So three to five objectives means you have focus? And we have fifteen, and the list is growing. This is another example of where we send the message, 'If a little of it is good, a lot of it must be great!' We lose focus by overdoing it; we take a strength and use it to excess, thus undermining its effectiveness." The people around the room nodded in agreement.

REVIEWING INDEPENDENCE'S MOJO

Each of the study teams gave their report to the leadership team about the insights they were gaining. Margaret Allavoine from the sales team prepared a summary report on the priority issues surfaced by the study teams:

- We think our customers buy from us because we are the best; however, they told us they buy from us because our competition is even more difficult to deal with.

- Our products are very high quality, but they have too many features, and our customers perceive our products to be complicated.
- We sell technical products; we do not sell solutions to customer issues.
- Major new sales opportunities exist if our organization could sell engineered solutions to companies in the Specialty Plastics market segment.
- Most medical component part customers buy primarily on price; quality is not a major differentiator, and all our competitors operate at a similar quality level. Independence was doing a good job in part of this market, but a significant percentage of it has almost zero profit margin.
- The maintenance product group was developing highly technical products that the customer base did not have the internal skills to use.
- On a more positive note, there might be an opportunity to create a new services business for the maintenance component customers (where Independence personnel could potentially operate the high-tech equipment for its customers).
- We have learned that the Rule of 16 pretty much applies to our business units: 50% of our customers only contribute 7% of our profits. So we have some customer service and pricing issues that require action.
- Finally, we looked at our Policy Deployment Matrix and our project list, which includes more than forty different teams in total. None of them are really working on the issues we just described.

Margaret closed with the following comment: "Independence does many things well. But it is obvious that we do not understand our key customers quite as well as we originally believed. And the work we did on Policy Deployment last year really did not provide the crisp focus we needed. There is still more to learn about value, and we can do a significantly better job of deploying this knowledge inside our business."

IDENTIFYING STRATEGIC VALUE AND IMPROVEMENT OPPORTUNITIES AT INDEPENDENCE

After listening to the report from Margaret and thanking the team members, Andy Fletcher turned to Ralph Voigt, the improvement coordinator, and asked, "Is this true? None of our process improvement teams (PITs) are working on issues related to what we just discussed?"

Ralph said, "Margaret is correct that we have forty teams working on projects, and none of them are strategically important. There is one team working on the new product development process, but they are primarily trying to fix some issues with the new Nimbus model we just launched."

Ralph went on: "As we were developing these insights, I went back to something Basem said. He stated that most companies only do an average job of improvement. I objected to that statement when he said it. But as I looked at our project list and even the action items from our Strategy Deployment Matrix, I realized that I could erase our name at the top of the sheet and put in any of our competitors' names, and they are probably working a very similar list, in very much the same way we are doing it. At that point, a light bulb turned on for me. We really do need to change the way we are going about improvement."

Mark Ekberg, vice president of Sales, jumped into the conversation and mentioned that his department was trying to address some of these issues, and that he planned to implement a new sales incentive system that would result in friendlier customer attitudes. Andy looked at Mark and asked, "What has been accomplished so far?" Mark looked around the room, paused for a moment, and then said, "Well we are really just getting started; not too much has been accomplished."

Andy thought back to his earlier conversations with Will Rasmussen, one of the company's directors. He thought perhaps this was the point Will was trying to make. Forty projects and none of them focused on critical customer issues! And even though the business is doing well, it seemed to be losing touch with our customers. Some of the projects were important for sure, but perhaps the company was missing the point with its improvement endeavors.

The leadership team had a very energized discussion in their next meeting, and several of the Value Team members attended the session. A major debate centered on the subject of incremental sales and the Ugly 50.

Mark Ekberg began the conversation on the Ugly 50 when he said, "I don't understand why you want to attack these customers. They are incremental sales. Their margins are all profit. If we have the capacity, we should make it!" Dana Herring responded to this by pointing out, "I'm not sure if this fits with what we're discussing, but a lot of the work we do in engineering seems to be for proposals that go nowhere, or we spend a lot of time doing designs for one-time projects, that in the end we don't win. And when we do win them, sometimes we wish we didn't because the customer demands all sorts of special changes that we do for free, because they were not taken into account when we did the proposal."

At this, COO Jack Morel spoke up and said there were valid points being made here from both perspectives, but this was not the forum to make a decision on this complicated subject. He charged Mark and Dana with pulling together some information and determining how to measure the benefit of an incremental sale.

The group also had an energetic discussion about the cross-functional PITs that were already working projects. They decided that 10 of the 40 teams were far enough along in their projects to see them through to the finish, and 5 were working issues that were important to address.

Jack Morel said, "This is great! I never liked the way we review our project list. It's like we stop doing our regular work and we review all of these projects. When that is finished, we go back to talking about 'what do we need to do with our businesses?' Even with our Policy Deployment matrix, we mostly had an internal view of the world. This approach forces us to look outside first and gives us an opportunity to better mesh our improvement activities with the things we have been trying to do in running our businesses. You know, I really did not want to do this review, because I thought we were doing terrifically! Now I'm starting to see just how much I did not know; we are going to be much better off as a result of this review."

SEEING REALITY: INDEPENDENCE ENTERPRISE'S IMPROVEMENT ACTIVITIES WEREN'T EFFECTIVE

Andy Fletcher arranged to meet with board member, Will Rasmussen. Over lunch, Andy told Will he had been right all along: the improvement activities at Independence were not highly effective. Andy shared much of what the Value Team members outlined. He indicated that Independence's improvement resources were to be redeployed against the list that Margaret Allavoine shared.

Andy said, "We have not finalized all of the goals yet. We plan to focus the new Policy Deployment Matrix on four key targets for driving change:

1. Determine what actions to take with the Specialty Plastics (medical) market, because it looks like significant growth opportunities exist. We set a goal to double sales to key customers over the next 4 years.
2. Look at sales to the Ugly 50 for all three of our business units. First, we want to determine if the Rule of 16 indeed applies, and then we need to develop a course of action for these customers with price increases, handing them off to someone else, or changing the service structures so that Independence won't lose money or spend excessive time.
3. Focus the Maintenance Controllers business unit (BU) objective on creating a new service offering to customers, using the sophisticated analytical equipment—essentially, to develop a new business model for this market.
4. Make sure both the Maintenance Controller BU and the Electronic Plastics BU focus on their new product development processes. The leadership team gave the leaders of each business unit 30 days to come back with a plan for addressing their process issues and improving results."

Andy challenged the teams to continue their hard work and to give consideration to each of the other ingredients that Basem Hafey indicated were weakly applied in most improvement recipes. Margaret said they would be looking at how employee performance is measured and how people are rewarded.

CHAPTER WRAP-UP: DEPLOYMENT ACTIONS TO APPLY CUSTOMER VALUE PRINCIPLES

Every organization does strategic analysis to a degree, some in a more sophisticated way than others. A multibillion-dollar global behemoth will do this differently from a regional 300-person or 30-person organization, but the core idea of positioning an organization for success with its key customers applies to *all* organizations. Strategies in all organizations should drive better thinking to differentiate an organization, and to help a company fulfill its reason for existence. The more an organization identifies strategies in harmony with its key customers (with its Mojo), the better it will do.

The strategy deployment example shown in the Independence story is explained more fully in Chapter 8, on the executive mindset. However, here are a few questions and/or actions that might jog deeper insights to get you started:

1. ***Make certain you have correctly assessed your value engine.*** You learn what this is by talking with customers. All too often, value is identified only with *inside* talk. Instead, everyone on the leadership team should have face-to-face talks with some customers. This adds a dose of reality that is priceless in terms of decision making. If your value proposition is wrong, nothing else is in alignment. It is critical to get this right!

2. ***Identify preferred or target customers or demographic groups that you currently serve, by applying the 80/20 Rule.*** A database and analysis should allow you to always have the answers to questions like these at top of mind:

   a. What percent of your customers contribute 80% of your *revenues?*
      - Who are these customers?
      - Are they individual entities or a demographic profile?
      - Are these customers that you can help grow their business?
      - What additional value can be provided?

   b. What percent of your customers contribute 80% of your *profitability?* In a manufacturing company, make certain to exclude overhead allocation formulae from these numbers. It is important to carefully analyze and understand how your costs add value (meet their requirements) for each key customer group on a periodic basis. Formulaic overhead allocations can provide very misleading information about true contribution margins; be careful in your analysis to make sure you understand how your direct costs add value to each customer group.

   c. Don't go nuts with the cost analysis. It is better to stay in touch with understanding customer needs and how you are performing. Work the key 20%. It would be crazy to rigorously go through and painfully analyze and break apart costs every year. Your costs per customer grouping will not change that much on an annual basis. Do this analysis if the market radically changes and periodically every two to three years.

3. ***Communicate what each major customer group values from your organization***. This helps everyone in the company be aware of how his or her own function might improve its contributions to the defined customer values. This helps to address unverified opinions or assumptions that people make over time. Can the CEO and senior leaders cite the top five things that bother them most about how customers are treated in your business? To ensure the quality and clarity (truth) of that information:

   a. Go out in the field to get it. Develop a deep understanding by having decision makers talk directly to customers; you do not learn it deeply by having third parties hand you the answers.

   b. Remember that customer requirements change over time, sometimes rapidly in today's world. Get clarity around the requirements by using Kano Analysis (shown in Exhibit 4.3) or some other vehicle. A slight variation on the Kano model would be to look at customer requirements from this perspective:

      • Specifications, that are typically written into the order or contract.
      • Expectations that are unwritten or unspoken. These can be deadly because people have begun to ignore them, although they may still be very important to the customer. Timely communications around the delivery point is an example of where customer–supplier relationships can accidentally go sour for lack of consistent attention.
      • Future requirements as yet unknown or unspecified. Thinking ahead, these can be planned for strategic advantage.

   It is very important to use data and analysis over opinion. It takes some effort, but will be worth the investment of time.

4. ***Make certain your strategies say something beyond simplistic motherhood-and-apple-pie statements like "be a low-cost producer."*** Your strategies should have a 3- to 5-year

time horizon. Great strategies come from doing something disruptive and challenging to the current way of operating. For example, think Chrysler and the minivan in the 1980s; Toyota and the Lexus (a brilliant new strategy that combined both business model and product excellence); and Microsoft and giving away free software (simple version of Word and Excel in the 1980s). These were bold new moves, and they were all truly strategic. And strategy making is not limited to the people on the top, especially in today's world. Powerful new strategies can come from any level of the organization (and we explore this concept more in Chapter 5, on engaging employees).

5. ***Identify operational improvement goals necessary to support the strategy.*** Several questions will help:

   a. What weaknesses need to be remedied to achieve the chosen strategy?

   b. What is being done to focus improvement and innovation activities on serving these customers better than your competition?

   c. What is being done to minimize or challenge costs and internal organizational resources for the 50% of customers who only contribute 5% of profitability (the Rule of 16)?

   d. How long is your critical list; is it more than 10 items? How much focus does a laundry list of 10, 15, 20 or more items provide? Can the leadership really pay close attention to that long a list? The longer the list gets, the more likely everyone on the leadership team is to have at least one item on it. A long list actually makes collaborating on the vital few items much more difficult.

Creating value for customers is not the type of improvement practiced in typical Six Sigma or Lean improvement initiatives. The hospital (mentioned in the section "An 80/20 Case Study" in this chapter) took a look at its basic business, not particularly using either one of these methodologies. Then it improved from a holistic business perspective, including marketing and business development as well as the operational portion of its business that directly serviced its patients.

Six Sigma and Lean both have vehicles to look at the voice of the customer. Lean advocates do this through a value stream mapping exercise, and Six Sigma typically has a voice of the customer/voice of the process analysis. But the improvements are looked at from an *operational* perspective, after first asking, *"Are we serving the right customers with the right products and services?"* When leaders gain more insight about their customers from a higher-level business perspective, and they learn more about the value their business provides, they can better align the overall organization. And the resulting improvement impact will be significantly greater.

As you will see in the next chapter, the way you treat your associates inside your organization will have a major impact on how they interact with your customers. If innovation and finding new value to provide to customers is important, then what actions are being taken to create a working environment conducive to that outcome?

Chapter 5

Ingredient 2: Engage People
Leaders Create an Environment Where People Can Do Their Best Work

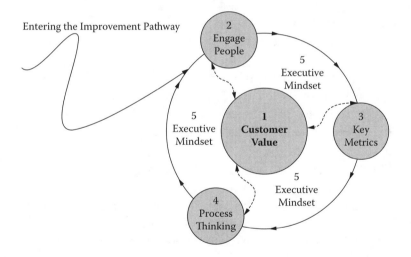

INDEPENDENCE ENTERPRISE EVALUATES HOW ENGAGED ITS EMPLOYEES ARE

Independence Enterprise's leaders felt pretty good about the company's level of employee engagement: they believed their employees were highly engaged in the firm and its mission. For the most part, the leaders interacted with smart, hard working, bright people on a daily basis. They felt they had a lot of trust in the employees who worked for Independence Enterprise, and they believed that employees had high levels of trust in the leadership team.

Then Kate Beck, vice president of Human Resources, gave a report to the leadership team about employee engagement at Independence. Kate said that they had a few questions in the company's survey that addressed engagement and that (only) 33% of the employees at Independence said they were highly engaged. She pointed out studies by Blessing & White, Hewitt Associates, and Gallup* pretty consistently show 29% of employees (in the workplace as a whole) are actively engaged in their jobs. The studies also show that organizations with high engagement have lower employee turnover, higher levels of productivity, less absenteeism, and more customer focus. Engaged employees are safer at work and have greater staying power in the face of business challenges. Engaged employees actively try to improve the business. The 33% engagement score at Independence was higher than the industry average of 29%—but not by much. The leadership team was surprised by this low score.

Kate explained that 18% of the employees at Independence were disengaged. But the challenge is to engage more people from the middle—that is, the 49% of Independence's employees who fell into the "not engaged" category. This group shows up for work, tries to do a decent job, but they are not passionate about the organization and probably feel it takes more effort than it is worth to make change happen.

Kate went on to describe how the studies emphasized a few key actions to increase engagement levels. Leadership should provide:

1. More clarity about what the organization is trying to do and why
2. More opportunity to use employee talents
3. More opportunity to develop new skills and capabilities
4. Less time spent working on meaningless tasks

Higher levels of engagement are reported by companies:

1. Where leadership demonstrates and values ethical and fair behaviors
2. That are seen as a leader in their field of expertise
3. Who maintain a strong, positive reputation with customers, employees, and shareholders
4. With a reputation for excellence and innovation
5. That act in a socially responsible way, especially those that do this during difficult times

---

* John H. Fleming and Jim Asplund, "Where Employee Engagement Happens." In *Human Sigma: Managing the Employee-Customer Encounter*, Gallup Press, November 2007. http://gmj.gallup.com/content/102496/Where-Employee-Engagement-Happens.aspx

Andy Fletcher, the CEO, took exception to Kate's findings. He claimed, "We would replace a manager who had only a 60% engagement score! In fact, if managers aren't working hard to exceed 80% and score in the 90% range in their employee satisfaction scores, they are viewed with disdain!"

Kate responded, "Andy, we're talking about two different metrics. Our employee satisfaction scores are much higher. An employee may be satisfied with the pay and perks, and even with the growth opportunities and with the job. But this does not guarantee an employee's unwavering commitment toward the job will take the company's performance to higher levels of excellence. Employees may be satisfied with the company and the work they do, but simply are not motivated to put forward their best performance. They are satisfied and yet may not be a willing team player. An offer of better pay, perks, or working conditions would probably lure a "not engaged" employee away from the company. Engagement is much different than satisfaction, but we have never really focused on that aspect of it in our metrics. It is buried within the satisfaction scores."

Jack Morel, COO, then jumped into the conversation. "Kate, are you saying we need to make this a happy place? I just don't buy that! We pay people a reasonable salary—that's why it is called a job."

Nora Schmidt, vice president of R&D, said, "I don't think that's what Kate is saying. She is talking about winning their hearts and minds. We all have people who work for us who we know are talented. Sometimes, they amaze us, like that young engineer Dana Herring periodically does. But do we have most of them fully and actively engaged? I don't think so. We may even make it difficult for people to tell us what they really believe; they revert to telling us what we want to hear, or at least what they think we want to hear, and we miss out on opportunities to get better, to gain new insights."

Kate said, "That is exactly the point! We have an opportunity right now as we assess the effectiveness of our improvement activities to better engage people we know are bright, people we know have high energy, people we know want to do the right thing. We simply need to create an environment more open to those behaviors. I'm not saying we are bad; we just could be much better!"

Andy thanked Kate for her report. He turned to the leadership team and said, "We have some work to do in this area. I'm not sure about the priorities or even which steps we should take." He asked Kate if she would be willing to continue working these issues and bring a report to the next leadership meeting. He also asked her to coordinate her activities with Lynn Shaunnessey's cross-functional team working on the strategic planning and customer value issues.

Jack stated, "I keep thinking we are so good, even a great company! But as we talk about these issues and different perspectives, I'm coming to appreciate more and more what Basem Hafey was talking about when he described 'average organizations' that think they are great.

Jack said, "It is hard work to gain these insights, but in the long run we will be better for it. Kate, if there is anything I can do or if anyone in my organization can help, let me know, and we will give you the support."

Kate was not at all surprised by the low score for Independence on employee engagement. Many of the people she spoke with seemed somewhat reluctant to say what they really felt, when they believed their thoughts conflicted with the view of their boss. Kate's initial findings are summarized near the end of this chapter. She did not want to prejudge the situation, so she went back to her files and reviewed the principles and ideas outlined in this chapter.

Principles to Consider Regarding Whether *Your* Organization's Employees Are Truly Engaged in Their Work

Peter Drucker once said, "Leadership's primary responsibility is to create an environment where people can do their best work."* What changes would an average organization need to make to accomplish this objective? What leadership and employee behaviors might change in this type of an environment? Drucker also said, "The most important, and indeed the truly unique, contribution of management in the twentieth century was the fifty-fold increase in the productivity of the manual worker in manufacturing. The most important contribution management needs to make in the twenty-first century is similarly to increase the productivity of knowledge work and the knowledge worker."† This will require redefining the normal way we manage work in most organizations.

Chapter 1 described the need to understand reality—quickly. From a strategic perspective, companies no longer compete against three other companies headquartered in the same city, all operating in a very similar fashion. Today, companies compete with established organizations spread all over the globe, as well as a constant influx of new entrants in many industries trying to redefine the industry. In the past, the normal practice was for leadership to develop a strategy for the organization. Managers were then responsible for making certain that strategy was efficiently and effectively deployed. They did this using a fairly rigid command-and-control management model. In a slower-moving world, with fewer competitors, perhaps this model was adequate. But in today's fast-changing global environment, this

---

* Peter Drucker, *The Essential Drucker*, HarperCollins, 2001.
† Ibid.

model will not work, especially if an organization wants to be in the top 20% of its industry niche.

Front-line workers who talk to customers, front-line people who understand the technologies, and people who do day-to-day work are much more likely to see the disruptions in process flows. People inside the organization see reality on a daily basis. They are in a position to share those insights, *when leadership shows an interest and willingness to listen.* Employees are actually becoming *more* important to an organization's success, not less. Organizations that more fully engage their workforce and coach their people to become more critical thinkers seize an opportunity to create a differentiator that is very difficult to copy.

Making the Case for Improving Employee Engagement

We intuitively know employee engagement is critical for improvement initiatives. Yet organizations continue to struggle doing this well. A senior operations executive in a successful Fortune 100 global manufacturing organization stated, "I have lived through a couple of major improvement initiatives at my company, and I can tell you, our latest initiative has taken years to gain traction (it is still struggling) in large part because employees didn't 'buy it.' Many of us still feel it was poorly introduced and then largely mismanaged."*

An important factor from our perspective is to avoid the issues discussed in the "Improvement Trap" section of Chapter 2. Rolling out improvement in the traditional way actually inhibits employee engagement over the long term because the improvement initiative runs alongside the regular organization. On the surface, establishing project teams and getting employee ideas seems like a great idea. But doing projects does not change the way we do business on a day-to-day basis.

Senior managers own the improvement process; if they do not create an environment where people look to improve on a daily basis, it simply isn't going to happen.

Formal project teams are certainly part of any effective improvement activities, but the real power is *engaging employees daily*, to use critical thinking skills to find better ways to get work done. That level of engagement will go a long way toward improving a company's competitive position. In his book *Good to Great* (2005), Jim Collins stated that if you have

---

* Private conversation.

the right people, in the right seats on the bus, they do not require much supervision. They will get it done. Don't require good people to overcome silly hurdles that make it difficult to be great.

Change management theories* state the importance of leadership creating a compelling case for change (i.e., a good story about why this change is needed). This is important, but it's not sufficient by itself. The CEO or leadership team may state a powerful reason for change, "We need to do this to survive." But those statements get filtered through employees' prior experiences with the organization. Employees may or may not trust leadership. Change theories assume people think in a logical fashion, and sometimes they do. But people often operate from "gut" feelings or a more emotional perspective.

A compelling statement may motivate some employees, but a broader perspective is needed to engage a critical mass of employees and to help them become passionate about the challenge. A key question for leadership embarking on a major improvement initiative is: "How many employees do you want to bring along to the new promised land?" If leadership desires to bring along a critical mass of employees, then right after they state their compelling case for change, they need to then zip their lips and start listening.

Research by a number of social sciences thinkers, such as Danah Zohar,[†] has shown that when managers and employees are asked what motivates them most in their work, they split their responses among five forms of impact:

1. Impact on the customer (e.g., value proposition, serving customers well)
2. Impact on the company and its shareholders (financial performance)
3. Impact on my team or department (effect on my peer group)
4. Impact on "me" personally (e.g., skills development, bonus)
5. Impact on society (e.g., focus on the community, the environment)

You learn what motivates people by talking to people. What the leader may care about the most, however, may not tap into issues that motivate a critical mass of employees. If the leader desires to inspire extra passion and energy to address key issues, she/he needs to tell a change story that covers several of the above perspectives. We certainly believe a story should

---

* John Kotter's *Leading Change* (1996) outlines the project management approach to change management. William Bridges's book, *Managing Transitions: Making the Most of Change* (1991/2003), focused more on the people side of change management. If you are interested in this topic, these are two outstanding information resources.

[†] Danah Zohar and Ian Marshall, *Spiritual Capital*, Berrett-Koehler, 2004.

include a customer perspective at a minimum, because without customers, nothing else on the above impact list will be very meaningful.

In some organizations, there may be a large group concerned about the environment; others may have more of a community or peer group thrust. Hitting several of the impact targets with a balance of negative (problems) and positive (opportunity) outcomes is a reasonable goal. This is another case of trade-offs. Although the leader may prefer to state a logical, concise business reason for change, one perspective probably will not go far enough. Determine which other perspectives are likely to engage as many people as practical.

This is a major challenge in highly unionized environments, where union leadership and company management have a long history of antagonistic behavior in their relationships. In some industries, this antagonistic behavior is turning into a death spiral for both sides. As we write this book, much of the automotive industry may not survive in North America. Both union leadership and management in that industry seem to have difficulty getting in touch with reality and with finding a pathway to future success. In this instance, both sides may wish to blame the other party for their problems. Unfortunately, placing blame will change nothing.

Union leadership has just as much responsibility as company leadership for getting employees in touch with the new reality. It is not about winning for your side—that will ultimately lead to a lose–lose scenario. It does include a sense of fairness (which is described later in this chapter).

Create an Environment of Trust

An organization needs to have an environment of trust before it can fully engage associates. It takes a little boldness to challenge leadership's assumptions. This does not mean the challenger is necessarily right. The question is, if someone doesn't agree with something important, is it safe for that person to voice his or her dissent? Does leadership encourage people to speak the truth to people in positions of power and to challenge assumptions that have been made? This is easier said than done. Innovation will happen more easily in organizations where leadership regularly has people challenge their thinking and openly debate reality.

Where does *trust* come from? Largely, it is experience based. Do people speak straight with one another, or is there a tendency to avoid conflict and tell people what they want to hear? People will often give you the benefit of

Exhibit 5.1 The trust model.

doubt at the start, especially in Western cultures. But over time, you prove yourself to be trustworthy or not. Trust can be broken into several developmental stages, as shown in Exhibit 5.1*.

Making and Keeping Agreements

This is the foundation of trust. A commitment to make and keep agreements is essential to all successful relationships, both personal and work related. To achieve this, there are four requirements:

- No fuzzy agreements are made.
- Agreements are clearly understood, realistic, and achievable.
- When an agreement cannot be met, those involved are notified.
- Broken agreements are cleaned up and put back on track.

Making and keeping agreements consistently leads to credibility.

Establish Credibility

Credibility means being believed. More often than not, credibility is built on experience; over a period of time, what a person *says* and *does* are consistent with each other. Credibility is linked to making and keeping

* This explanation of the Trust Model was influenced by work Cumberland did with the Atlanta Consulting Group, more than 25 years ago.

agreements, but it also includes a relationship dimension. People who possess credibility are worth listening to because they have shown in the past that they reflect on issues and offer ideas, which moves everyone forward with the task at hand. Credible people get the right thing done, in the right way. They have proven their skills and capability.

Internal (to the company) social networking software is beginning to offer insights regarding who the key credible players are inside an organization. Leadership needs to know these people. Some credible players are obvious; others maintain a very low profile. The better job leadership can do in providing opportunities for people to establish credibility, the more leadership can relinquish the traditional command-and-control model of management. Credible people do not need close supervision; they only need clarity on the targets and freedom to do the right thing.

Ensure Openness

This is a higher level of interaction between people. People share information. Each person is receptive to others' ideas, willing to say, "I don't know," and interested in finding the "best" way of doing things, regardless of personal ownership. People who are open with each other are not afraid to get involved, and see participation as necessary for success. If they see something being done in the wrong way, they can point that out.

Toyota does this through asking questions. The outstanding managers inside Toyota do not tell people what to do. They ask questions to broaden a person's perspective, to help people better understand process connections, and to help them think about problems more deeply. We'll show you two other companies that do this: W. L. Gore (described in this chapter) and Cisco (described in Chapter 7, on process thinking) highlight two different approaches that leaders are pursuing to create a more open environment.

Trust Is Developed as a Result of Three Behaviors

When people relate to each other with openness and credibility, and learn that each one can be depended on to make and keep agreements, there is trust within the relationship. Honesty, integrity, and respect characterize the feelings each person has for the others. There are no lies and no exaggerations; there's no need for them. This sort of environment eliminates the need for bureaucratic oversight. It can eliminate much excess overhead, which primarily exists to make sure things are done right.

This is very common in high-performing teams, but it is very difficult to do from an organizational perspective if command-and-control is the typical management style.

Challenge People to Improve Their Critical Thinking Skills

High-performing leaders know there is more than one way to reach a destination. When a candidate is up for promotion to a leadership position, a review board might ask a question like, "How would you deal with this scenario …?" Some people have a great first answer, but the real challenge is the thinking skills they use when asked, "And if that did not work, what would you try *next*?" The best candidates display multiple ways to get something done, just like the best taxi driver knows six ways to safely get you to your destination in heavy traffic. Obviously, this is a variation of the "5 Whys" Lean analytical tool. This sort of thinking and probing (where leadership is open to multiple possibilities) is more likely to engage a critical mass of people in improvement.

Exhibit 5.2 is based on Maslow's hierarchy of needs. It points out that organizations have a major impact on the four foundational levels of motivation, which ultimately lead to self-motivation.

If the foundation is strong and sustained, people can move to higher and more passionate levels of engagement. In the current economic environment, even healthy companies are finding their employees regressing to the lower-level need for security. Employees are less engaged, and they feel more uncertainty and lack of control due to external variables impacting the economy. Many seem to feel that if they hide in the corner long enough, all this will blow over: in other words, they do not want to be noticed, even if they have good ideas. Through proper messaging, leaders must focus on getting their employees back to the self-motivation stage.

This is all about the law of numbers. Any single individual may or may not adhere to the hierarchy of needs sequence. There are always exceptional people who rise above their circumstances. If an organization's leadership desires to more actively engage a broad number of employees, it needs to ensure that the foundation is strong. And the foundation strengthens when employees' needs are consistently met while moving up Maslow's hierarchy.

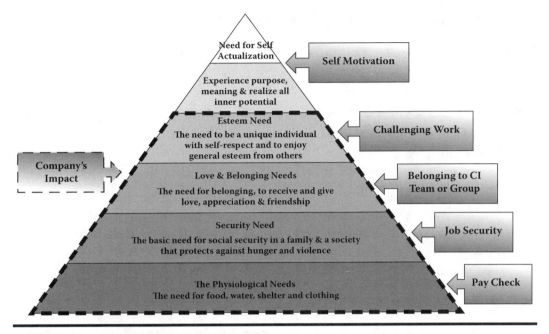

Exhibit 5.2   Maslow's hierarchy of needs.

So what exactly is engagement? Employee engagement is defined* as: "the ability to capture the heads, hearts, and souls of employees, to instill an intrinsic desire and passion for excellence." Engaged people are passionate and enthusiastic about their work environment. It is a place they go to develop, to learn, and to do meaningful work.

Scott Smith, president of High Performance Systems (based in Kitchener, Ontario, this company is a pioneer in forming business consortiums that MIT has called "leveraged learning networks") defines engagement in the following way:

"Engagement = Motivation (desire) + Focus (direction). I have found this to be useful. The company is responsible for the focus through vision and alignment. And if you are an advocate of Maslow's theory of personal needs hierarchy, the company is responsible for physiological needs up to esteem needs, which creates a strong foundation for self-motivation. I have found it is easier for companies to understand as well as to develop an improvement plan, when they have some understanding of the Maslow Model."[†]

---

* John H. Fleming and Jim Asplund, "Where Employee Engagement Happens." In *Human Sigma: Managing the Employee-Customer Encounter* (Gallup Press, November 2007).
[†] Personal communication.

Surveys Conducted on Employee Engagement

Employee responses to a Gallup Survey done in October 2006* were pretty typical:

- 29% of employees said they were "engaged" at work; engaged employees work with passion and feel a profound sense of connection to their company
- 56% were "not engaged" at work; they put in their time, try to do their job in the right way, but there is not very much passion about their work
- 15% were actively "disengaged" from their jobs; on a daily basis, they act out their unhappiness, and they undermine or at the very least passively support what their engaged coworkers are trying to accomplish

One of the survey items was to comment on how strongly the following statement was true: "At work, we give our customers new ideas." Of engaged employees, 74% strongly agreed that they share new ideas with customers; contrasted with just 13% of actively disengaged employees.

If approximately 30% is the *normal* engaged survey score, what kind of a competitive advantage might an organization have if *60%* of employees were actively engaged? Might this type of an environment require less supervision and be more likely to innovate? In fact, employees at Toyota and other Level 4 and 5 companies have more than 50% of their workforces actively engaged in the business.

The Corporate Leadership Council's Managing Director, Jean Martin, says that "increasing an employee's level of engagement can reduce employee turnover by 87% and improve employee performance by 20%,"[†] based on studies the council has conducted.

In a BlessingWhite[‡] study, only 53% of employees said they trust their senior leaders. Lack of trust presents a major obstacle if leadership is trying to engage employees, especially during tough economic times.

---

* Gallup Study: Engaged Employees Inspire Company Innovation," *Gallup Management Journal*, 12, October 2006.
† Tekrati: The Industry Analyst Reporter, "Upgrading the Organization's Employee Engagement strategy," Corporate Leadership Council, 2007. Available at http://cio.tekrati.com/research/8645/.
‡ BlessingWhite, Inc. "Employee Engagement Report, 2008," April–May 2008. Available at http://www.blessingwhite.com/EEE__report.asp.

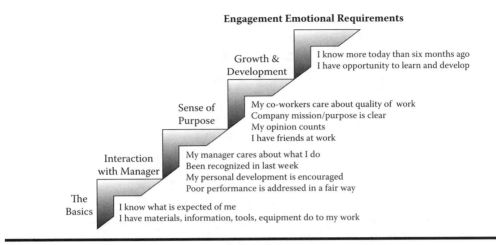

Engagement Emotional Requirements

Growth & Development
- I know more today than six months ago
- I have opportunity to learn and develop

Sense of Purpose
- My co-workers care about quality of work
- Company mission/purpose is clear
- My opinion counts
- I have friends at work

Interaction with Manager
- My manager cares about what I do
- Been recognized in last week
- My personal development is encouraged
- Poor performance is addressed in a fair way

The Basics
- I know what is expected of me
- I have materials, information, tools, equipment do to my work

Exhibit 5.3   Levels of employee engagement emotional requirements.

What's Needed to Increase Employee Engagement?

A core set of emotional requirements must be met to ensure high levels of employee engagement. As shown in Exhibit 5.3, they include:

- Fairness
- Opportunities to grow and develop
- Trust in leadership and with coworkers
- At the most basic level, people have the tools, information, and equipment necessary to do their best work

This list of emotional requirements mirrors Maslow's hierarchy; it describes key characteristics of an environment where people can do their best work. Engaged people want their organization to succeed because they feel connected emotionally, socially, and even spiritually to its mission, vision, and purpose. This sets the stage for innovation.

Employees Who Are Engaged in Their Work Will Actively Innovate

According to Arie de Geus, author of *The Living Company: Habits for Survival in a Turbulent Business Environment,** the only sustainable

---

* Harvard Business School Press, 1997.

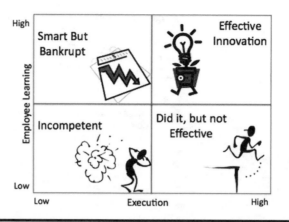

Exhibit 5.4   Innovation and execution.

competitive advantage is the ability to learn faster than your competition. Execution and learning are keys to effective innovation, as shown in Exhibit 5.4.

- ■ ***Incompetent:*** These companies don't understand customer requirements, and the stuff they do does not get done very well; for example, this is the reputation (justly or unjustly) of many governmental bodies around the globe.
- ■ ***Smart but bankrupt:*** For example, think of the original dot-com companies and many small start-up companies. They had loads of venture capital and very smart people, but most did not execute their vision in a way that allowed them to survive and prosper
- ■ ***Did it, but not effectively:*** These companies start off with a really great plan, but as Dwight Eisenhower once said, "Plans are useless, but planning is indispensable."* The thinking and reacting to learning and reality is critical to success. Plans alone will not suffice. For example, think of Home Depot's attempt to enter the market niche for upscale home appliances, lighting, floor coverings, and bath and kitchen fixtures. In their new Expo Design Centers, they had in place all of the physical products needed to succeed. But Home Depot's leadership failed to plan for the level of employee engagement that was required to play in this more demanding market. The upscale market needed employees with more experience and capabilities than the skill levels of employees who worked in Home Depot's building supplies stores.

---

* Quotation # 18611. "The Columbia World of Quotations". Bartleby.com

■ ***Effective innovation:*** These companies recognize that their plans will likely need to change along the way. Employees who experience rapid learning and then apply that knowledge to improve the end result are more likely to win over the long term. For example, think of Amazon. com, which redefined the book market. "In the end, scarcity can be pretty good at prompting new ideas. Constraints drive innovation,"* says Amazon's CEO Jeff Bezos.

So the innovation challenge includes actively engaging people and at the same time having support mechanisms in place to surface and fully bake good ideas quickly. (Support Systems are more fully discussed in Chapter 7 on process thinking.)

Employee Engagement at W. L. Gore: A Case Study

Terri Kelly, the CEO of W. L. Gore & Associates, gave a presentation at the MIT Sloan School of Management. She stated that the company's corporate culture has a lot to do with its ability to innovate:

> A lot of companies ask about "How do you innovate? What do you invest in R&D?" They're not really the right questions to ask. We would flip that and talk more around "How do we create the right environment where collaboration happens naturally—that people actually want to work together, that they actually like to be part of something greater than just the individual contribution?" And if you get that part right, all the other pieces fall in place that allow us to create this great innovation cycle within Gore.

Gore has been called the most innovative company in the world by *Fast Company* magazine. It is mostly known for Gore-Tex outdoor all-weather fabrics, but it manufactures many types of materials and products. Gore is consistently listed as one of the best places to work (by *Fortune* magazine). Gore's culture, like Toyota's, has evolved over a 50-year period. Another organization cannot simply copy what Gore does and suddenly replicate its success. Terri Kelly points out in her speech that the company's corporate culture has a lot to do with its ability to innovate: "It all has to work as a

---

* Jena McGregor, "The World's Most Innovative Companies," *BusinessWeek*, April 17, 2008.

system. As the CEO of W. L. Gore, I spend as much time making certain the system works (the way people work together) as I do on the business side, making certain the organization has the right strategies and executes them well."*

At W. L. Gore, associates (the company's term for employees) are granted *dabble time*. They can devote a half-day per week to something they want to work on, so long as their primary commitments are met. As a result, innovation in its initial stages is very inexpensive. The first test for an idea is whether other associates will invest their personal dabble time in moving the concept forward. One associate turns into a small group of two or three people working an idea. Ideas progress through a rigorous, but informal, peer assessment.

The dabble time effort can continue in an ad hoc manner for weeks, months, or even years until the group believes the idea is fairly well thought-out and can then progress through the organization's more formal review processes. Only at that point is any significant investment in the idea actually considered. Innovations that had their birth in this fashion include Gore's guitar string and dental floss businesses.

The culture within Gore de-emphasizes leadership hierarchy. Terri became CEO after her peers nominated her, a very unusual CEO selection process. You are only a leader at Gore if people decide they want to follow you (a "pull" method versus directive command-and-control "pushing"). Every day you need to prove yourself. To maintain their culture and to stay in touch with reality, senior leaders are rated by their leaders, peers, and subordinates on a five-point scale. The leader's assessment includes commenting on the accuracy of the following statements:

1. I feel he/she creates an environment of trust
2. Culture is valued as a critical means of achieving business results
3. Accountability and decision making is clear within the division
4. Associates and teams feel empowered to make decisions
5. Associates can speak their mind without fear of retribution
6. I feel he/she seeks appropriate input when making decisions
7. Diversity of thought and perspective is encouraged
8. I feel he/she creates a healthy balance of challenge and support
9. I feel he/she is approachable

---

* This is a great presentation and available on the MIT Web site: http://sloanreview.mit.edu/improvisations/2009/02/13/creating-a-culture-of-innovation/

Leaders do not decree actions within the Gore world. They need to explain their reasoning. And every topic is debated. The organization believes that although this may initially take more time, in the end, the actions are improved and there is more ownership of the actions as a result of engaging associates. Implementation is much faster and much better as a result of engaging passionate people in the planning stages.

Before we leave the Gore story, think again about two aspects of it: First, true leaders rise to their positions only if their coworkers have been convinced that those leaders are worth following, based on previous demonstrated actions. That creates tenacious, quality-oriented ownership of workforce roles and responsibilities that are far beyond what can be expected in a command-and-control organization. Innovation happens spontaneously in that kind of a motivated workforce.

Second, leaders in an engaged organization think first about how to provide the support systems needed for an environment where people can do their best work—including continuous, incremental innovation. Then they react to the larger ideas percolating up that need corporate sponsorship for major R&D resources. Meanwhile, many ideas have already been implemented by a fully engaged workforce. Both aspects—"pull" leadership and support systems management—are keys to the workforce engagement and productivity of Level 5 companies.

The W. L. Gore story is very much at the other end of the spectrum from how most organizations treat their associates. For example, several years ago we worked with a manufacturing company in Shreveport, Louisiana. We were facilitating a Kaizen team focused on operational improvement. The team did a great job implementing improvements to several workstations and developed a process for faster changeovers. At the end of the week, after the Kaizen team members had made their presentation to the leadership team, we asked them a question: What did they get out of this experience? We went around the room and received interesting comments from all participants. Then we came to Pearlie. She said, "I have worked for this company for more than 32 years. This is the first time they ever asked me to *think*." Then she paused and finished with, "And I really liked it!"

So many North American and European companies miss this wonderful opportunity to show respect and to honor peoples' capabilities. If leaders help their people grow and treat them fairly, they can compete with anybody.

In John Shook's book *Managing to Learn* (Lean Enterprises Institute, 2008), he translates a 1997 quote about respect for people from Fujio Cho, past chairman of Toyota:

> We want to not only show respect to our people, the same way we want to show respect to everyone we meet in life. We also want to respect their humanity, what it is that makes us human, which is our ability to think and feel. We have to respect that humanity in the way we design the work, so that the work enables their very human characteristics to flourish.

Ensure Fairness in Compensation and Rewards

Compensation and rewards are not good things when they are given for the wrong reasons. The financial services meltdown in 2008 was partially due to inappropriate compensation for innovative but risky and inadequately regulated financial products. At some level, there was an element of a good idea: for example, create leverage and allow more people to own a home. But what may have been a good idea at the start certainly turned into a disastrous idea in the end. At the very least, the financial markets took a strength (leverage) and carried it to an extreme that was not just a weakness, but an outright disaster. And it's likely that the way people were compensated drove a lot of the misguided behaviors.

The same arguments can be made about senior executive and CEO compensation. In 2005, the ratio of CEO pay to average worker pay was 411:1, according to a report by the Institute for Policy Studies and United for a Fair Economy, two groups that focus on social justice issues.* That compares with a 1980 ratio of 42:1, as calculated by *BusinessWeek*.† And on a global basis, CEOs in the United States are compensated considerably higher than in any other country. The closest statistic we could find was a 60:1 ratio in Germany (similar to the U.S. ratio in 1980). Did something happen between 1980 and the year 2005 that all of a sudden makes U.S. CEOs that much more valuable to an organization?

Even when organizations are failing, CEO compensation has seemed increasingly excessive over the last two decades. Quite a bit of work has been done on fair executive compensation by Elliott Jaques regarding fair

---

* Sarah Anderson, John Cavanagh, Chuck Collins, and Sam Pizzigati, "Executive Excess," Institute for Policy Studies and Mike Lapham, United for a Fair Economy.
† "Special Report: Executive Pay," *Business Week*, April 19, 1999.

pay in general and Mark Van Clieaf on executive compensation in the United States. They surveyed the performance and executive pay over 5 years for 3,000 of the largest U.S. companies. They found that 60 of the worst-performing companies lost a total of $700 billion in stock market value, but those same companies paid their executive officers $9 billion to $12 billion during the same time period.*

Excessively high compensation puts an almost unbearably high price on ethical behaviors. When compensation gets that out of whack (out of balance), it is nearly impossible for a person to make an unbiased decision regarding an action that is good for the company versus personal compensation. Personal greed is part of this problem, but a more important issue may be the loss of a sense of purpose that is greater than one's self. (And we return to this theme in Chapter 8 on the executive mindset.)

Greed is actually a weakness of character, and it happens when people put their own personal satisfaction far above everyone else's. Unfortunately, once you start down this slippery slope, there is no end in sight. How much is too much? More than a 400:1 ratio seems pretty excessive, but what is the limit once a person starts down this path? There isn't one really, until the individuals involved decide to address this major character flaw. Certainly, corporate boards should play a role in moderating this issue, but so far they have seemed reluctant to do so. If leadership desires to mature to Level 4 and 5 company performance in a sustainable way, there needs to be more fairness in compensation practices.

Several of the companies in Jim Collins's book, *Good to Great* (2005), have stumbled over the last couple of years in major ways. But the people who were leading those organizations when they experienced more than a decade's worth of success were said to be "Level 5 Leaders." These were people with a fair amount of humility. That does not mean they were quiet. For example, Ken Iverson, the retired CEO of Nucor Steel, was a scrappy fighter against the rest of the steel industry and against Congress when it was giving handouts in the 1980s. These leaders did not maximize their personal compensation, nor did they try to take the major amount of credit for their organizations' successes. Instead, they invested in the people inside the organization to develop their capabilities and to grow their organizations in a meaningful way for long-term competitive success, not short-term, manipulated payoffs.

There are a handful of individual CEOs who did come into large problematic global organizations and inspired major turnarounds, including Lou

---

* Mark Van Clieaf and Janet Langford Kelly, "Myths of Executive Compensation: Returning to Basic Principles of Pay for Performance," *Corporate Governance Advisor,* September–October 2005.

Gerstner at IBM, Carlos Ghosn at Nissan, and a very few others. They did not do the turnaround single-handedly, but they certainly aroused people's passions, and they actively engaged energetic people to get in touch with reality and to use their critical thinking skills to act and radically improve those businesses.

But many CEOs are more like bureaucratic landlords. They preside over a great empire, but do they really create that much new value? Outsourcing to reduce costs or making an acquisition where someone else created the original value—are these really the actions of leadership at its best? Is it something so valuable that it is worth making the total compensation spread between the highest paid and the average person's pay go from a ratio of 42:1 to 411:1? This holds especially true for Level 2 and 3 organizations, which are merely average in terms of how effectively they improve.

More important, in this type of an environment, will an organization's leaders perceive employees as their most important asset in creating value-adding services for customers? *Probably not!* Are leaders who are paid so disproportionately more than their average employee able to truly engage most people to improve the business? *Probably not!* Do these extremely high compensation packages make a leader more concerned about their compensation or more concerned about the long-term health of their business? It would certainly seem to emphasize the short term over the long term because that is how their performance is measured.

Leaders and boards who let compensation schemes get so far out of balance as related to the average person's pay do a major disservice to employees, to shareholders, and ultimately to the long-term viability of an enterprise. It is a serious morale affront to the kind of inspired workforce engagement that's needed to compete in the new global marketplace. In a recent Berkshire Hathaway annual meeting, CEO Warren Buffett stated:

> The CEO has had too much say in determining their compensation. They pick their own compensation committee. I've been on one compensation committee out of nineteen boards because these people aren't looking for Dobermans; they're looking for cocker spaniels. It's been a system that the CEO has dominated. In my experience, boards have done little in the way of thinking through *as an owner* what they ought to pay these people.*

---

* Liz Wolgemuth, "Warren Buffett on Executive Compensation" *U.S. News and World Report,* May 4, 2009.

Fortunately, a few companies are doing something about it, because it's critical for the long-term competitive health of American businesses. For example, John Mackey, the CEO of Whole Foods, reported* that his company had made adjustments to keep the external and internal equity perspectives in balance:

> We have a salary cap—the maximum allowable ratio of the highest cash compensation to average employee cash compensation—to address internal equity. But that cap has increased over the years so that we can help avoid the loss of valuable executives. Twenty years ago, when we were only a fraction as large as we are today ($40 million in sales then compared to $8 billion now), the salary cap ratio was 8:1. Today it's 19:1. That puts the maximum cash compensation anyone can make at Whole Foods at about $650,000.

This example does not include noncash compensation like stock options, but even if you triple the spread, it is much more reasonable than many U.S. companies.

Volkswagen is another company that has been working to transform its competitive position. It is too early to tell if VW can sustain the gains on changes that have been made to its operating practices. The company recently changed its executive compensation practices to focus more on long-term results.

Starting in 2010, VW will introduce a so-called "long-term bonus" plan, in which managers will be rewarded according to customer and employee satisfaction, as well as their achievements in sales and the company's rate of return. In addition, VW will no longer offer stock options.

Horst Neumann, director of Human Resources at VW, confirmed that the new system, developed over the course of the past year, has already been agreed on. "We want there to be a close relationship between bonuses and strategic objectives," he said.†

In 2008, VW's top five managers earned base salaries worth a combined total of €5.3 million, €12.5 million in bonus money, and millions more in stock options.

---

* John Mackey, "Why Sky-High CEO Pay is Bad Business", *Harvard Business Review* Guest Blog, June 17, 2009. (http://blogs.hbr.org/hbr/how-to-fix-executive-pay/2009/06/why-high-ceo-pay-is-bad-business.html).

† Vanessa Johnston, "Large German Companies Reform Bonus Systems" © Deutsche Welle, December 18, 2009 http://www.german-info.com/press_shownews.php?pid=2010.

Under new company regulations, however, the fixed components of their salaries will account for about 30% of their remuneration, and any extra pay will be contingent on performance over a span of four years. There will also be limits to how much bonus money is paid.

If business is bad, managers won't be able to expect any extra euros to flow into their pockets. "If we don't earn any money, that means the performance results can't be very good, and there will be no bonuses," said Neumann.*

It will be very interesting to see the results of the VW experiment. From a global competition perspective, VW compensation practices were not nearly as disproportionate as U.S. automotive companies. Yet VW is taking action to address the issues. Perhaps there is a lesson here for many North American organizations.

Executive compensation metrics related to the current business should attempt to measure true value creation from the company's operations using value-based performance measures, such as economic profit, economic value added (EVA), free cash flow, and return on invested capital (ROIC). Companies should avoid measures that can be easily manipulated, such as earnings per share, which do not reflect the level of capital efficiency in value creation.

This book has nothing to help you defend against the financial machinations behind executive compensation excesses. Instead, we are focused on helping you build value-based organizations for long-term competitive leadership. The ideas expressed are intended for CEOs and boards of directors who care about real value creation—and care enough about the customers, employees, and shareholders involved to fix and guard against this problem.

Profit-Indexed Performance Pay Systems

For management teams that are serious about providing a solid support-system foundation for inspired workforce performance, a profit-indexed performance pay (PIPP) system is an especially effective solution. We have long been proponents of PIPP systems, such as those pioneered by Dr. William Abernathy (now part of Aubrey Daniels International). When done well, a PIPP system can be a primary, driving support system for an entire organization intending to focus the business culture on continuous business performance improvement for competitive advantage.

---

* Vanessa Johnston, "Large German Companies Reform Bonus Systems" © Deutsche Welle, December 18, 2009 http://www.german-info.com/press_shownews.php?pid=2010.

As we'll discuss in the next chapter, appropriate business process metrics are critical to guiding performance improvement efforts effectively. As Dr. W. Edwards Deming often said, "If we don't measure it, then we're unlikely to improve it." The challenge is to determine the *appropriate* metrics—not counterproductive ones—and then tailor reasonable near-term goals for the process metrics so the work team has a clear focus on what's important to accomplish next. That's a tall order, as many of you may have already learned from your own efforts to build or improve your business performance metrics systems. The potential rewards of doing well are enormous, but the potential pitfalls of doing it poorly are truly scary and debilitating. An efficient, powerful fact about a PIPP system is that it's a multidimensional solution that directly includes:

- A balanced scorecard for measuring performance
- Metrics reflecting customer and business values
- Recognition and rewards for performance above expectations
- An appropriate balance of rewards for the whole team and individuals

Imagine a carefully planned, validated, balanced scorecard with graduated performance goal scales that recognize performance levels from subpar through extraordinary, and then applies a monetary bonus based on the individual performance factored by whole business-unit profitability—so the participants are always aware of both their individual contributions and that they're still "all in the same boat." You can see that PIPP metrics and bonuses have the active attention of all involved.

Additionally, a well-designed PIPP system can include other operating elements of a mature continuous improvement process:

- Integration in routine operations planning
- Quick feedback for corrective and improvement action
- Visual performance metrics presentation
- Active collection of improvement opportunities ideas
- Work-team collaboration for daily optimization of the metrics

Suffice it to say that it's a powerful business tool that should be considered by any management team with a holistic view of how to enable and support an inspired, team-based culture, including a fair compensation system as a key ingredient. Bottom line, PIPP is a comprehensive way to head off an accidentally misaligned compensation system that can scuttle otherwise well-planned improvement efforts. You can refer to Dr. Abernathy's book, *Managing without Supervising* (2000), for further information.

Chapter 7, on process thinking, will provide more information on recognition and rewards, as well as how other elements of business-process support systems come into play in the Business Process Model.

When Employees are Engaged, Phenomenal Results Can Occur*: A Case Study

The management of Orem-based Mity-Lite, Inc. was resigned to the idea that it soon would have to arrange for the company's new "Mesh-One Folding Chair" to be manufactured offshore. The new product (refer to Exhibit 5.5) was expected to be a game-changer. It's 20% lighter than most other chairs, takes less storage space, and the breathable rip-stop nylon mesh seat and back conforms to the shape of the sitter.

One of the company's internal manufacturing teams, though, had a different idea. They approached CEO Randy Hales and asked if they could submit a bid on the project just like the factories in Asia would.

Hales said, "I had faith that the team could get there eventually, but our continuous improvement plan was new and the teams only had about four months of experience with it. We've challenged them to make significant differences, and now they're coming to us saying, 'We can do this.' It wouldn't support what we'd asked them to do if we didn't give them a shot. They had convinced us that they could, on paper. But there was a fair amount of risk. There's a big gap between making it look good on paper, and practically applying those principles and being able to do it."

But the team had done its homework. Not only did the team members have the passion and the desire, they were also able to speak the language of finance. They gave consideration to the complete cost of manufacturing and procuring the product, its total landed cost. Major components of the decision were lead time, cycle time, carrying cost of inventory, and communication hassles. Although you can't put a dollar figure on the communication challenges, they certainly play into the whole perspective when you are evaluating this type of a decision.

---

* Drawn from two sources: Steve Overbeck, "Shining a Light on Innovative Utah Companies," *Salt Lake City Tribune*, November 5, 2009 and Karen Wilhelm, "Lean Team Competes with Asia and Wins," Lean Reflections Blog, November 23, 2009.

Exhibit 5.5 Mity-Lite's new chair.

Hales said, "They were very well prepared to make their case. Well-armed with facts and figures, they knew what we would have to spend in order to upgrade facilities. They had a plan as to how they would get there. It turned out they were right! Our team submitted the low bid." He continued, "They've done a fantastic job! They were so motivated to prove that it could be done. I knew that there was some risk, but it was minimized by their level of interest."

So how did Mity-Lite's leadership and front-line employees get on the same page so effectively?

Before taking the helm at Mity-Lite, Hales had seen the results of Lean initiatives in manufacturing facilities around the world. Nevertheless, his view was from an arm's-length perspective, leaving the improvement process to others. He describes one reason for that distance as "Not feeling like I could contribute, I was standing back and watching and saying 'Hey, you guys go do it!'"

Hales began to think differently as he talked to others who had undertaken similar transformations. Then what he heard when he arrived at Mity-Lite gave him his "ah-ha" moment. Employees had already gone through two failed attempts at Lean. They described senior management saying, "Go do that and let us know how it goes." Employees told Hales they didn't feel like they had the commitment of senior management. Management didn't understand why changes had taken place in the facility, sometimes with some capital required.

This brought home to Hales that it's very difficult to go through a transformation if senior management isn't committed and doesn't understand what's going on. He realized that management must help set the metrics, work on the plan, and watch what happens. He said, "I wanted to be very involved, hands-on, with the sleeves rolled up, and to be part of the planning process and execution."

Lean practices are quickly spreading throughout the company. Hales said, "It started out as an isolated group on a small project or two. But it spread so quickly through our facilities that we found people saying, 'Hey, we want to do this. We want to be a part of it.' We're hearing great things, we're seeing big changes. It has moved through our entire facility. And we're hitting on all fronts. There isn't an aspect of our domestic manufacturing any longer that isn't in the middle of a continuous improvement."

Hales said, "Any under-optimized company—and in my mind that is any company that that hasn't gone through a continuous improvement program—has the responsibility to create their own recovery. Rather than waiting on a macroeconomic recovery, we should be creating our own recovery, regardless of what's going on in the economy right now.

"We have doubled our EBITDA in the last twelve months. Every bit of that is due to the continuous improvement and Lean transformation and becoming more efficient. You can do that if you really embrace what continuous improvement means, and you get it implemented accurately. All companies are disadvantaged if they are not focused on this kind of transformational change right now."

ASSESSING THE ENGAGEMENT LEVEL OF INDEPENDENCE EMPLOYEES

Human Resources vice president Kate Beck had continued to work on her report on employee engagement. She decided to get some input directly from employees to see if what people said matched what she interpreted from the surveys she had read (described at the beginning of this chapter). Most employees said they really liked working at Independence; however, there were a handful of employees who were bold enough to share a few concerns:

- A lot of people expressed frustration about customer relationships. The company would develop new products that customers did not seem to want. A lot of the customers were very hard to deal with, for seemingly small amounts of business. Several people thought there might be a correlation between how little business a customer did and how much extra stuff or time they wanted for free from Independence.

- People expressed frustration over how difficult it was to lay out a plan for developing new skills and capabilities. They were willing to create a plan on their own, but the organization seemed to thwart their plans by sending them to seemingly random training sessions, where employees obtained training on things they never used.
- They also wanted leadership to hold people more accountable for non-performers in management, on project teams, and in functional support departments.
- There was a general feeling that a lot of game playing went on between departments, and although no one would directly sabotage a project, support was often passively withheld.
- Although project teams seemed to work okay within Independence, many people felt the organization did not do a very good job of launching teams. The sponsor's role was rarely clear, and the people on the team had varying degrees of commitment and time available to be on a team.
- A smaller group also voiced some concerns over employee versus management compensation. There was a feeling that it was not fair. Employees were doing the bulk of the work on several projects while the overall leader seemed to reap most of the credit and most of the compensation benefits.
- A few people also wanted more participation in determining whom to hire for their teams or departments.

Leadership learned pretty quickly that highly engaged managers tended to have highly engaged employees. It was also pretty obvious that some people were not in the right jobs. They might be good people, but they were not a good fit with their current responsibilities. COO Jack Morel recalled that Jim Collins, in his book *Good to Great*, wrote about the "the right people on the bus, in the right seats" as one of the key principles for moving from average to great levels of performance.

Andy Fletcher said, "Let's set a goal to increase the company's score of highly engaged employees from 33% to 60%." He wanted to get this done in the next 2 years. Lynn Shaunnessey, CFO, responded to Andy, "That is a noble goal, and we can certainly strive to do it, but should we set a more realistic but still stretch target of 40%?" Andy looked around the room and asked what the consensus was. Several people said 40% was too low, because it was only 7% higher than the current baseline. The group also felt the 60% target was too aggressive for a 2-year time frame. The consensus ended up being to go for a 50% level of employee engagement. Everyone realized engaging more people was vital to reduce turnover of valuable employees, and the company needed active engagement to deal with important customer issues.

The meeting finished with a discussion of the customer issues surfaced from the work done under the strategy umbrella. Employees in the Medical Devices Unit were already very excited about moving away from commodity to higher-value-adding products. Lynn had cautioned the Value Team and the related subteams to have some patience. First, everyone seemed to be quickly locking in on specific solutions. Lynn wanted to know their thoughts on these questions:

- How would their proposed changes affect performance measurement?
- What was the impact on roles and responsibilities of existing and any new players?
- What steps had they taken to obtain buy-in and support from people who had changing roles and responsibilities?
- What was the team doing to make cross-functional cooperation more likely in the future?
- What consideration had they given to actions needed to sustain the gains from any changes made?

Each team agreed to put together a baseline metric for how the organization was performing on employee engagement at this point in time. (Metrics are discussed in the next chapter.) They also committed to develop at least three workable solutions in order to maintain a more open mind about business improvement possibilities.

CHAPTER WRAP-UP: DEPLOYMENT ACTIONS TO ENGAGE EMPLOYEES

It is easier to engage employees if the organization has its act together from a strategic perspective. Does leadership clearly understand the value proposition? Have meaningful strategies been put in place and clearly communicated? In part, this means permitting people to redefine the value equation as they gain new knowledge and insight.

Here are a few actions to better engage employees:

1. ***Set a multidimensional, measured baseline.*** One of the biggest challenges to higher levels of employee engagement is unlearning what you think you know. We mentioned this Satchel Paige quote earlier in the book, but it also fits here: "It ain't what you know that gets you in trouble, it's what you think you know, that just ain't so." Before you progress forward on encouraging more engagement, it's probably best to do some type of a baseline assessment to better see your starting point. The leaders at Independence were using several internal study teams to

do this. You could also do an overall assessment of the missing ingredients (Chapter 9). Most organizations perceive their level of employee engagement to be much higher than it actually is. Determine which questions in your employee surveys relate to engagement. Separate those scores to help establish a baseline.

2. ***Communicate a clear value proposition.*** Engage people by having a clear understanding of customer value. Nothing cuts through organizational inside talk faster than having a true understanding of real customer needs. It makes it much easier for functional departments to cooperate when they have a similar view of what the customer needs. There is a direct correlation between non-value-adding work and lack of value clarity. Make sure the customer value proposition is known—and that it's correct. Make sure it is kept fresh, because it does change over time.

3. ***Listen more than you talk.*** Leaders typically begin to buy in to the need to change before the rest of the organization, as they develop the initial change plan. They are ahead of the rest of the organization in understanding the new reality. Leadership should go and listen to employees. What is on their minds, what concerns do they have? Then restate the compelling case for change, taking into account the viewpoint of people in the organization. Perhaps even include views from people in the greater supply chain, beyond the walls of the organization.

4. ***Identify three important behaviors for leadership to change:***
   a. Find someone to give you honest feedback, rather than polite praise and agree on one behavior to change for improving your effectiveness.
   b. Discuss, as a leadership team, actions taken that inhibit employees' ability to do their best work. Ideally employee feedback will guide you to these issues. Identify specific actions and behaviors that need to stop and those that need to start. Incorporate this into the leadership team's improvement plan.
   c. Learn how to do a 'Gemba Walk' to get more in touch with reality (which we'll discuss in Chapter 8 on the Executive Mindset). Use those walks to better understand what is happening in your organization, your function and your work area.

5. ***Create a more open environment.*** The stories from W. L. Gore and others emphasize the need for an open environment where people can safely discuss the real reality, not some fictitious reality that is frozen in time like a leadership "brain cramp." What steps can you take to build an environment of trust and encourage people to challenge assumptions?

6. ***Let go of overcontrol.*** Traditional leadership operates under the belief that leaders can control what is happening and simply tell people what to do. If this was ever a truth, it certainly is not true in today's complex, environment. Focus on effective execution, but make sure leaders have a process thinking mindset as they hold people accountable for results.

7. ***Operate with a few meaningful guiding principles.*** Principles are easy to write, but they only develop deep and real meaning when times are tough. Does your organization repeatedly and daily live according to the principles professed? Do leaders walk the talk, or is the talk cheap? (This subject is discussed in more detail in Chapter 8, on the executive mindset.) The best example of this type of behavior has to be Johnson & Johnson. If you have never read it, check out J&J's "Credo Values." During times of crisis, J&J has lived up to these powerful words. Refer back to the P&G case study in Chapter 4 on customer value for examples of a few principles to guide employee engagement.

8. ***Simplify the need-for-change message***. People hear only what they understand, and they hear it only when they are ready to listen. That is why understanding reality can be such a challenge. When leadership talks about the need to change, are the messages simple enough that a sixth grader can understand them? Are they stated over and over and over again? The simplicity is not intended to be a slam on employees. Simplicity makes certain the message is not overly complex and full of jargon.

9. ***Spend time on employee engagement.*** Leadership needs to spend just as much time making certain the employee side of the business is working as successfully as the product and service side (reference the W. L. Gore case study in this chapter). Eiji Toyoda once said, "A person's life is an accumulation of time. … [E]mployees provide their precious hours of life to the company,

so we have to use it effectively. Otherwise we are wasting their lives." What a profound statement. What steps does leadership need to take to operate this way? The business support systems relate to this thought (and there is more information on this topic in Chapter 7 on process thinking).

10. ***Ensure fairness at all employee levels.*** Do employees feel they are treated fairly relative to the senior leaders in the organization? Or do they perceive leadership as a bunch of greedy pigs, taking all the spoils and showing little concern for everyone else? If greed is rampant in the halls of your organization, we commend you for reading this book, but we have little confidence in your organization's ability to survive.

We want to close this chapter with a very short story about one person who is making a difference in the world by increasing people's self-esteem and giving people more critical thinking/understanding skills.

Greg Mortenson, the author of *Three Cups of Tea* (2006; we encourage you to read this book) is at the center of this story. Greg's mantra is, "One Man's Mission to Promote Peace … One School at a Time." Greg has helped to establish more than 130 schools in Afghanistan and Pakistan. He has focused on rural areas and believes that educating children, especially girls, is key to long-term peace in that region of the world. At a much more rudimentary level, Greg is seeing that children are given an education so they can be more critical thinkers and not subject to demagogues who prey on people's illiteracy.

If you think *you* have problems, think about what Greg is trying to accomplish. This is a very different world from the Independence Enterprise story and the business examples we share in this book. But the core concept—which is to help people become more critical thinkers and to become more active in controlling their destiny—is not that far removed from the message we try to share in these pages.

As you will see in the next chapter, the metrics you use can make it easier or make it more difficult to engage people inside your organization.

Chapter 6

Ingredient 3: Key Metrics
*Focus on the Vital Few,
Meaningful Metrics; Avoid
Drowning in Irrelevant Details*

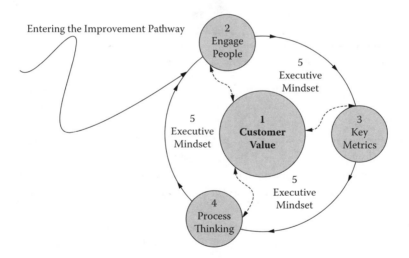

INDEPENDENCE ENTERPRISE EVALUATES ITS
KEY PERFORMANCE METRICS

The leaders at Independence Enterprise felt they were doing a pretty good job on their key metrics. They used red, yellow, green reporting to keep the department and functional managers focused. See Exhibit 6.1 for an example of one of their reports (here, red is shown in a black background, yellow in gray, and green in white).

Leadership met once a week to review performance and provide feedback. Department and functional managers' performance reviews and bonus dollars were

Rating R/Y/G	Process Element	Metric	Previous 3 months history			Performance Criteria	Remarks
			M-2	M-1	M		
			Apr	May	Jun		
Y	On-time delivery	Items Shipped on/ Before O.S.D.	G	Y	Y	G = 1000 Y < 1000 R < 900	Shipping Tickets and Report
Y	On-time delivery	Total Number of Items Shipped	Y	Y	Y	G = 1200 Y < 1100 R < 1000	Shipping Log
G	On-time delivery	% on Time	Y	Y	G	G = 100% Y < 98% R < 95%	Report
G	On-time delivery	Fill Rate % Key Customers	G	G	G	G = 100% Y < 99% R < 98%	Report
R	On-time delivery	Number of Late Orders	G	R	R	G < 10 Y < 20 R < 30	Report
G	Completeness/ accuracy of data	Incorrect Shipments	R	G	G	G = 0 Y > 10 R > 20	Returns Report – Reason Code

Exhibit 6.1   Red (R), yellow (Y), green (G) reporting.

largely based on the results in their areas of responsibility. No one wanted to lose face with the Big 3 (Andy, Jack, and Lynn). COO Jack Morel was famous for dressing down managers at the staff meeting if they failed to meet their objectives. The unwritten philosophy was to operate within ethical boundaries but do whatever it takes to meet your numbers. If that made other departments look bad, that was their problem. The people who made their numbers were the people who got promoted.

CFO Lynn Shaunnessey issued monthly financial reports using traditional full absorption costing. Operations people tried to avoid negative labor variances, and the other functions operated in a similar fashion. The organization had been working to improve two numbers for the last couple of years: on-time delivery and meeting the launch date for new products. They were doing better with on-time delivery; it had jumped from 85% to 93%.

Bill Kennedy from the Finance Department was given leadership responsibility for a cross-functional team to improve the effectiveness of performance metrics inside Independence. The team members started their work by sending a survey to each department head, a random selection of employees, and to members of the leadership team. The employee responses to the survey are shown in Table 6.1.

Table 6.1   Independence Enterprise Surveys Employees Regarding Its Performance Metrics

1. "The people in my Business Unit clearly understand the linkages of the work they do to one or more key organizational strategies or business goals/objectives."

1	2	3	4	5	Score	Mean
10%	25%	40%	15%	10%	Results	2.9

2. "Our unit's performance metrics provide visual, timely, meaningful information for controlling business process results and implementing sustainable gains."

1	2	3	4	5	Score	Mean
15%	35%	35%	5%	5%	Results	2.4

3. "The performance metrics used in our Business Unit help us to fully cooperate with other departments/units."

1	2	3	4	5	Score	Mean
0%	25%	40%	25%	10%	Results	3.2

4. "The performance metrics used by other business units (departments) help them to fully cooperate with our unit (department)."

1	2	3	4	5	Score	Mean
30%	40%	30%	0%	0%	Results	2.0

Legend:
1 = Very Low Effectiveness
5 = Very High Effectiveness

The team was a little surprised by the results of this survey:

- People were evenly split on linkages to the organization's strategic objectives.
- 50% of the respondents felt the metrics used in the department were not visual, timely, or meaningful.
- 75% of respondents thought their metrics helped them to cooperate with other departments.
- At the same time, 70% of the respondents thought other departments did not return the favor; other departmental metrics made their lives difficult.

Lynn Shaunnessey reviewed the results of this assessment with Bill and told him, "Independence cannot launch any additional improvement teams on this topic. Your team needs to figure out how to positively influence the department leads."

Bill's team had more work to do. The team members realized that good metrics would drive more spontaneous, companywide performance improvement, and that wrong or bad metrics would hurt the organization. The team wanted to make certain that it could help the leadership to better understand the difference. Bill's team planned to present a summary of its findings to the leadership team after giving some consideration to the principles and ideas outlined in this chapter.

Getting the Metrics Right: What You Can Learn from Baseball Stats

There is a wonderful baseball sports metaphor to summarize problems with performance metrics. You do not have to understand the game of baseball to appreciate this story. Here is a very simple situation and question.

A pitcher throws a ball. Your only objective is to get to first base. There is no one else on base, and you cannot go any further than first base. You have two choices on how to get to first base. One way is to hit the ball, no one catches it, and you quickly run down to first base, and you are safe. The second way is for the pitcher to throw four bad pitches, which you do not swing at. If that happens, you get a free ticket to first base, called a *walk,* and you trot down to first base.

The question is, "Which way would you rather get to first base? Would you rather hit the ball or take the free ticket (a walk)?"

Most people (more than 95%) say they would prefer to hit the ball. And that is how most major league players feel as well.

But the second question is, "If you are standing on first base, does it make any difference how you got there?" And of course the answer to that question is, "No!" Now let's look at the baseball analogy more closely before we compare it to business metrics. Trust us, the comparison is disturbing—or enlightening—depending on how you look at it.

Michael Lewis's book, *Moneyball* (2003), tells the story of Billy Beane, General Manager of the Oakland Athletics baseball team. Billy discovers work being done by a statistician, who asked the question, "Is there any correlation between the statistics collected by baseball teams and the number of wins that a team could be predicted to win during the course of a season?" At the time (1990s), baseball teams measured performance using the traditional statistics shown in Exhibit 6.2.

No one had really run an analysis to see if those numbers had a high correlation to the number of wins during the course of a season. In terms of *a single game performance*, home runs could result in winning that night; therefore, the metrics traditionally collected were assumed to be good. But it

Hits	Runs	Errors	Home Runs	Triples	Walks	Saves	Left on Base	On Base Percentage
Doubles	Singles	Innings Pitched	Sacrifice Bunts	Ground Outs	Total Bases	Lead Off Hits	Full Counts	Slugging Percentage
Sacrifice Flies	Fly outs	Extra Base Hits	Strikes	Balls	Total At Bats	Complete Games	Pitches Thrown	Fielding Percentage
Team Batting Average	Team Pitching Average	Stolen Bases	Walks to Hits Ratio	Strikes to Balls Ratio	Night vs. Day Record	Won-Loss Record	Strike Outs	

Exhibit 6.2   Traditional baseball statistics.

turns out that traditional metrics did not have a high degree of correlation to winning games *over the course of an entire season.* In that broader view of baseball team performance, the important metrics included these:

- The ratio of walks to hits (in other words, don't swing at bad pitches)
- The number of pitches thrown (for example, if a pitcher throws too many pitches early in the season, he is not as effective at the end of the year)
- Errors per opportunity to make an error (which differed somewhat from the traditional statistic)

Billy Beane used these metrics to create a new mental model for the Oakland Athletics. When the batter got a walk, he was told "Great job!" It was not a mistake by a pitcher; rather the batter did not swing at a bad pitch. The batter earned the walk! With a team payroll at the low end of the league, Oakland was able to consistently make the playoffs at the end of the season and won a world championship. One of the biggest differences between this ball club and the rest of the league was the fact that this team had identified and used *process metrics that were more predictive of winning games.*

Other business models exist in Major League Baseball. The New York Yankees hire the most powerful hitters in baseball, have player salaries higher than most other teams, and have won a number of championships based on talent. But most teams cannot afford the New York Yankees' business model; their local markets are smaller and they could not generate the same number of advertising and TV revenue dollars.

You might now ask, "So how does this story relate to my world?" Here's how: Baseball is a metric-driven industry that's more than 100 years old. If, in a *hundred years,* baseball managers and players hadn't identified the correct metrics in a simple game like baseball, where it is very obvious at the end of day whether you won or lost, then where does that leave the rest of us? How often do people inside a business even know what a *win* is? Many companies and organizations are clueless. People think they are measuring the right factors, but in fact, their metrics could be causing dysfunctional behaviors, and in some instances, actually suboptimize business results.

It took more than 10 years for most other baseball teams to begin using the metrics described in *Moneyball*. In today's world, major league teams commonly look at on-base percentage (a variation of the walks-to-hits ratio) and pitch counts (another key metric). But for more than a 10-year period, teams that got an early start using these metrics had a competitive advantage. Now that most teams use them, a new more refined data set will be needed to create a new competitive edge. Teams actively look for this information, and most now have statisticians on their payroll.

We need to do the same thing in business, in government, and in the not-for-profit worlds. The metrics you have traditionally used may not get you to where you need to go for future success!

Principles to Consider Regarding How Well Your Organization's Key Metrics Reflect Overall Performance

Improving process effectiveness and understanding process capabilities is more important than ever in these tough economic times, when sales are scarce and margins are thin. Metrics should make it easier for cross-functional cooperation; they should not make cooperation more difficult due to competing or conflicting functional department performance requirements.

Metrics inside an organization should help people in a department or functional group know how well they are doing. This is a challenge if the metrics are inwardly and backwardly focused. It is too easy to get caught up in doing activity counts (e.g., how many products did we make?). A department's customer does not care how many products you manufactured; that customer only cares if its needs were met. Ideally, metrics guide the department/function toward a win that has been defined at some level higher than the group being measured. It helps minimize inward focus. *Forward-looking* numbers are better. For example, profit per customer looks *backward* at a lot of history; the number of high-value customers acquired last month is more *forward* focused.

But numbers never tell the total story, so in Chapters 7 and 8 (on process thinking and the executive mindset), we will emphasize the importance of going to the source to see with your own eyes and always, always, always trying to have a process view of the world.

Metrics should be close to the source where action needs to happen, they should be visual, and there should be a clear line of sight in operations where people can easily see how they are progressing against customer commitments. The further up inside the organization a metric has to go before a corrective action is taken, the less effective it is in facilitating high-performance business operations.

From a management perspective, metrics typically serve one of two purposes:

1. *Identify actual and potential problems.* This requires some detective work. Just because you *can* measure something does not mean that you *should*. Gather some evidence of the issue(s) you are trying to address. This is rarely just one thing. Simple tools like asking "Why?" five times can sometimes reveal deeper, more meaningful issues rather than just the symptomatic surface issues that first come to mind. Once you have a tentative metric, ask the following questions:
   a. If this metric goes up or down, would that drive certain actions?
   b. Does this seem appropriate?
   c. Is the implied action unambiguous, or could people have significantly different interpretations of what to do?
2. *Understand performance levels.* Metrics can facilitate:
   a. *Evaluating* how well we are doing
   b. *Controlling* how much of something is OK
   c. *Learning* how or what needs to be done better
   d. *Motivating* to take action
   e. *Comparing* performance levels
   f. *Obtaining feedback* and asking are we getting better; was the gain sustained?

True North Performance Metrics

When people reference Toyota and performance measurement, they often use the expression "True North." Like most things at Toyota, True North has multiple meanings. A basic definition is *a common direction*. It certainly can help define what winning means. If you apply a time dimension to the expression, it can also include a longer-term view of where you are headed and what you need to accomplish moving forward. Probing still further, it can begin to incorporate stretch performance targets.

Businesses are complex places with many variables. If senior managers try to manage with too low a level of detail, they miss trade-offs that take place inside the business and lose sight of overall process performance, which is the only thing customers care about. The temptation to optimize metrics focused on an isolated part of the process is too great to have that level of detail on high-level scorecards. Senior leaders need to focus on True North–type metrics that are important, including customer value, real costs (versus allocated costs), total cycle time, on-time delivery, productivity, quality and safety (in a manufacturing plant), and people development. It's important to improve these performance indicators without making any of the others suffer.

Although the metrics will certainly differ for various industries, there are some core concepts that apply to most. True North metrics for your organization should incorporate some form of the elements described in the following sections.

Measuring Customer Value. As discussed in Chapter 4, this pertains to how to measure your value engine. The 80/20 Rule helps you to find your Mojo 20 (i.e., your key customers). Value is why this group buys from you. However the organization chooses its value targets, it should be done through the eyes of those key customers. Many organizations only seem to share tactical customer metrics (e.g., on-time delivery) at lower levels. If you desire people to better understand value from a customer's perspective, share something about value: market share for key markets, proposal win rates, and so on. How do you know if you are winning the competitive challenges in the marketplace? Share that information, and use it as an improvement challenge for further progress.

Measuring People Development. As discussed in Chapter 5, this pertains to the importance of measuring employee engagement and their passion for the business. An indirect measure of engagement is how many Kaizen or rapid-improvement teams people have participated in. Note: people generally need to participate on at least three process-improvement teams before their perception of how improvement happens begins to change. The first time they mostly learn the tools. Subsequent practice helps them to see the amount of change possible. Everyone on the senior executive team should participate on at least three improvement endeavors: this will go a long way in helping them learn to see the magnitude of improvement that is possible. So in your first and second year of an improvement endeavor, a metric might be executive participation. The number of improvement ideas submitted and implemented by employees can also be useful, if it is not simply an activity count.

Measuring Time or Velocity. This is one of the most powerful metrics you can use. Lead time is a key metric that measures the time from the beginning point of a process to the completion of a finished output. This is still a very strong competitive differentiator and one of the best metrics you can use for driving out waste because with a focus on continuously reducing overall process lead time, we are constantly asking what portions of it add value and which do not. Over time, we find ways to drive out the waste steps and streamline the rest. That makes companies with a focus on lead time *always faster* in serving customer demands, *usually cheaper* because waste costs have been wrung out, and *often better* because there is an undistracted focus on the remaining value-adding steps that meet the customer requirements. (Several time-related metrics are discussed in Chapter 7 on process thinking.)

Measuring Real Cost. Most organizations measure *allocated* costs, not real cost. (We touch base on this concept further in a couple of places: target costing and Lean accounting are discussed later in this chapter, and total cost is discussed in Chapter 7 on process thinking.)

Bill Waddell* has a great description of cost that we paraphrase slightly here: The only meaningful measurement of *real* cost is on a cash basis. All money spent on manufacturing must be summarized, and the total compared to the previous period—not to a flexible budget or a plan. What matters is whether the *real* cash spent on manufacturing was more or less than it was in the previous period. It is important that this cost figure is exclusive of all allocations, and does not exclude sales, general, and administrative expenses.

The only exceptions are that major capital investment spending is excluded, and expenses are adjusted for accounts receivable and payable. Although these amounts must be added back in to create a total Lean-accounting-based income statement, manufacturing performance should be measured as if payment were made at the time materials and services were delivered, and payments were collected at the time finished goods were shipped to an outside customer.† Significant fluctuations in raw material costs

* Lean consultant and co-author of *Rebirth of American Industry* (Vancouver, WA: PCS Press, 2005).
† Bill Waddell, "Five Golden Metrics," 2009. Available at http://www.sme.org/cgi-bin/get-newsletter. pl?LEAN&20061010&2.

could cause an adjustment to this number, and it would need a link to sales volumes if they are changing significantly.

To further understand costs, you may want to look at two numbers that have a very high correlation to costs: productivity and value-added time. Cost, for the most part, is an estimate, so it should be supplemented with reality whenever possible. So let's take a closer look at measuring productivity and value-added time.

Measuring Productivity. This still does not get sufficient attention. All too often, this degenerates into an activity metric. At the most basic level, this is an inputs-to-outputs metric—that is, how much went in versus how much came out. In reality, this is the primary metric of wealth creation. How fast and how well are you doing it? Look at it from the perspective of total inputs (capital, labor, and commodities), not just people. Productivity is something the customer cares about from a cost (price) standpoint, not just cranking things faster into inventory. If you can double your productivity, you decrease your cost by 50%. You need to develop a meaningful number for your organization. This will be easier to do for an individual value stream, and more difficult for multiple value streams and staff support departments.

Normally, the input part of the productivity equation is dollars or hours worked. For example, use hours even at a company level (actual hours for production on time-clock employees and 40 hours assumed for salaried employees), then compare the hours input to either units or dollar sales output. At lower levels of business, the units metric works well; at higher levels, you usually end up measuring dollars due to product mix issues (i.e., simple, low-cost orders mixed in the same production flow with complex, high-cost orders). If using sales dollars for the output metric, you should adjust for inflation in prices or deflation in prices, as these are not productivity changes. Again, an adjustment may also be necessary for major capital investments or automation expenditures. If they are intended to improve productivity, they should be part of the input resources.

Senior managers do not spend enough time trying to understand how to measure productivity. And few organizations set serious targets for productivity improvement. "Yet productivity is the single major controllable cost driver that can determine long-term competitive advantage."* Along with that statement, Art Byrne, retired CEO of Wiremold, said, "Productivity = Wealth."

---

* George Koenigsaecker, *Leading the Lean Enterprise Transformation,* (Boca Raton, FL: CRC Press, 2009).

Productivity is a key economic factor in terms of fighting inflation, staying competitive on a global basis, and promoting business growth. This is what the Toyota Motor Company has done so well year after year. In order to be competitive, all organizations need to work with an ongoing sense of renewal, where they *expect* to continuously find ways to produce more value with less input cost, and thereby outdistance the competitors.

Measuring Value-Added Time. This is a time- and cost-related metric, so it could reside in either category. Most organizations look at value-added versus non-value-added time when examining a process. Most do not use it as a monthly metric. Value-added times can help leaders learn to better see waste. Value-added versus non-value-added time should be a general metric, measured on a monthly or at least quarterly basis. Value-added time is typically 5 to 15% of overall process lead time. If the actual value-added time were posted monthly for key processes, it would help people observing the process realize how far short of the ideal they fall. An ideal process would be 100% value-added time; we hope to see one of those someday.

After writing the above paragraph, we noticed that Bill Waddell talked about the same subject in his Evolving Excellence blog. Here is what Bill had to say on this subject.

> Nevertheless, there is one number—a percentage really—that goes a long way toward quantifying whether the business is getting leaner or not. It is the measure of value-added expenses to total expenses. If the business spent $20,000, for instance, and $12,000 of it was on value-adding things while the rest was on management, supervision, material handling, inspection, and generally pushing paper around, the Lean ratio would be 60%; or it could be expressed as 3:2 if you like looking at numbers that way better.
>
> I like the percentage approach better because it is easy to graph and track on a month-to-month and year-to-year basis to see if the business is actually making progress toward the elimination of waste. Note that it is a useless benchmarking tool. The fact that one company may have a 60% ratio while another has a 45% is meaningless. All that matters is that the 60% company becomes a 61% company then a 62% company and so forth.
>
> It seems pretty straightforward. The objective is to continually improve the percentage of money spent on useful endeavors—making sure more of it is going to things customers perceive to be of value and worth paying for, and less of it to waste. The rub is

that very few companies really know what adds value and what does not, as important as it is to know. One of the most important, interesting, and probably contentious discussions you and your management team can have is the one needed to build consensus on defining value adding.*

Measuring Quality. Although the quality gap is perhaps not quite as big as it used to be, it is still a major determining factor of customer loyalty. There was a wonderful study published in 1987 by Bradley Gale and Robert Buzzell,[†] who pointed out the linkages between quality, market share, and profitability. It is still meaningful and often mentioned as a seminal work in business strategy. There is a proven link between quality and profits. For your business, how can you measure external and internal quality? Senior leaders should primarily be looking at the external perspective. Work cell, department or value-stream levels should have internal quality metrics. Like most things in life, your quality is probably not nearly as good as you think it is. How can you better understand your real quality levels and focus improvement on this important differentiator?

In most industries, if you evaluate the top five competitors, there is almost always a perception in the majority of customers' eyes that one or two have much better quality than the others, and the bottom few are not perceived as all that great, so they usually have to give away margin dollars in lower pricing to maintain market share. For that reason alone, leadership should maintain a vigilant focus on quality, especially in the service industry. However, the profit impacts on quality are broader than they are on sales margins, as illustrated in the following thoughts.

There has been some interesting research done over the years on quality issues with customers. It has been verified with work done by the Washington D.C.–based nonprofit organization, Technical Assistance Research Program (TARP).

Most customers do not complain to an offending supplier. However, they do talk a lot to other potential customers. So for every one complaint you do receive, you do *not* receive a complaint from 7 to 9 other customers, who simply took their business elsewhere.

---

* Bill Waddell, "The Lean Ratio, " Evolving Excellence blog, December 16, 2009.
† Robert D. Buzzell and Bradley T. Gale, *The PIMS Principles: Linking Strategy to Performance* (New York: Free Press, 1987).

Now, how do these numbers play out? Let's assume you have 1,000 customers and 1% of them are unhappy with something your organization did, but they didn't send you a complaint. The numbers play out like this:

- You have 1,000 customers.
- Ten of them (i.e., 1%) complained to the offending organization.
- Ninety others did not complain (this corresponds to the previous information that for every person who does complain, 7 to 9 don't. In this case, it's 10 who do and 90 who don't); however, *90%* of the people told 7 other people about their issue.
- Therefore, 630 potential customers (90 x 7) heard about a quality issue with your company.
- Ten percent of the people who did *not* complain actually passed along their gripe to 20 other people or potential customers. To keep this simple, we will simply say this is 9 people.
- Therefore, 180 (9 x 20, above) additional potential customers heard from the heavy complainers.
- In total, roughly *810 potential customers* (630 + 180) heard about quality problems pertaining to your organization's products or services, even when you only have a complaint rate of 1% of 1,000 customers.

If we wanted to maximize the statistics from this research, the ultimate number of people that hear about a complaint actually *exceeds* the size of the customer base. But based on our experiences and other studies, the 810 is a reasonable approximation. Whatever the exact number is, this is still a very big number. And the organization only officially received 10 complaints.

The next ugly aspect of this problem was dubbed, "the Hundredth Monkey Syndrome" by Chuck Chakrapani in his article, "Why Is Management Always the Last to Know?"* If a critical mass of customers begins to believe something, the word spreads and many customers then believe it, even though they have no personal experience with the situation. This is actually a problem for the traditional U.S. automotive manufacturers. In the not-too-distant past, the quality difference between a U.S. manufactured car and a car made in Asia or Europe was significant: in short, the cars made outside the United States were higher quality. Today, that gap is very small, almost nonexistent, yet the perception lives on that Japanese (and even some European) cars are

---

* *Professional Marketing Research Society Magazine*, November, 1990 (http://www.chuckchakrapani. com/Articles/PDF/90110656Chakrapani.pdf)

much higher quality. What this reveals is that if you sink that low in your customers' eyes, that perception is very difficult to overcome. A bad reputation has a long life—even beyond when the problem may have been corrected.

This is why *quality* is still a very important metric!

True North metrics need to go deep inside your organization. Most of those metrics are easy to measure as a finished result for the overall business. But what does quality look like for Sales or for the IT Department? How important is quality in the work done by those functional departments for the other people they need to play with to get work done? Going deep with the previous metrics is what makes them True North. They drive behaviors at multiple levels of an enterprise. Defining what a win means in your organization then gives you an opportunity to run a correlation analysis and better align your *upstream* operating process management metrics with increasing your number of *downstream* business results wins. Just like our baseball story.

How Do Goals Fit into Performance Metrics?

If the above classifications are True North metrics, where do goals fit in? Most organizations do not set their goals nearly high enough. The first rule of thumb is: If it is bad, cut it in half; if it is good, double it! Level 5 organizations are multiples better than Level 3—for example:

- From a quality perspective, the multiple might be a 10:1 ratio.
- From a productivity perspective, Level 5 companies are 400% more productive than Level 3.

If leaders don't realize that level of improvement is possible, it is easy to become complacent and to accept incremental levels of performance improvement. If you scored less than two stars on the simple assessment in Chapter 1 (Exhibit 1.5), you are average, and that magnitude of improvement is realistically possible for your organization. You should strive for stretch goals in overall business results (growth, return on investment, etc.), but to get there, you need to focus on specific customer values and upstream process capabilities, not just a simple business results number (downstream) pulled out of the air.

George Koenigsaecker was a pioneer in the adoption of the Lean methods often called the Toyota Production System at several companies in the United States. He is also the retired president of Jake Brake (Danaher),

HON Industries, and a consultant, mentor, and/or board member for several organizations that are undergoing Lean transformations. George very much understands how Level 4 and 5 companies operate. In his new book, *Leading the Lean Enterprise Transformation*, he states, "I have yet to meet an executive who comes into a Lean transformation thinking that it will be possible to increase the organization's productivity by fourfold, reduce quality errors by 99%, or reduce lead time by 95%. Yet those are the documented norms for a true enterprise transformation."*

George also cites a number of transformational statistics:

- Improve inventory turnover by 3 to 30 times.
- Reduce lead time by 95%.
- Increase productivity by four times (400% increase).

Furthermore, George points out the relationship between True North metrics and financial performance, when he shares the results of a firm that had been walking the Lean transformation pathway for 7 years:

- Recordable accident rate: decreased by 81%
- Warranty costs: decreased by 69%
- Complete and on-time delivery: improved from 84 to 98%
- Inventory turnover: improved by 171%
- Sales per square foot of space: improved 131%
- Operating income percentage: increased 221%
- Return on assets: improved 237%
- Cash flow: improved 519%

So transformation is indeed possible. Leadership and the associates who work for an organization must learn to see the waste. Once people can see it, they can do something about it.

The actual metrics people use will differ by industry and by your competitive situation. Paul O'Neill, former CEO of Alcoa, used safety as a key employee development metric to drive change and more critical thinking. O'Neill was notified within 24 hours whenever a safety violation took place, anywhere in the world. You might guess that this caused a lot of executives to look a lot more closely at what was happening in the world of safety. For

---

* George Koenigsaecker, *Leading the Lean Enterprise Transformation*, Boca Raton, FL: CRC Press, 2009 p. 37.

an extended period of time, Alcoa was much more diligent in improving employee safety than most of its competitors, and it did help people focus on the *process* of safety.

Interestingly, when O'Neill became secretary of the U.S. Treasury, he again tried to use safety as a key metric. However, *in a service business, it bombed completely!* He did not adequately adjust to the new environment and the needs of that organization.

Therefore, you need to find competitive differentiators for *your* business. There may be some industry-specific metrics where you need to perform well, but for the most part, if everyone else is looking at the same metric, it will not differentiate your business. For example, many large corporations look at some variation of return on investment (ROI), perhaps economic value-added, total return on capital employed, and so on. Normally, these metrics will not foster a competitive advantage; they are an after-the-fact measure of how well you did. You need to identify True North metrics that will have a positive influence on those important results. By the time you know your ROI, it is too late to act! We make several suggestions in this chapter on where you should look for upstream metrics that will positively influence these important indicators of effective results.

Metrics can drive both positive and negative behaviors inside an organization. Because it is simpler to point out something that is ugly and harder to create something elegant, let's look at the ugly side of metrics.

The Ugly Side of Performance Metrics

Most organizations do several things that are supposed to provide focus, but the results can be negative when applied without deep thought about the cause-and-effect relationships involved:

1. They have a set of business strategies they hope to accomplish, but (as discussed in Chapter 4 on customer value) these strategies are typically not crisp or clearly defined. Key objectives and strategies often exceed more than thirty items, so attention is dispersed broadly. Lacking focus on the important few, it's likely that the most important objectives will be missed.

2. They have some type of management by objective, where each department has a set of performance goals (perhaps linked to a budget

process). Each department's objectives are independent of other organizational departments. A unifying set of metrics and objectives does not exist, so each functional silo attempts to optimize its own numbers and the organization as a whole suffers from a lack of coordinated effort.

3. They have a long list of things that are either broken or in need of improvement. Working them piecemeal, one at a time is very inefficient, so the list grows, while key overall process improvement opportunities continue to be unaddressed.

And there may be other priority/alignment actions in addition to those mentioned previously, where leadership says, "These are important things to do." The end result is that it is not easy to decide which to do first and which to put aside. The multiple actions taken to provide clarity and provide focus actually send conflicting messages: "We want to do it all." So people fall back to doing what makes them look good, because they are not certain about higher-level priorities.

If we simply react to a number, without understanding the reason behind that number, we can unintentionally make a situation worse rather than better by doing the wrong thing. In today's stressed economy, organizations should *not* be reducing costs in a traditional way. For example, a 10% across-the-board cost reduction may sound reasonable, but that approach undermines an organization's value engine and misses a golden opportunity to prune unnecessary legacy costs that get funded year after year in good times. An organization may need to reduce costs by 10% overall, but how you should get there is to whack away at costs for the Ugly 50 and perhaps even increase investment for your Mojo 20. Don't try to avoid conflict by pursuing the simple-minded path of universal cuts. Better information is needed to make decisions for future competitive advantage.

Performance measures should obviously measure the right things and foster appropriate behaviors, but many metrics do not do this. For example, in our baseball story (at the beginning of this chapter), if hitters are only rewarded when they get hits, they will swing at bad pitches that are close to, but not over, the plate. As a result, they are more likely to strike out, thus statistically decreasing the team's opportunity to win. Ask yourself if any of *your* organization's metrics foster those types of behaviors? *Possibly!*

It is very easy to slip in this arena. For example, a major global manufacturer of heavy capital equipment has adopted the Toyota Production System as a key goal. It has mastered many of the tools in its Lean activities. However, one of the eight classic wastes is overproduction. In the words of a senior executive from this company, "Unfortunately, while we claim the principle 'don't overproduce,' we measure efficiency in terms of machine base hours, and that is a critical metric for our production personnel. In order to meet the goal for this metric, they continually overproduce parts to keep their base hours up. In this case, the metrics clearly don't match the intended cultural change and the metric 'trumps' the cultural change."

Metrics should guide us to learn better ways to serve customers and improve returns to shareholders. Unfortunately, the way many organizations deploy metrics, this does not happen. The previous example is a classic case of trying to do the right thing with an improvement initiative, but getting held back by traditional patterns of behavior focused on optimizing functional areas of responsibility instead of the whole. The theory is that if every functional department optimized its performance, customers would be served well, and financial performance would be great. Unfortunately, you cannot optimize the component parts and have harmony across the whole. Yet that does not stop organizations from managing this way.

These types of inconsistencies happen all of the time inside organizations, large and small. It is another factor that traps so many at an average Level 3 of improvement maturity, relative to their industry, and inhibits a true transformation to Level 4.

The Month-End Panic

Here's another simple example: In order to make their numbers, salespeople push to get sales made before the end of the quarter. A gigantic load of orders is handed off to manufacturing to make the product. We saw one example where more than 25% of sales were being manufactured and shipped in the last two weeks of a quarter. Uneven order flows of that magnitude cause expensive chaos in operations. Do any of your metrics cause friction between functional departments? *If the answer is yes, you need to do something more to provide focus, something more to tell people what is happening across the business!*

Metrics cause people to behave in certain ways. For example, ask yourself these questions about how your organization responds to performance results:

■ If the numbers look good, is this person a hero? That certainly drives people to make their area of responsibility look good.

- Do you punish people who have bad metrics? If so, you should realize that punishment might encourage people to *hide* problems and hope that they can fix them later, instead of bringing problems quickly to light so they can be addressed.
- Do *any* of your metrics encourage heroic behavior or reluctance to spotlight problems? *Possibly!*

The Purpose and Use of Metrics

A famous quote attributed to numerous people runs along the lines of "What gets measured is what gets done."* A corollary to that expression could be, "What gets measured is what gets reported." Dr. W. Edwards Deming[†] said many things about measurement in numerous presentations, and two of his quotes influenced our thinking about performance measurement:

1. 95% of all troubles in an organization are the result of the system (processes) and only 5% are the fault of people, and
2. Over 97% of the circumstances that affect an organization's results are immeasurable, and a disproportionate amount of management's time is spent on the 3%.

If you are a control-type person (and most of us in leadership positions have this trait to some degree), it's pleasant to think that you could measure your way to greatness. But if you look at the second part of Deming's quote, and if you look at the reality of most measurement systems, greatness is not a likely outcome of the performance measurement system. GE probably does a better job on performance metrics than anyone else in the word, and it is a very good company, but even mighty GE is struggling to continue its high levels of success.

In this book, we have described three critical factors to successful performance improvement:

1. How well your organization delivers *value to your customers* (as *they* identify what is valuable to *them*)
   a. The 80/20 Rule
   b. Net Promoter Score (loyalty metric)
   c. Target costs

---

* Paraphrasing of a quote from William Thomson (Lord Kelvin), 1891.
[†] W. Edwards Deming, *Out of the Crisis*, MIT Press, 1986.

2. How well your *employees are engaged* in their work and the organization as a whole, and
3. Process thinking metrics
   a. Process capability
   b. Variation (common and special causes)
   c. Leading and lagging indicators (correlation analysis)

So if you plan to improve the way you measure performance, perhaps these are three places to focus. Let's take a closer look at each from a metrics point of view.

Customer Value and the 80/20 Rule

In Chapter 4 on this topic, we shared several thoughts about customer value. Essentially, we believe that your customers should be segmented into several groups:

- Key 20% of customers who represent 80% of profits (Mojo 20 or the Vital Few)
- The 50% of customers who represent 5% of profits (the Ugly 50)
- Future value customers

You had better know what is happening with those three groups and have metrics for each set. The Mojo 20 customers should be the focal point for innovation and improvement activities. In contrast, the Ugly 50 cause complexity in your business, distract resources from taking care of the most valuable customers, and take time away from searching for a few new key customers.

Thinking based on the 80/20 Rule is all about focusing on the important few out of the trivial many elements of your business. The same 80/20 thinking can be applied to the products and services you sell. It works the same way as 80% of your profits typically come from 20% of the things you sell. Determine a reasonable approximation of profitability, but don't use standard costs for this analysis if you are a manufacturing company. The overhead allocations are very likely to provide a misleading picture of reality. And when you bury your overhead costs inside a product as an allocation, it makes it more difficult to manage those costs. It's much better to look at sales minus direct product cost and compare that contribution margin to the overhead that needs to be covered. You will work much harder to reduce overhead cost with that perspective. Look at where the overhead is really used. You do *not* need a monthly report to figure this out, and it will not change that much from year to year. Periodically sit down and have someone do this analysis (every 2 to 3 years). (We touch on the topic of Lean accounting near the end of this chapter.)

When you compare the company's performance to your industry, if you are not in the top 20% (and obviously most companies are not), what can you learn from the top performers? Where can you use metrics to help close the gap between your desired performance and today's reality? If you are a small company, modify this thinking to your key customer groups:

■ Are you in the top 20% for the customers you serve? Do they go to you before they go to a competitor?
■ Can you actively engage employees in developing metrics to gain their ownership and buy-in?

And finally, take the same 80/20 concept that has long been used in the quality movement,* and look at your sales force: 20% of your salespeople, or sales distributors, or sales territories most likely generate 80% of your profits. In this instance, you first want to take a process perspective:

■ What are the key 20% of salespeople (or sales territories) doing differently from the rest of the pack?
■ To what extent are some salespeople or sales distributors caught in a process trap, where they are largely at the mercy of the system?

Then, you need to analyze the data *before you take any action*. For example, a bank looked at checking and savings accounts and realized it had many small-balance accounts. A senior executive ordered all of the accounts with a balance under $300 to be closed. What the bank did not realize was that most of those accounts belonged to the children of people who had larger balances in other accounts. Many of them were so upset with the bank's handling of their children's accounts that they switched their business elsewhere.

In other words, you never want to *automatically* react to these numbers! But when you dig into the Ugly 50, you are going to find many problematic customers, problematic products and services, and problematic activities. The Ugly 50 increases complexity and increases overhead costs. Once you have segmented this group, dig in to determine how to simplify your life and your

---

* Dr. Joseph Juran actually coined the phrase "the vital few."

organization; wave the magic wand and make the ugliest of the ugly disappear! Use the overhead resources freed from this complexity to work innovation and growth opportunities. Focus sales activities on the key customer groups. You may find that some people cannot make the change. You must address those issues, or you will find that the ugly you thought you eliminated is reborn.

Customer Value and the Net Promoter Score

There are also steps to take on the customer loyalty side. Many organizations have frequent buyer tracking, and a reasonable tracking program can provide very useful information. General Electric has carried this a step further using a formula called the Net Promoter Score (NPS). The formula is based on a book by Fred Reichheld entitled *The Ultimate Question* (2006). The research has been around for some time. In the 1980s, research was published that showed unhappy customers were ten times more likely to complain to another person about poor products or service than happy customers were to tell another person how pleased they were. At a leadership team meeting in 2006, Jeff Immelt, CEO of GE, said, "NPS is the best formula I have seen. … and I want to get it on our scoreboard."

Determine your Net Promoter Score. Reichheld's key customer question is, "How likely are you to recommend [*company name*] to a friend or colleague?" Customers respond with a 0–10 point rating, with 10 being extremely likely to recommend. You then create three categories of customer loyalty based on the scores, which is shown in Exhibit 6.3 and explained below:

- Promoters (scores 9–10) are loyal enthusiasts who will keep buying and will refer others.
- Passives (scores 7–8) are satisfied but unenthusiastic and will consider competitive offerings (they don't count in this scoring).
- Detractors (scores 0–6) are not satisfied and feel no loyalty to your company.

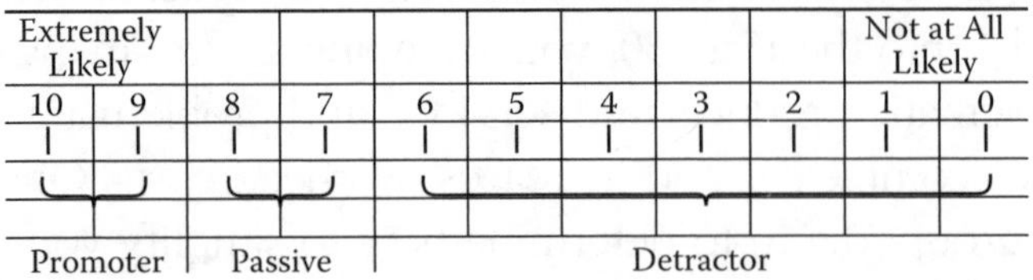

Exhibit 6.3 Net promoter score.

Your Net Promoter Score = %Promoters − %Detractors

The logic behind the NPS calculation is that promoters will keep buying and referring others to fuel your growth, while detractors damage your reputation and impede growth through negative word-of-mouth.

For example, if your promoter score is 55% and your detractor score (percentage of people who rate your organization lower than a 7) is 25%, your NPS = 30%. A score of 50% or higher is considered a good score. A world-class score would be in the 70 to 80% range. However, most organizations score less than 15%!

When you do the customer survey, don't just ask one NPS question. Formulate up to six additional supporting questions to help determine where to focus your attention for improving customer loyalty and NPS performance. Keep it simple; don't ask too many questions.

While the score is interesting, it's more important what you do *after* you receive the feedback. Call customers that rated you 9 and 10 and find out why they would refer your organization to someone else. What strengths can you use and do more of it? You should also call your detractors, because they obviously represent improvement opportunities. If you did this survey only for your key 20%, imagine the importance of this feedback.

At the same time, don't be a pest with these surveys. You may love the surveys you get from automotive companies and automotive dealerships, but we tend to find them annoying, largely because we don't believe any corrective actions are going to take place as a result of the feedback we provide. When we have seen organizations share the results of their surveys with their customers and share the actions they plan to take as a result of the feedback, their survey response rates have climbed significantly higher. This is especially true in business-to-business surveys.

Keep in mind that if the ratings are not confidential, you may bias people to respond more favorably. The NPS ratings may hold truer for consumer ratings than for business-to-business ratings. In the latter situation, an organization is typically selling multiple products and services, so customers may feel one way about product/service x and another way about product/service y. Business-to-business relationships also frequently have multiple people within a customer's organization. Some of those folks may be promoters and others detractors. These problems are one of the reasons NPS effectiveness has been challenged. But the same problems exist to some degree with all surveys. And although we think Reichheld's premise that this is the ultimate question is a tad presumptuous, we still think it is useful information to know.

The one fact that holds true is that NPS is a very high-level survey; not detailed enough to discern the root cause factors. Therefore, you must dig more deeply to gain meaningful insight. There is a great quote from Alan Lafley, former CEO of Procter and Gamble, "You need to know who your consumers are—intimately! You need to understand not just their habits and practices but their needs and wants, including those they can't articulate. Then you've got to delight them with your brands and your products."* In your survey questions and follow-up homework, this is what you are seeking to learn. Then put metrics in place based on what you learn that will help your organization drive in the appropriate direction.

Customer Value and Target Costs

The target cost formula is a different way of thinking model. It goes to the core of customer value first and asks, "What would the customer be willing to pay?" Then it considers the profit percentage necessary to justify providing the product or service. Target costs are calculated by a formula that looks so simple that people underestimate the power of the concept:

Estimated Market Price – Required Profit Margin = Targeted Cost

People equate the above to this formula:

Costs + Required Profit Margin = Sales Price.

But they are two very different ways of thinking. The latter formula is traditional *cost plus* pricing. Costs in the latter example include, as a given, all the wasteful activities that occur inside an organization (e.g., scrap, looking for things, inspection, rework, underutilization of people's ability to improve, etc.). Businesses that have sold to governments around the world have used that formula, as did many companies in the private sector.

In contrast, selling price minus the profit percentage leaves a targeted cost. Total cost to make the product must be less than that target for a company to make an adequate, sustainable return on invested capital. Cost will typically be lower following this model because the business

---

* Ram Charan, *What the Customer Wants You to Know*, Penguin Books, 2007.

proposition starts out with the customer value in mind rather than accepting the inherent wastes in a legacy production process. And it's a more realistic customer-oriented and globally competitive way of pricing rather than inside-the-business "cost plus" thinking. Target costs analysis typically includes a supply-chain view. Typical steps include:

■ Conduct a value engineering/value analysis of all product component parts (e.g., quality function deployment [QFD] methods).
■ Design for manufacturability (DFM) methods—make sure the production, preparation, and process take into account manufacturing constraints.
■ Apply Lean tools and concepts to the production process before they are hard-wired in place and difficult to change.
■ Focus on cross-functional and supply-chain handoffs to make certain they maximize value flow.

Analytical work is typically done by some type of cross-functional team with knowledge of current practices and process issues, which is open to finding new methods. Target cost is typically applied to new product development, but it can also be used to redesign an existing process to meet new target cost requirements as a market evolves.

In the world of new product development, target cost is important to do well, because 70 to 80% of a product's life-cycle cost is determined in the design stage. It is much easier (though we're not saying it's easy) to take cost out in the design stage than it is to try to reduce cost after the design is completed. If design engineers focus only on traditional form, fit, and function, and do not look at cost until late in the design stage, the major opportunity for reducing costs is lost. Too much cost is locked in after the design is complete. And targeted cost should be a holistic view covering the complete value chain: suppliers, internal operations, service providers, distribution, and customers.

For example, Boeing pulled significant cost dollars out of its airplanes when the company started to share with its customers how much requested custom features cost. Prior to that, Boeing gave them a total cost of the plane. Once customers could see how much unique items cost (which made no real difference to the airline's customers), they adopted more standardized products.*

---

* An article by Swenson, Ansari, Bell, and Kim titled, "Best Practices in Target Costing" provides useful information and a few company examples.

Engage People Metrics

The W. L. Gore case study (in Chapter 5) describes a leadership effectiveness survey. Studies have shown that engaged leaders are more likely to have engaged employees. Engaged employees are also more likely to go the extra mile for the organization and its customers, so it's important to gain useful insights about the levels of engagement.

Employee engagement differs from employee satisfaction. The intention of measuring engagement is to measure something more meaningful, very similar to organizations moving from customer satisfaction to customer loyalty metrics as a more insightful metric. There is not universal agreement on what engagement means. But we can probably break it down in a few key components.

While satisfaction is certainly a component of engagement, so are many other things: trust, company pride, feeling valued, commitment, and feeling your work is meaningful or relevant. Given those elements, it's easier to see how someone could be satisfied, but not engaged. Satisfaction is an interesting, too often inert, *attitude*. But employee engagement—like customer loyalty—indicates a *behavior* set that's valuable to both parties.

One way to look at employee engagement is to measure the four key elements shown in Table 6.2.

This will probably need to be done through some type of employee survey. Most engagement surveys cover the first three elements, although element 3 is worded differently. Element 4 does not seem to be covered in most engagement surveys we reviewed, but it seems critical to being fully engaged.

Metrics that should have a direct favorable correlation to high levels of employee engagement include:

- Customer satisfaction and Element loyalty
- Absenteeism and employee turnover
- Quality and safety
- Employee referrals of new employees

And there are others. Work by Hewitt Associates,* a global human resources consultancy, found that companies in which at least 60% of the workforce was engaged showed an impressive average total shareholder return of 20.2% between 1999 and 2003. This was significantly higher than the average results generated from companies with a less engaged workforce. (That's also very similar to the information from Gallup discussed in Chapter 5.)

---

* Best Employers Setting the Baseline," *Hewitt Quarterly Asia/Pacific*, Volume 7, Issue 1, 2009.

Table 6.2   Employee Engagement Questions

	Element	Example
1	Commitment	At my company I feel a strong sense of belonging.
2	Ownership	I understand the company's strategic direction and believe this is an important thing to do.
3	Sense of Purpose	My work is meaningful and important to the company's success.
4	Trust	If the company is doing something I don't agree with or I see a better way, I am comfortable expressing the thought.

The most important aspect of good survey practices is that once your survey results are in, you share them with employees. You don't want your associates thinking their concerns are falling into a "black hole." Go beyond sharing and engage employees in a *dialogue* about the survey responses so they can help determine the causes of the issues raised.

Surveys alone rarely provide the level of detail necessary for impactful action. For example, you may find out that your employees feel they are not appropriately recognized for their work, but you won't know what specific actions cause this impression until you engage them in a dialogue. We are not talking about PowerPoint slides with too many bullet points, where management talks *to* employees. You need to talk *with* your associates, which means asking a question and then listening.

Obviously, to maintain credibility, you actually need to do something about their key concerns. Communication is critical here; it's not enough to simply act on those concerns; be direct and tell them that the reason you're taking these steps is based on their input from the survey: "You said *this* was a concern, so we're doing *this*."

Compelling research shows that surveying employees and *not* following up (by sharing, listening, and acting) has a *negative* impact on engagement. In other words, you'd be better off not surveying them at all.

Finally, look at your talented employees. Do you keep the ones you want to stay without having to do something ridiculous? There is quite a bit of work being done on network connections and social networking. We have not done enough in this arena to have an opinion yet, but it is coming. IBM looks at who is connected to whom. Are there key people in your organization who maintain a low profile, but when an associate has a question or problem, they get in touch with this person? The mere number of connection points is not sufficient because a considerable number of people on Facebook, Twitter, and other social networking sites are simply trying to make connections with as many people as possible. You want to know where the solid connections are. Explore this arena for useful knowledge about employee relationships.

Process Thinking Metrics

One of the most important deliverables of your metric system should be improvement in process thinking and understanding, at all levels of the organization. Process thinkers should ask, "Why am I doing what I am doing, and what does it mean for the experience that our customers are having or for the effectiveness of our business operations?"

Process metrics may cause more change to the way you do business than anything else we describe in this book. A key piece of knowledge for senior leadership is process awareness. There are three very important pieces of information for managers to understand about processes.

1. What is the process capable of doing?
2. What is the breadth of variation in the process?
3. What type of variation is currently taking place?

Most organizations have way too many goals inside the business. Dr. Deming addressed this issue many times:*

> If you have a stable system, then there is no need to set a goal. You will get whatever the system is capable of doing. A goal beyond the capability of the system will not be reached. And if you do not have a stable system, then again there is no point in setting a goal. There is no way to know what the system will produce, it has no capability.

What a profound and insightful statement.

Leaders in Level 4 and 5 organizations understand process capabilities. In contrast, when average organizations talk about processes, they have project teams improve processes, but leadership in an average organization does not have insightful understanding of process capabilities.

---

* W. Edwards Deming, *Out of the Crisis*, MIT Press, 1986.

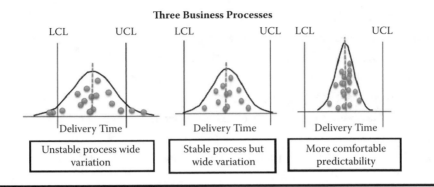

Exhibit 6.4   Breadth of process variation.

In Exhibit.6.4, the process on the left is not predictable. Performance is beyond the upper and lower control limits. The middle process is predictable, but although the variation is in control, it is very wide. The graph on the right should be the capability target for key processes. This is not the same thing as setting an arbitrary performance goal. The process on the right has been redesigned to operate much closer to the mean (average).

So the real goal is to gain better understanding of process capability and improve the capability of the process to meet customer specifications. Dr. Deming emphasized the importance of understanding (through proper statistical methods) the degree of common cause variation that is a natural part of a repeating process, and special cause variation. Deming once said, "If I had to reduce my message to just a few words, I'd say it all has to do with reducing variation."* Let's take a closer look at variation and how it relates to metrics for business performance improvement.

1. ***Common Causes of Variation Are Always There.*** They impact the output of the process on a daily basis. They are inherent in the design of the process (e.g., unclear procedures or requirements, outdated procedures, wrong drawings, people fiddling with machine controls, poor maintenance, poor lighting, cleanliness, normal wear and tear, insufficient time to do the work, etc.)

   Actions to take:
   - **Avoid trying to explain differences between high and low data points.** An unbelievable amount of time is wasted in management and operating team meetings making up stories,

---

* Mike Bock and David Weekley, "The Deming Tape", *WCEA News*, June 1992.

trying to explain the differences between high and low data points. Stop it!

■ **Improve the capability of the process.** In the example in Exhibit 6.4 on the right-hand side, narrow the bandwidth of variation. This is accomplished through standardizing work practices, clearly defining requirements, leveling workflows, improving skills, and so forth.

2. ***Special Causes of Variation Arise on a Periodic Basis***, and they knock a process out of control. Special causes are somewhat unpredictable. In the example in Exhibit 6.4 on the left side, there is an unstable process with wide variation beyond the control limits that are the result of special causes (e.g., broken tools, new procedures introduced, new person doing the work, power outage, machine breakdown, etc.). Special causes *can be fixed or prevented* by going after an individual problem. Fix the broken machine, have a special process that is used when a new employee is doing a job or a new procedure is introduced.

Actions to take:

■ Quickly understand when a special cause occurred.

■ Determine what was different when it happened; the longer you wait, the less likely you are to know.

■ Identify how to prevent the special cause from recurring.

The important reason for understanding the types of variation is that common-cause variation is beyond the capability of one individual to fix. And common causes of variation are much more frequent than special causes. Deming said, "Ninety-five percent of all variation is due to common-cause variation."* Management owns responsibility for process design. Therefore management, not an individual worker, is responsible for 95% of all process variation. This has been a primary focal point of Dr. Deming, Russ Ackoff, Dr. Joseph Juran, Peter Drucker, and many other improvement icons over the last 50 years. This concept of process ownership and responsibility is well understood by Level 4 and 5 companies. In contrast, leaders in average organizations do not have deep understanding of process capabilities and process ownership.

That does not mean you need a statistical process control (SPC) chart for every process. People went nuts with SPC charts in the 1980s (another strength used to excess that sometimes became a weakness, or at least an unnecessary overhead cost), and ultimately the fad died. Which processes

---

* W. Edwards Deming, *Out of the Crisis*, MIT Press, 1986.

are important to better understand at this point in time in your world? Which are the critical few? Start there, both at a macro (overall) business perspective and deep inside the business.

In our baseball story at the beginning of this chapter, gaining an understanding of what behaviors contribute to winning was critical. It turns out that walks were important to success. The walks-to-hits ratio is a key indicator. That meant the manager needed to reinforce the importance of patience at the plate (i.e., don't swing at a bad pitch). Change the mental model. When the player comes back to the dugout, the desired new behavior was reinforced. "Great job! You did not swing at a bad pitch. You earned that walk."

To gain better understanding of process variability at the leadership level, pick two or three key business processes to measure; for example, the delivery process or new product development process (if new products are a frequent occurrence). Look at the statistical performance of those processes in order to gain a better understanding of process capabilities and the inherent breadth of variation. It is a valuable investment of time and will create more profound knowledge about your business.

Cascading the Metrics from One Level to the Next

Often in business, governmental units, and nonprofit organizations, as you move down inside the organization, a win is a trade-off. For example:

- Is a sale a win? For the Sales Department perhaps, but what if it causes problems in operations or other parts of the business?
- Is the funding of a research project a win for a charitable foundation? Are all research projects equal? Do all researchers have equal capability? *Probably not!*

So what exactly does *win* mean for your world, for your area of responsibility?

Everything starts with a good understanding of customer value. Strategy deployment (which was discussed in Chapter 4 on customer value and will be further discussed in Chapter 8 on the executive mindset), ideally cascades from the top of the organization. It is very much like a fractal, a repeating pattern:

- Define what is important.
- Determine the target.
- Determine how to measured it.

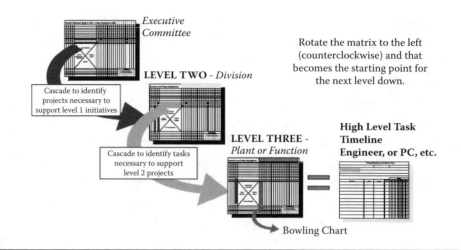

Executive
Committee

Rotate the matrix to the left
(counterclockwise) and that
becomes the starting point for
the next level down.

LEVEL TWO - *Division*

Cascade to identify
projects necessary to
support level 1 initiatives

LEVEL THREE -
Plant or Function

**High Level Task
Timeline
Engineer, or PC, etc.**

Cascade to identify tasks
necessary to support
level 2 projects

Bowling Chart

Exhibit 6.5   Deploying the metrics to lower levels.

- Measure progress.
- Adjust based on what you learn.
- Repeat.

Each lower level takes the handoff from above and adds information appropriate to its area of responsibility; each time, the new level discusses the goals and metrics with the people impacted by the improvement initiatives to make sure they are addressing real business issues. Exhibit 6.5 shows a cascading deployment.

Although it is nice if the overall organization adopts strategy deployment at the top, it can actually be started at any level and should help whoever uses it to get a better focus on what is important. For example, the "Bowling Chart"* shown at the bottom of Exhibit 6.5 is simply the weekly, monthly, and quarterly measures shown against the improvement plan. It typically includes expected results (plan) and actual results, perhaps monthly and on a year-to-date basis.

Get the Right Metrics

How do you get the right metrics? A simple way is to start with a hypothesis. For example, Emerson Electric felt it needed to sell more new products

---

* It is called the Bowling Chart because these reports end up looking like bowling score sheets that were used to keep score before most bowling alleys became automated.

in order to improve its profit margins and to accomplish several key business objectives. So the company required all business units to measure the "percentage of revenues from new product sales," and everyone had a target number. (One can argue whether that is the appropriate thing to do for all business units, but let's just let this slide for the moment.) After two years of using this new metric, the margins had not substantively changed and business growth was less than expected. So the original hypothesis was in question.

The company was using surface-level thinking. Whenever you believe you have a key metric, you should dig more deeply to gain more understanding by probing and asking, "What drives performance of this metric?" This is a simple variation of "Asking Why? five times."

So Emerson leaders dove more deeply to see exactly what people were measuring as new product sales. They discovered people were counting four things as "percentage of revenue from new products":

1. Existing products with minor improvements (we made blue ones, now do red)
2. Existing products with major improvements (we made small ones, now big ones)
3. Products new to Emerson (a competitor perhaps had the original idea)
4. Products new to the world

The facts showed that margin growth primarily came from the last two types. Once Emerson's leaders realized what was really driving revenue and profitability growth, they redefined the metric to count only new lines of business and products new to the world. This was a better metric, and it *did* correlate over time to margin growth, new revenues, and increased customer value.

Leading Indicators

You can also search to find meaningful leading indicators, especially important at a department or subdepartment level, by asking the same question, "What drives the performance of this metric?" Do this several times, plumbing down beneath the surface to gain more insight and deeper understanding. This simple method often reveals powerful leading indicators that can foster early corrective action.

Let's look at an example in the world of equipment maintenance. Outcome metrics might be: equipment reliability, downtime, and wrench time (time that maintenance personnel spend doing maintenance work). Potential leading indicators *might* include:

- Age of equipment
- Tools or materials available for scheduled tasks
- Qualified/skilled employee availability for assignments or specific equipment
- Workforce capacity utilization percentage
- Percentage of preventative maintenance targets (schedule) met, etc.

How do you know which of these are valid? You start with a reasonable hypothesis (an educated guess), and you test the correlation over time. Is the situation improving as a result of the insights provided by those metrics? If enough data is available for all the indicators, you can do a statistical analysis (using Mini-Tab or similar software) to identify the indicators with the most direct correlations to the end results.

Maintain a Process Perspective

It is also important to maintain the process perspective discussed earlier in this chapter, especially if you are an internal department supporting other internal departments.

For example: Purchasing can buy the least expensive material, but it may be more difficult to work with. Or to get it slightly cheaper, they purchase lots of it, which then needs to be stored, paid for as part of carrying costs, runs the risk of obsolescence, and so on. The actual purchase price is only one segment of the materials supply process. If purchasing is only measured on its independent performance, and the organization does not understand the total costs of buying, storing, and using materials, poor decisions will result. (See total costs in Chapter 7 on process thinking.)

An internal department should look at its key goals and metrics and ask, "Does this help the people I serve win in their work?" Even better, they should try to go one level beyond the department they serve and look at their internal customer's customer. If they have a goal or metric that makes the next two departments look good, it is probably a good metric.

Visual Methods

When you get down to the shop floor or operational level, the right measures must provide rapid feedback, as close to real time as possible. That pretty much eliminates monthly accounting reports from the equation. By the time they arrive, the month is finished and it is too late to act. So there should be more use of visual controls and white or electronic boards with useful information.

Key performance indicators (KPIs) are the main ingredients of a visually managed company. Without these goals, a company may never reach its potential. Empower people by setting the correct goals that motivate a team, taking into account several different perspectives.

Many companies view these goals through the rearview mirror. But you need to look *ahead* through the windshield to drive a car. Use metrics that not only look at history but also forward to improve before results are created. For example, if you track recordable accidents as a metric and take action or countermeasures because of the results, then you are viewing what has already happened (the rearview mirror approach). The results are important, but they are typically too late for early action. In contrast, upstream metrics (leading indicators) might include: safety violations, near misses, safety audit results, and so on. When these metrics start to get ugly, the likelihood of your having a serious accident is increasing. Take action or improve *before* the poor results occur. Think about your metrics or KPIs and determine if your company is looking through the windshield or the rearview mirror.

Metrics should positively motivate people and drive alignment. Key performance indicators should roll up to higher levels of the organization, as we referenced cascading metrics earlier in this chapter and in the True North discussion. For example:

- A cell's KPIs should roll up to the focus factory or value stream.
- The focus factory's KPIs should roll up to the plant's KPIs.
- The plant's KPIs should roll up to the supply chain's KPIs.

If everyone has different goals, then you will not accomplish your potential. It is like tying the supply chain to six cars and watching them all drive in different directions. *Focus your supply chain!*

When you drop inside the organization, there is a need to shift the measurement paradigm. Most of us have been trained to measure performance in dollars, but work gets done in a physical or a mental (thinking) fashion.

Department KPI Board

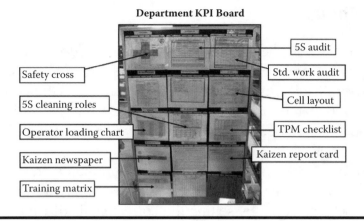

Safety cross
5S cleaning roles
Operator loading chart
Kaizen newspaper
Training matrix

5S audit
Std. work audit
Cell layout
TPM checklist
Kaizen report card

Exhibit 6.6   Cell-level visual metrics.

What the customer wants and how efficiently and effectively the process can deliver that product or service is better defined in terms of quality, timeliness, productivity levels, improvements made, and so on. Only physical action can change the relationship of work inputs to work outputs; you cannot do this through financial engineering. Process doers can understand and control metrics that measure physical things better than dollars.

Exhibits 6.6 and 6.7 refer to visual (key performance indicators) metrics for departments/cells. Cell-level metrics in a factory might include several categories:

- Safety (would come first in a manufacturing environment)
- Quality
- Delivery
- Cost (Productivity)
- Innovation
- People development

Hopefully, you have observed some similarities between the preceding list and the True North metrics discussed near the beginning of this chapter.

Environmental Health and Safety (S)

S—Number of OSHA recordable incidents (cell level)
S—Number of lost-time injuries (cell level)
S—Number of near misses (accident possibilities)
S—Environmental compliance

S—Safety Audit score
S—Preventative maintenance schedule compliance (%)

Quality (Q)
Q—Cost of quality (dollars; sell level)
Q—Finished Goods Audit (defect parts/million units) (cell level)
Q—First time through yields
Q—Standard work compliance in cell or 5S Assessment Score
   (cell level)

Time (T), Delivery (D) or could also be Customer (C)
D—Takt time compliance (%)
D—Change over time versus target (cell level)
D—Ship promise or target compliance (%) (*even better to know how late*)
D—Complete shipment (%)
D—Plan or schedule compliance (%) (cell level)
D—Past due (cell level) (*even better to know how late*)
D—Lead time (activation to time shipped)

Cost (C) and Productivity
C—Inventory ($)
C—Inventory days on hand
C—Capacity utilization for bottleneck operations
C—Production conversion cost
C—(Sales $ – Purchased Materials)/Paid hour or per employee

Innovation (I)
I—Number of best practices innovated and implemented
I—Improvement performance implemented vs. improvement performance sustained
I—Number of ideas implemented per employee
I—Customer satisfaction scores (may come from an internal customer)

Employee (E)

E—Employee new skills or capabilities added and used

E—Employee participation on improvement teams

E—Employee engagement scores from surveys

E—Employee turnover

E—Internal employee promotions

E—Employee referrals for new hires

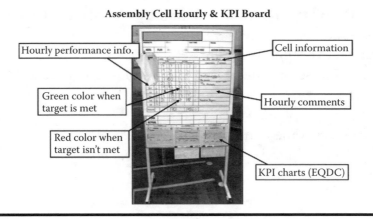

Exhibit 6.7   Visual department-level metrics.

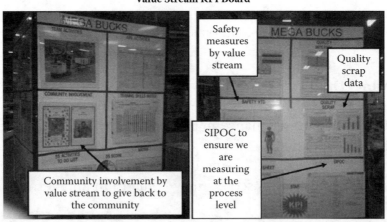

Exhibit 6.8   Value stream KPI board. (EQDC is a variation of the above classifications.)

This is definitely a laundry list of metrics; therefore, your focus should be on the handful that can drive the most positive change in your organization. For example, a cell might decide to focus on a few key metrics, without changes, for a given period of time while evaluating the correlations to overall process results. For example:

- Near misses (safety)
- Takt time (match production pace to the customer's rate of demand.)
- Cost of quality
- Production conversion costs
- Ideas implemented per employee

If that is the case, these metrics should be the most visual. Exhibit 6.8 shows one organization's key visual indicators for the overall value stream. Others could also be tracked, but they should receive more focus only if issues arise; otherwise, they might be reported on monthly versus daily or hourly basis for the key metrics.

As in Exhibit 6.9, you may also choose to use happy and sad faces or other simple visual methods. Some levity in the displays can help people remember that, although the metrics are often critically important, they're not personal and we're all in the same boat, trying to best understand how to improve the business processes and our ultimate business destiny.

Visual communications and feedback can come from Microsoft Excel worksheets, rapid reports from enterprise resource planning (ERP) systems,

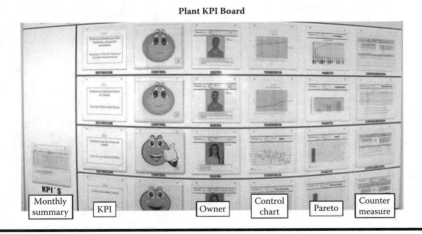

Exhibit 6.9 Plant KPI board.

kanban cards, and visual methods where customers pull orders; wherever possible, replace complicated-to-produce reports on forecasts, how much did we make, or did we test in the last hour, and so on. Using Takt times (production rate or pace needed to match customer-order pull levels) can visually and instantly show if there are problems that need to be addressed.

Rapid feedback can also be provided by the use of box scores that are kept locally on electronic boards or whiteboards (as shown in Exhibit 6.9). The metrics would be nonfinancial: they might capture customer service (could be internal), productivity rates, flow rate of work or cycle times, defect or error reduction, and so on. There could be several types of box scores kept in a business: operations, customer, and employee views. Exhibit 6.10 shows a typical operational box score card.

The important point is to do only what you will use. It may require some experimentation to figure it out. A learning curve may be necessary as new behaviors get developed over time: that's why it's sometimes nice to have an outside set of eyes show up periodically to place a spotlight on the

Box Scores (Often Visual Displays)

Box Scored		Metric	Last Year	Goal	Jan.	Feb.
	Operations	Units/Person				
		On-time, complete Shipments				
		First Time Through				
		Lead Time				
		Etc				
	Capacity	Productive		Could have several of these:		
		Non-Productive		Customer		
		Available		Employee		
		Bottleneck flow rate		Financial		
	VSM Financial	VSM Revenues		Value Stream		
		Materials				
		Conversion Costs				
		Operating Margins or Ovhd Contribution %		*Are these leading or lagging indicators?*		
	Total Financial	Cash Flow				
		% Sales new Products				
		ROA				
		Working Capital				
		EBITDAT				
		etc.				

Exhibit 6.10 Box scores.

new actions. If one experiment does not work, try something else. Let the people who are going to be measured figure out how best to do this; don't impose a rigid solution from the outside. As best practices develop inside an organization, share them by having people visit or audit what is being done elsewhere.

Metric Development Tools

There are two fairly simple tools that could be used to help determine which metrics are most important: a metrics map, shown in Exhibit 6.11, and a metrics relationship matrix, shown in Exhibit 6.3. Both tools require dialogue with people who understand the business.

The categories in the example shown in Exhibit 6.11 come from an organization's balanced scorecard. They track to a key set of KPIs, and then upstream metrics are identified that impact those KPIs. This tool could help to surface metrics important enough to go in a Strategy Deployment Matrix. The matrix helped this particular organization to

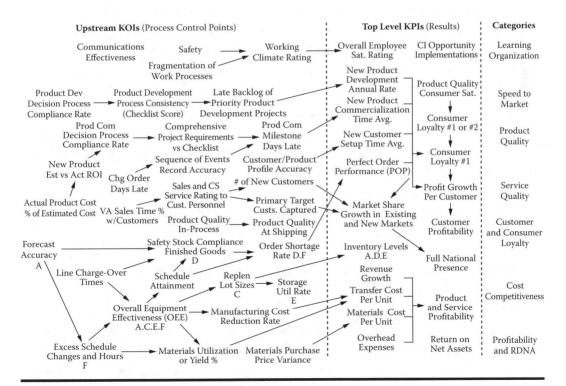

Exhibit 6.11   Metrics map.

Performance Indicators Map for Xxxxxx Proposals Process
(Initial working draft – To be further developed and validated.)

Input Indicators (Upstream)		In-Process Indicators (Upstream)		Overall Process Results (Downstream)	
Input Quantities		**Throughput Quantities**		**Output Quantities**	
XX	% Client-specific new contracts	XXX	Test Scenarios per month	10	Customized proposals/month
XX	% RFPs re-submitted w/ changes	XXX	# Qualified customer bids	20	Std product proposals/month
Quality		**Quality**		**Quality**	
XX	Info shortages in RFPs submitted	XX	Scenarios w/ DB input defects	X.x	# of issues per implementation
XX	% RFP Forms not-in-good-order	XX	Last 24 hour changes	XX	Net promoter score
XX	% Data-base audit errors				(Customer Loyalty)
Time		**Time**		**Time**	
		X	Rework hours in Xxxx group	XX	Hours avg TAT, unsigned forms
		X	Rework hours in Zzzz group	XX	Hours avg TAT, signed forms
					(TAT = proposal turnaround time)
		XX	Total hours in Xxxx group		
		XX	Total hours in Zzzz group	60	Total staff proposal hours
Productivity		**Productivity**		**Productivity**	
		X.x	Scenarios per proposal iteration	2.0	Staff hours/proposal
				$130	Staff $/proposal

Exhibit 6.12   Metrics map development worksheet.

surface metrics that caused conflicts between departments. One of this organization's goals was to decrease inventory levels; another was to improve customer service levels. If the functional managers of those two departments simply tried to maximize their numbers with no regard for the other perspective, customer service would be negatively impacted. Therefore, they used this worksheet to force a dialogue with higher-level managers about that conflict.

You could also use a worksheet to develop a more simple metrics map as shown in Exhibit 6.12. The indicators to left and above (upstream) in Exhibit 6.12 cause (i.e., map to) the Overall Process Results in the right-hand column (downstream). If overall results are inadequate, look for causes in the upstream indicators. Identify the true cause-and-effect correlations (versus coincident relationships); if possible, use statistical analysis. Manage the upstream indicators to optimize routine overall results. This exhibit has been modified somewhat, but it is an early draft from a real company.

A second tool to surface potential metrics is a relationship diagram, as shown in Exhibit 6.13. This is a fairly simple weighted matrix. Each of the measures are weighted in terms of importance, as are the goals. Each measure was given a high (2), medium (1), or low (0) rating against each goal. That rating times the goal's weight determined the contribution value. The

Measures and KPIs	Importance Rating	Learning Organization	Speed to Market	Product Quality	Service Quality	Customer and Consumer Loyalty	Cost Competitive	Business Growth and Final Results	Contribution Rating	Tracking Cost-Admin. Effort	Priority Rating
KPI Weights		4	5	2	2	3	3	2			
External Indicators											
Consumer Loyalty	9	1				1		1	9	1	81
Product Quality, Consumer Satisfaction	10	2		1		2		1	18	1	180
Profit Growth Per Customer	6	2						1	10	1	60
Customer Profitability	6	2			1	1	1	1	18	2	216
Market Share Growth	10	2				1	1	1	16	1	160
Revenue Growth	10							1	2	2	40
Support Practices and Systems (name resp.)											
Leadership Effectiveness Score	10	2	1	1	1	1	1	1	25	2	500
Safety	10	2					2		14	2	280
Employee Engagement Score	8	2	1		1	1		1	20	1	160
CI Opportunities Implemented Value		1	1		1	1	1	1	25	1	0
Product Development (name)											
Prod Dev Decision Process Consistency	5	1	2			1	1	1	22	1	110
Late Backlog of Priority Prod Dev Projects			2					1	12	1	0
New Product Development Ann. Rate	9	1				1		1	10	1	90
Product Commercialization											
New Prod Act Cost $ vs Target Cost	9	1	2		1		2	1	24	1	216
New Prod Act ROI vs Est ROI	6	1	1				1	1	14	1	84

Exhibit 6.13   Metrics relationship matrix.

administrative effort was similar: easy to gather (2), some work (1), lot of work (0) points. The contribution weight × metric importance × administrative effort resulted in the overall priority weighting. Blocks with a score of more than 200 points were considered significant. There is nothing magic about the above formula; you might even debate it or change it to suit your situation. The important activity was the dialogue that took place, on the individual line items and the individual goals, about what was more important, relative to the other columns or rows.

Lean Accounting

This topic requires more explanation than we have space to give in this book, but we cover it briefly here because it can have a very favorable impact on developing more effective performance metrics. There is a fabulous quote from Stewart Witkov, CFO at Ariens (a North American manufacturer of snow-removal and landscaping equipment) that truly captures the essence of the Theory of Standard Cost practices inside manufacturing companies:

Your setup cost is an estimate. Your budgeted hours are an estimate. Your materials are based on a quote. Your lot size is based on a guess. And the time scheduled for manufacturing is from a forecast. So you have an estimate, an estimate, a quote, a guess and a forecast. How accurate is that going to be?*

Lean accounting concepts are designed to better reflect the financial performance of a company that has implemented Lean manufacturing processes. Lean accounting might include organizing costs by value stream, changing inventory valuation techniques, and modifying performance reports to include more nonfinancial information. All are aimed at simplification of a business to the essential elements, with an eye toward meeting the requirements of the customer in a more effective, and therefore profitable, manner. Lean accounting can help organizations to better identify value in the eyes of the customer, organize by value streams, apply flow and pull processes in operations, empower employees, and pursue process perfection. This definition is adapted from an article by Jan Brosnahan.† Suffice it to say that once an organization begins to adopt Lean operations practices, it should follow on the accounting side to ensure harmony and alignment. A very real danger is that newly improved Lean operations can be accidentally pushed back to old non-Lean ways, if the accounting and other metrics don't keep people focused on the big picture, not irrelevant details.

Lean accounting draws on many principles of *direct costing*, which tried to avoid the problems of excessive overhead allocation (irrelevant details). Direct costing was popular for a brief period of time during the 1960s and 1970s. In that same vein, do not get lured into the trap of *activity-based costing*, which goes through an even more detailed set of procedures to allocate overheads. Many people express concern about dropping standard cost systems and not allocating overheads to individual products. They are worried that the overhead costs will not be covered. Lean accounting principles actually do the opposite. They bring allocated overheads out of hiding, into the spotlight, and organizational leadership needs to better manage those costs.

---

* Richard Schoenberger, *Best Practices in Lean/Six Sigma Process Improvement*, John Wiley & Sons, 200.
† Jan P. Brosnahan, "Unleash the Power of Lean Accounting," *Journal of Accountancy*, July 2008. Available at http://www.journalofaccountancy.com/Issues/2008/Jul/UnleashthePowerofLeanAccounting

To pursue this topic more fully, we suggest you seek out the very useful information published in books and on the Web by Brian Maskell, Bruce Baggaley, Orry Fiume, and Jean Cunningham.*

INDEPENDENCE ENTERPRISE DEVELOPS NEW INSIGHTS INTO THE USE OF METRICS

All Independence department leaders had recently attended a one-day workshop by Basem Hafey, their external consultant, titled Developing More Effective Performance Metrics. In that workshop, Basem shared a metric worksheet, which Bill Kennedy's team decided to use for the next round of analysis.

Exhibit 6.14 was pretty typical of the responses. Most metrics were lagging activity counts (e.g., which tracked metrics like "How many did we do?"). Several important categories of the business, such as Employee Development, did not show up as sublevel metrics on any departmental worksheets. And the way people rated the relationship of the metric being used to customer satisfaction, key strategies, and goals was questionable. The ratings tended to overstate the importance of the metric, which meant people did not have a deep understanding of the interconnections.

Bill's improvement team members summarized in a report the number of metrics that were leading and lagging and they also pointed out key strategies and key goals for which no sublevel departmental metrics existed. They then asked for each department head, on a voluntary basis, to look at the metrics they were using and to have two separate conversations:

- The first conversation was with the internal customers they served and was designed to get feedback. Is this a good/mediocre/bad metric from that customer's perspective? If it was not good, could they suggest some alternatives?
- The second conversation was to be with the employees in their department. Revisit the purpose (the aim) of that department, review the organization's key targets, and share the information from the customer dialogue. Then ask the employees what/how to measure. About 50% of the departments seriously tried to do this. The results were quite startling!
- For example, the maintenance department had been having problems for years with having everything they needed when they went to a work site to do a maintenance job. They had a list of problems.
  - A complete set of parts or right parts would not be there.
  - The equipment was not where the drawings said it should be, or major modifications had been made to the equipment.
  - The time scheduled to do the work had been changed by operations, but maintenance did not know.

---

* Brian H. Maskell and Bruce L. Baggaley, "Lean Accounting: What's It All About?" Available at http://www.maskell.com/subpages/lean_accounting/articles/Lean_Acctg_Whats_It_All_About.pdf

Functional Responsibility (Summary or Mission):	Department/Group:	Contact for this worksheet:
The project dep't...we deliver what you request and then some		

Metric Classification(s)

Metrics	Customer Sat.		Timeliness		Quality		Productivity		Cycle Time		Employee Development		Cost		Risk	
	Lead	Lag	Lead	Lag	Lead	Lag	Lead	Lag	Lead	Lag	Lead	Lag	Lead	Lag	Lead	Lag
1 # projects Completed								■								
2																
3																
4 # projects completed by original request date	■		■							Ø				Ø		
5																
6 % of requirements charged during the project	Ø		Ø			Ø			Ø					Ø		Ø
7																
8																
9																
10																

Medium Relationship Ø
High relationship ■

	Key strategies (for example)	Metric Linkages	Key Goals (Hoshin/Policy Deployment) for example	Target	Links
1	Describe the primary responsibility or mission				
2	Enter key metrics currently utilited, do great metric test (4 attributes)	Increase sales from products new to the world, or new to organization	% Revenues from Products New to Market	30%	Ø
		Ø			
3	Determine if the metrics are leading or lagging indicators by category – some may belong to several classifications	Launch new Governance process	Governance Process fully deployed	100%	
		Focus Value Proposition on Key Customers	Increase sales penetration key customers	20%	Ø
4	Decide if your metrics are approximately linked, a balance of views and a few early warning indicators	Build a High Performance Organization	Reduce product portfolio 'C' items	20%	
			Double 'employee engagement' survey score by XX	60%	

Exhibit 6.14 Metrics worksheet.

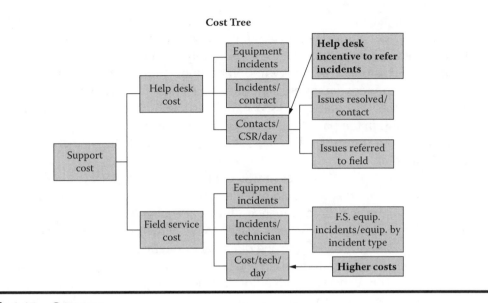

Exhibit 6.15   Cost tree.

There were a number of process issues that needed to be fixed. Out of this list, the lack of parts availability was the most frustrating. Maintenance personnel met with the purchasing department, and they jointly agreed on an interim fix. Purchasing personnel knew when they were making a maintenance-related buy, but they did not know when the job was scheduled. Maintenance personnel agreed to add that information to their purchase requests. In response, purchasing agreed to track maintenance purchases in its computer reports, and if the parts did not come in on the scheduled date, purchasing would give maintenance a 24-hour heads-up note, so that a crew would not be sent to site when the parts were not available. It was not a perfect solution, but it did eliminate a lot of wasted time sending a team to do a repair, realizing the parts were not there, and then a mad scramble to figure out where to send the crew next.

A similar set of improved/clarified agreements took place across the organization. The ability to discuss real issues as problems added a new element of reality to the improvement opportunity list. Several issues that had festered in the background were now seen, and plans were made to more fully address them.

The Customer Services Department took this opportunity to address issues it had been experiencing with the call center and the field services team. Some of the department members put together a simple diagram, shown in Exhibit 6.15, to highlight their cost and key metrics.

After doing the analysis, they realized they had conflicting metrics for customer support. One of the key metrics for the help desk manager was customer service representative (CSR) calls per day. If her team handled complex phone calls that took a while to resolve, she would not be able to meet her daily number of calls per CSR. So whenever her team members had a complicated call, they would simply transfer the issue to field service. The field service manager would send a technical associate to fix the issue in the field, which of course was a much higher cost. The field people had griped about this for some time, but nothing changed. This new focus allowed the issue to be seen, and they changed their metrics.

The team also looked at factory floor reporting. There were all kinds of variances being reported—labor efficiency, materials purchase price, standard cost variance, overhead variance, and so on. Bill had sat in on quite a few variance review meetings in the past. People always had a story about why the variance happened, and it was never their fault. People would work the metric, rather than do the right thing.

Just looking at labor variances, it was pretty obvious the factory supervisors knew how to find parts they could manufacture to keep people busy and to avoid getting hit with negative labor variances. It was also obvious this was anti-Lean behavior, because they were using capacity to make things that were not ordered by customers. And they were moving direct labor operators to indirect activities whenever they needed to reduce the total direct hours number. The whole concept was silly. The workforce on the floor did not change from month to month. In reality, there was no labor variance. And the way overheads were allocated had no relationship to the real world. The team had not studied this issue enough to make a specific recommendation. They were going to need to address this in future work with this cross-functional team, or tell Lynn that another team was truly necessary.

In their report to the leadership team, they suggested:

- Leadership should use the metric worksheet in reviews with every department. Make sure each department has a balanced set of metrics, and ask which internal customers they have used as a review resource. Learn what, if any, changes were made to the worksheet as a result of those discussions.
- Encourage more use of leading indicators at the department and subdepartment levels. Share the results of selected indicators in the leadership teams' monthly report to the organization.
- Use the Simple Metrics Survey over the next three years to see if there is a shift to high effectiveness in terms of metrics effectiveness.
- Run a correlation analysis across the organization to learn if there is any linkage between leading indicators in use at a department level and overall margin growth; try to get a better handle on just which metrics are indeed the vital few.

The next challenge for Bill Kennedy's Metric team and the Customer Value Team launched by Lynn Shaunnessey was to look more deeply at cross-functional process performance and customer alignment. Bill felt they were about to get swamped with improvement opportunities. Lynn tried to reassure him that the leadership team would do a better job of agreeing on key priority targets, so that people would not be overwhelmed by the opportunities. Bill believed her, more or less. The leadership team certainly did not have a good track record for that sort of thing. But Bill felt that maybe this time it would be different.

CHAPTER WRAP-UP: DEPLOYMENT ACTIONS FOR BETTER (MORE USEFUL) METRICS

Don't try to reinvent the metric system all at one time. Keep in mind that *perfection is the enemy of good enough.* Sometimes it is difficult to obtain correct, reliable data. Unfortunately, the perfect number does not exist. All data is ultimately flawed. So don't waste a whole lot of time trying to find the perfect number. If it is difficult to gather the data, people are less likely to do a good job of entering information. Experiment with a reasonable (80%) level of confidence, and try it. If it does not work over time, find a new one. How the measure is used is more important than what the measure is.

Start with what you already have. Leadership should define a set of True North metrics. Don't have too many categories. Metric classification might include: customer value, people development, process capability, quality, time, and cost categories. Cascade metrics down through the organization to drive/guide alignment. Make certain a portion of the metrics provide a process focus to look beyond the performance by a single functional group.

METRICS EVALUATION CHECKLIST

Review and evaluate your existing metrics before you start doing something new. See if they provide a clear understanding of what the unit (organization, business unit, department, function, work center, or activity) being measured is trying to accomplish in relationship with the other units trying to serve the organization's customers. What is the primary purpose, what is the aim, what is a win?

1. *Customer value:* Do you have metrics for the value proposition that are accurate and easily understood throughout the organization or value stream? Consider using:
   - Demand drivers, customer value, and business growth for the Mojo 20
   - Identify the Ugly 50 and apply the Rule of 16 to eliminate laggards
   - Some type of customer loyalty metric (e.g., the Net Promoter Score)

- Target costs for new products or the redesign of old products/services
- Performance and improvement against the priority customer requirements

2. ***Employee engagement***: If you believe people are important, you had better do a good job measuring their level of engagement and development. Give consideration to:

- Leadership surveys (e.g., W. L. Gore model)
- Employee engagement survey
- Leader's capability for developing successful new leaders
- Employee participation in Kaizen teams or rapid improvement events (including the number of times a person has done this)
- Look at metrics related to employee engagement (absenteeism, turnover, etc.)
- Critical thinking skills (organization's ability to promote learning, quality of problem solving). Figure out how to get a handle on this in your environment.
- Are you keeping the employee talent you wish to retain?
- Do you know the key employees that people in the organization seek out for advice and guidance?
- Employee referrals for new hires (even better if friends rather than relatives are referred)

3. ***Process focus***: Process thinking and understanding is a critical element of Level 4 and 5 companies and should be used to help define wins in the organization. Give consideration to:

- What is the process capability? This does not need to be done for every process; use it for problem areas, critical processes, and those that consume a lot of resources (i.e., a request for quote process, complex or customized products/services).
- Test inside wins against overall cross-functional process performance results. Often a trade-off is necessary. How will you decide between functional department performance trade-offs versus overall process performance?
- Definitely develop a few high-level organizational process-wide metrics to foster this type of thinking/knowledge at an executive level.

- For internal function-to-function relationships, how does performance favorably impact your internal customer's customer?

4. ***Overall business performance***: How well are you performing and improving against the priority business requirements? And do these metrics foster cross-functional cooperation?
   - Effectiveness against policy deployment targets
   - Quality performance
   - Timeliness performance, giving special consideration to lead times
   - Productivity performance
   - Cost performance, giving consideration to target costs and total costs

5. ***Macro to micro linkages***: Do the metrics cascade from the macro overall business level to the micro department level?

6. ***High goals and expectations***: Most people like challenges and they will find ways to achieve them if they are perceived to be fair.
   - Have your metrics set the bar high enough to encourage people to use the best of their abilities?
   - It is totally arbitrary, but the Toyota expression makes practical sense: "If it is bad, cut it in half; if it is good, double it."

7. ***Common analytical tools***: To help determine which measures are most important, simple, familiar tools should be used to show the relationship between the output performance measures and key input and process measures to help determine which measures are most important. Many examples of these are on the Web, including:
   - Cause and Effect Diagram (fishbone)
   - Metrics maps and map worksheet (see Exhibits 6.11 and 6.12)
   - Relationship Matrix (see Exhibit 6.13)

8. ***Vital few identified***: A handful of metrics are better than a bucket full of metrics. Organizations often drown in data and starve for knowledge. What are the vital few metrics that provide focus for your current situation? If you have too many, they will

provide conflicting signals, drive inaction, and destroy credibility of the metric system.

■ Emphasis is on the things you are trying to change.

■ For each metric considered, ask "What drives the performance of that metric?" Keep doing this until you dig down to true key indicators. Discuss the relative merits of each proposed indicator. Weed out those that are redundant.

9. *Actionable*: Metrics should drive/guide action and prevent us from acting when we should not. If the metric is too broad, it may apply to multiple departments, many options may exist for correction, and it can be difficult to decipher which action to take. The number should have some context related to trends or time. Single-point numbers, while easy to gather and look at, can drive firefighting and dysfunctional behaviors.

10. *Credible and not complex*: The data needs to be accessible and trustworthy, otherwise numbers will be seen as arbitrary and unreliable. The formula to calculate a metric should be transparent, not confusing. The more we build in assumptions, the less likely the data is to apply to a given situation. When you look at a report, it should not be too complicated to figure out what you need to do. Metric operational definitions help to clarify what metrics mean.

11. *Timely*: If the information comes too late, you are cooked. One of the primary purposes of a metric is to facilitate timely, informed decision making. Are the metrics you generate driving instant action or are they instantly ignored? *Metrics also have a life cycle.* The same set of metrics that applied to your function, department, or organization three years ago probably does not apply today. Has the business, the competitive climate, the technology, the people, or the nature of products or services provided changed? If yes, then your metrics should also be evolving over time.

METRICS DEVELOPMENT STEPS

If your metrics evaluation (from the checklist above) turns up deficiencies to be corrected, or if you are ready to build a new metrics set for a

new or redesigned business process, then use the steps below to guide
your work:

1. ***Draft a metrics map model:*** Start with a two-dimensional
   model similar to Exhibit 6.11 with the process flow from inputs
   on the left to outputs and overall process performance results
   on the right. Below are metrics categories starting with flow
   activities and quantities at the top, down through quality, time,
   productivity, and cost metrics. Notice that the flow is top left to
   lower right, similar to how a profit and loss (P&L) financial statement foots to the lower right-hand corner. Also, you might notice
   some similarities to the old DuPont RONA (return on net assets)
   wishbone format, because in the end, everything we do in an
   enterprise has to contribute to common-good value returned on
   invested capital, and human effort.

2. ***Define the key results metrics:*** Those few key performance
   indicators (KPIs) in the right-hand column should be visible to
   everyone involved in the cross-functional business process to
   be measured. Use the previous checklist to plan for a balanced
   range of indicators.

3. ***Identify upstream process and input metrics:*** For each
   of the KPIs, identify at least two upstream process metrics
   that should be monitored and managed to ensure dependable
   downstream results. This will require significant discussion with
   process doers who are very familiar with the details of process
   operations. The best process metrics are those that have direct
   cause-and-effect relationships with the KPI outcomes.

4. ***Identify leading indicators:*** These may be indicators of
   environmental change, developments, or preparations that would
   affect routine process operations (+/−) in the near future. For
   example, customer promotions, new product introductions, process team training, and so on.

5. ***Select the few metrics most correlated to the KPIs:***
   Vigorous debate within the stakeholder group is usually
   adequate. A relationship matrix like Exhibits 6.12 and 6.13
   is often helpful. In rare cases, there may be enough process
   data available to use statistical analysis software to identify the

high-correlation upstream metrics and separate them from the less-useful coincident indicators.

6. ***Validate your selected metrics with a metrics worksheet***: Use a worksheet like the one shown in the Independence Case Study (Exhibit 6.14), and ask the following:

   a. Do some metrics relate to external customers and to higher-level organizational goals or strategies?

   b. Is there a blend of perspectives (quality, inputs, outputs, etc.?)

   c. Is there a balance of leading and lagging metrics?

7. ***Evaluate the practicality of the selected indicators***: Before finalizing which indicators you will use, ask the following questions to see if the measurements you've chosen are feasible and easy to work with:

   a. Where will the data come from?

   b. How often will measurements be taken?

   c. Can you use trends rather than just a single number?

   d. Who will do the actual measuring?

   e. How will the data be presented?

   f. Who will see and judge the significance of the data?

   g. What actions might be taken as a result of changes in this number? Are those appropriate behaviors?

As you will see in the next chapter, business process metrics are a critical ingredient in the support systems of the Business Process Model, and history has shown that bad or missing management metrics are a common cause of business process failures. We recommend that you spend as much time as necessary to establish good metrics to support high-performance routine operations and continuous improvement of them.

Chapter 7

Ingredient 4: Process Thinking

Maximize Cross-Functional Process Performance and Foster Deeper Process Understanding, Innovation, and Execution of the Best Work Practices

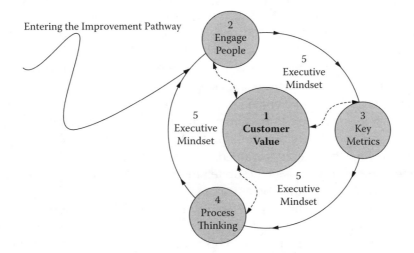

INDEPENDENCE ENTERPRISE'S FUNCTIONAL GROUPS DID NOT WORK TOGETHER

Independence's Maintenance Controller's Division (MCD) was not in dire straits. Its numbers were OK, but it had lost four points of market share during the last 12 months. In many ways, the division was at the leading edge of technology development. But when the customer value team members took a hard look, they learned customers were buying 15-year-old technology from their competitors.

They shared this information with the leadership team for this business unit. The leaders felt the nine new products currently under development were too far along to cancel, so they continued investing in product development and marketing materials.

When the sales force went out to get customer orders, only one customer placed an order for the new products. This was a painful wake-up call for the senior executives. They knew problems existed with their new product development process, but they did not realize how out of sync they were with their customers. When CEO Andy Fletcher and COO Jack Morel learned about the decisions made by this division, they fired the division president and his second in command. They promoted Margaret Allavoine, the sales manager on the customer value team, to lead this unit.

The customer value team had already reported that the older-technology products sold by competitors were simpler to understand, easier to install, and much easier to maintain. MCD delivered technical products, but it did not deliver customer solutions to problems. MCD had no clear agreement across functional lines of authority on what a solution needed to be. So MCD was often its own worst enemy as different functional groups lobbied for their view of the world during product development. Without a clear set of guidelines, unnecessary features would creep in, and features truly important to customers would be overlooked.

Seventy-five percent of MCD sales were to the custom design controllers market. So in addition to the problems with new product development, MCD also had major problems in this market segment because it won only 12% of its proposals. Therefore, engineering was spending a lot of time working on proposals that did not result in any business for the company. Meanwhile the sales people believed they were developing long-term relationships with potential future customers. Sales also felt that engineering overengineered the proposals, so in the end, the costs were too high for customers to make the purchase. Engineering felt the salespeople were proposing on projects they could not win and that sales did not do a good job of specifying what the customer wanted. Both departments argued that their processes were under control. Each group felt the other department was the primary cause of the issues facing their organization.

Margaret met with her new direct reports and shared the work done so far by the customer value teams. She reiterated that 85% or more of all organizational performance problems were process problems, not people problems, and that the value teams would be looking at the key processes used inside MCD as well as the rest of Independence Enterprise. She emphasized the importance of moving quickly and that the MCD team needed to have more in-depth understanding of requirements for its Mojo customers. She also said they would have to address issues with the Ugly 50 in their customer base.

Margaret asked her leadership team to figure out a better way for Sales, Engineering, and Operations to cooperate more effectively. Emphasizing this was an important action for all three major business units at Independence. Margaret said, "Everyone needs a practical mental model for thinking about how business processes work, learning how to do a better job of finding and eliminating waste, and doing it as a key part of their daily activities." This chapter outlines a few principles and ideas for making that happen.

Principles to Consider Regarding Whether *Your* Organization's Departments Are Truly Working *Together*

There is a basic flaw in the way Level 3 organizations go about finding and selecting processes to improve. That is part of why they get trapped at the third level. Leadership decides there is a problem in the business. Someone who owns a piece of a process is appointed as a project sponsor who *pretends* to own the overall process, and a team is selected to work the issues. Too often, there is not a business owner who will have responsibility for ongoing performance of the improved process after the project team is finished doing its work. Therefore, the organization struggles to maintain the gains.

Contrast this with a system where different members of the leadership team have end-to-end responsibility for process performance for a key set of customers. The term *end-to-end responsibility* is significant, because there really isn't a *beginning-to-end responsibility*: all processes are interrelated with other processes. A change in one can impact many others. The idea of end-to-end responsibility means where you start is a handoff from another process, a transition zone. It is important to have the handoff roles and responsibilities clearly agreed on; the transition zones between processes are usually stuffed with improvement opportunity. The leadership team should then routinely look at process performance metrics for critical cross-functional transition zones and the value-creation processes that serve key customers. This is one of the primary purposes of value stream identification. The Cisco example discussed later in this chapter provides an example of how to have end-to-end process responsibility. You do not need to go through a major reorganization to do this.

If people have end-to-end responsibility for a process that truly serves external customers, you have leaders saying, "Please take me! Let me have the resources to improve X process." The process owner will routinely report on the performance of that overall process, in leadership team meetings, rather than spending time talking about functional departmental performance, which by definition is only a piece of a process. Process owners will have a much higher level of concern for the cross-functional effectiveness of the total process, rather than simply stating, "It ain't my problem." When the focus shifts to process performance, leaders do not report on project savings; instead, they report about process performance in their business. On an ongoing basis, there is a built-in incentive to improve performance and to maintain the gains when cross-functional processes are routinely managed. This is a very different leadership team discussion.

When resources are allocated to work an improvement project in a process thinking/understanding environment, the owners are pulling the resources in to meet a business need, not to fix an isolated something that is broken. The challenge for the leadership team in this type of environment is to allocate those resources based on business needs. This is where tools like Hoshin planning or Strategic Policy Deployment can help.

Get the strategic part of process thinking right. Then dig down a little more deeply and start to look at process effectiveness. It's hard to discuss process thinking without touching on some of Dr. Deming's work.

Deming emphasized that parts of an organization should always be considered in relationship to the other parts. Long before people started discussing supply chain relationships, Deming was pointing out the importance of cooperation with suppliers and customers to optimize overall value. Every process is connected to another process. When a change is made, it has ripple effects beyond the borders of the process being worked. To maximize value, it's critical to recognize the interdependencies within and between organizations and the potential of these relationships. In other words, the whole is greater than the sum of the parts.

Deming suggested that "key parties involved with the organization (including shareholders, personnel, customers, suppliers, and the broader society) should be better off than they would be if the organization did not exist."* This is a different philosophy than win–lose because if you follow Deming's philosophy, *everyone gains*. It is impossible to optimize every component part of a system by itself; there needs to be a sense of balance (creative tension) between the parts. If each component tries to maximize its individual performance, the overall system flow will break down. This is one of the reasons so much care needs to be taken with reward and recognition systems. It is not difficult to optimize a *piece* of a process for the short term. If people are incentivized to do this, they are rewarded in the short term—however, *they are hurting the overall process in the long term.*

---

* W. Edwards Deming, *Out of the Crisis*, MIT Press, 1986. Chapters 2 and 3.

Understanding how a process works and the capability of a process moves leadership beyond a simplistic view of the world. Understanding process capability for strategic business processes also gives an organization's board of directors much greater insight about what is really happening inside a business.

In contrast, leaders who lack a deep understanding of processes have a simplistic knowledge of how things really work. If a process is not important, this is not an issue. But it is important for the entire leadership team to have a deep and clear understanding of key value-adding and key support processes for the value engine of their organization. Otherwise, decisions will be made in ignorance.

The mental model for someone without a deep understanding of how a process really works looks like the high-level process map shown in Exhibit 7.1.

In a simplistic view of the world, these blocks look like they all work together to serve the customer in relative harmony. But in real life, they are often independent fiefdoms (silos). For example, the sales manager sets goals for the salespeople and is measured for sales performance. The sales department does not have any significant responsibility for the other blocks because they are outside of the walls around sales. Sales is held accountable only for sales results. And the same story is true for every other functional responsibility block.

Even though people *intellectually* understand there is an input–process–output relationship between the blocks, leaders still often try to manage their

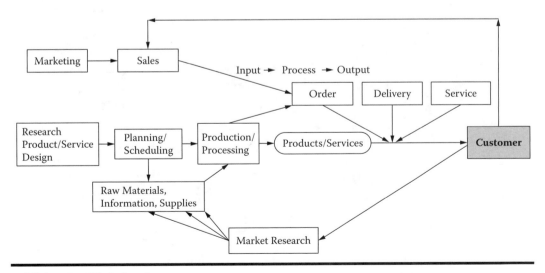

Exhibit 7.1   High-level process map.

blocks as independent from each other. Senior leaders reinforce this thinking by challenging each block to optimize its particular area of responsibility. That view of the world makes it nearly impossible for these blocks to work in harmony. You cannot optimize each individual block in isolation; every block needs to work in harmony with the other players to best serve customers.

Contrast the preceding view with the way a process looks in the real world. This is still a simplistic map; it does not contain numeric information and the real world is uglier than we have shown. Exhibit 7.2 shows the software development process inside a major financial institution.

This map shows just a few problems: every arrow after the initial customer project request causes rework, wait time, quality errors, and a host of other problems. Customers change requirements at each step along the way due to a variety of factors. For example, just think about Microsoft's Office products: What percentage of the features of Word or Excel do you actually use? Most people say they use less than 15%. We are not making this point to attack Microsoft's strategy; the company had its reasons for doing it that way. However, let's apply that same logic to IT systems developed for *your* enterprise or department. Do the software programs you use have many more features than you use?

IT typically gathers too many requirements, many of which are not important or urgent. IT personnel then create features no one will use because the internal customer was asked to state everything he or she might possibly need. Customers are incentivized to do this because they finally have attention from

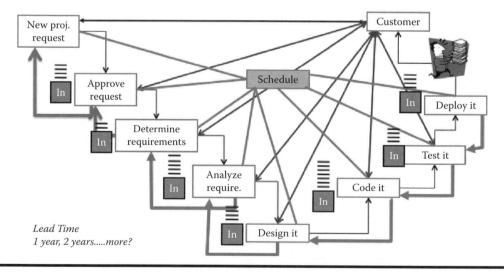

Exhibit 7.2   Software development process map.

IT, so they want to put as much stuff (requirements) in the basket as possible. Who knows when they will ever have an opportunity like this again in the future? But each of those requirements or features needs to be tested and linked to other parts of the system, and that complexity is awfully cumbersome (overhead), expensive, and frequently totally unnecessary. Every step of the map shown in Exhibit 7.2 becomes more and more complex because requirements are being flushed through the software development system, many of those "requirements" are not important, and the customer does not really care about them. This is the equivalent of batch manufacturing in the IT world.

The longer the project takes to finish, the more other issues arise. For example, an internal IT schedule shifts resources between projects as priorities change, so a new group of people needs to become familiar with an in-progress work package. And of course, each time one functional group hands off to the next functional group, the receiving party says, "What were you smoking when you did this work? This is not what the customer is telling us they want! You need to redo …" By the time the software is actually developed, the internal customer has probably changed, and the response of the new internal customer is, "Why did you give me this? This isn't what we need!" The map shows reality—everyone is so busy doing, no one has time to fix it or ask, "Why the heck are we doing this?"

So let's look at how process improvement *should* work.

Stretch Your Thinking beyond Your Direct Roles and Responsibilities

Business process improvement work *is not complicated* rocket science, but it *is complex* because there are many pieces involved that have to be handled in context to make sense of the whole. Unfortunately, in the case of process thinking, the complexity problem is compounded by the fact that few managers have any experience or education for it. The business schools give it scant coverage, if at all. And most managers, even at the top, are too burdened with managing the current situation to get much experience with practical process improvement concepts or methodologies. So it's a blind spot in modern management.

This is in direct violation of Dr. W. Edwards Deming's exhortations to managers to seek "profound knowledge"* about the business processes

---

* W. Edwards Deming, *Out of the Crisis*, MIT Press, 1986. Chapters 2 and 3.

they manage, as they consider potential actions without much regard to impact on the overall organization. For example, consider the purchasing department, which is typically held accountable for buying prudently, using low-cost procurement practices, and perhaps playing one supplier against another to get the best deal. But what is *low cost*? And what is *prudent*? What responsibility does a purchasing manager have to more deeply understand:

- The impact of erratic schedules or change orders on suppliers
- The cost of maintaining or the complexity of servicing purchased equipment or parts
- How to work with suppliers to raise their level of performance
- Cost drivers in their organization that cause higher costs to suppliers
- Cost drivers in the suppliers' organization that should be improvement targets

A *traditional thinking* purchasing manager calls suppliers to demand price reductions. In contrast, a *process thinking* purchasing manager will focus on the value-creation process and how to eliminate waste while improving responsiveness and quality. But it's common practice in our modern cultures of impatience to just do the easy thing, even if we don't have the facts and are unknowingly headed over a cliff.

Supplier performance metrics in today's world should focus on a combination of delivery, quality, and contribution to total (overall) cost reduction, rather than just the cost of a single purchase looked at in isolation. The new thinking is to *consider suppliers as business partners* and to get away from the adversarial relationships of the past based exclusively on the low cost of procurement (as a stand-alone issue). Your suppliers could help you succeed in your business if they understood your needs (the same way you most likely emphasize understanding your customers' needs). For example, suppliers might consign inventory, fill your shelves, and better educate you on their products and their application. These are nontraditional ways in which suppliers could add value to your business success. More and more, the overall supply chain is being looked at from a value added to the chain as a whole model, rather than a single-purchase transaction in isolation from the rest of the business.

Define a purpose for the process that goes beyond the walls of functional responsibility. For example, a credit manager might perceive the process purpose for that department to be "avoid incurring bad debts for credit transactions." And from a Credit Department perspective, this holds true. But what about the cross-functional process purpose? Especially for a process that directly touches customers. Would the purpose or aim of the process be better stated as "To approve transactions as quickly as possible for credit-worthy customers?"

Both purpose statements want to avoid doing a losing transaction, but the perspective differs. The first is inward; the second is outward and productive, not narrowly restrictive. And the metrics used to measure performance would differ. The credit department shifts from being *the credit police* to helping another department get its work done. What do *we* need to do to get appropriate transactions done as quickly as possible? This is a subtle but significant shift. This type of a purpose statement helps a functional department define a better win.

Redefining Our Mental Models for Business Processes

Business processes are complex because of the multiple people and organizational structures involved. Organizations often have problems sustaining the gains when they try to improve a process. One of the major reasons for this conundrum is that *organizations often go about trying to improve the process in the wrong sequence.* They try to solve the problem from the bottom up, rather than from the top down. This phrase needs explaining, because we are not talking about the boss telling people what to do. First consider the Business Processes Model in Exhibit 7.3.

The appropriate sequence for improving a process is shown as the ABC development sequence:

1. **Clarify Customer Requirements:** Eliminate assumptions and gain an understanding of the "real" customer output requirements (value) for the overall process before considering internal process improvement possibilities.
2. **Streamline Value Creation Processes:** Eliminate waste and undesirable variation. Design the process so customers pull work. Make things better, faster, and cheaper by eliminating interruptions to the flow of customer value. In most businesses, the actual value-added work is a small amount of the overall time it takes to deliver a product or service. And a lot of time is spent doing non-value-adding work activities because "that's the way we have always done it" and no one has taken

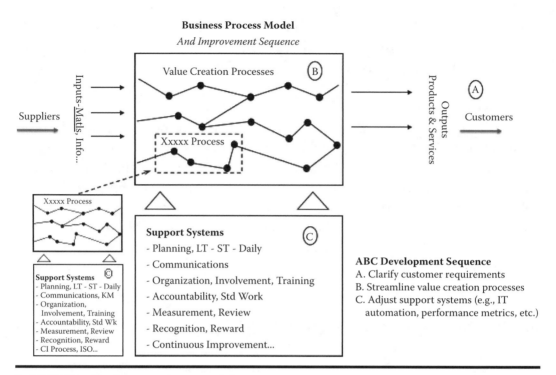

Exhibit 7.3   Business process model.

time to look at the overall process to strip out the wasted steps and streamline what's left.

3. **Support Systems:** Make certain the support systems maximize performance of the overall value creation process, not just some of the players inside the process box. The five missing ingredients we discuss in this book are primarily support-systems related issues.

Now let's go back to the *wrong* sequence. Unfortunately, the normal practice for improving process performance is done backward, in exactly the opposite sequence of what should happen. We are not referencing process improvement teams with that comment. Instead, we are talking about the far more frequent way most companies try to address process problems. Companies make changes to the *bottom* of the model (Block C) first and hope those changes make the things above it work well. Just consider one support system example—implementing an automated information system.

This has probably never happened in your organization, but have you ever seen a company try to fix a process problem by installing a new computer system? (You're allowed to laugh derisively at that thought.) Companies implement automated systems hoping to solve process problems without cleaning up the process first. But if the value proposition (purpose) of the process is not clear and waste is not eliminated, then we end up automating a poorly designed process rife with exceptions. That complexity more than doubles the cost and time it takes to automate. This is like putting the cart before the horse—and if you have ever ridden in a carriage, you can imagine that it wouldn't work too well with that arrangement.

To make the situation even worse, because the project started with an IT trigger, the clock starts running immediately based on an IT implementation schedule. There is never enough time or focus on determining the real process requirements before the IT hard-wiring begins. It's then too late to go back, so no real process improvement is done, and the end result is whatever IT can do with limited consideration for what the real process should be. The business press has been full of disaster stories along those lines.

We picked on IT, but we also could have used new performance metrics systems (fix the process with metrics), new human resources compensation or performance review practices (fix the process with better performance reviews), or many other systems. Support systems adjustments should always be *last* after the first two steps of the ABC development sequence have created a process worthy of IT automation or whatever other support system investment is justified. That is why our first missing ingredient is customer value.

Before we leave Exhibit 7.3, take a look at the small dashed box labeled "Xxxxxx Process" inside the Value Creation Processes box in the model. It could be any one of the value processes in a business that produces value to customers. In the subimage shown on the lower left, notice a smaller Support Systems block under its Value Process segments block. The concept here is that every process—from enterprise to business units, departments, and work groups—has local versions of the Support Systems. To fully support its local operations, each process owner must manage its local Support Systems.

The next sections in this chapter look more deeply at each of the ABC process development sequence steps.

Step A: Clarify Customer Requirements

This must happen before we look at anything inside the process. That seems obvious, but the real customer requirements (shown in Exhibit 7.3) are rarely known well enough in the current situation to know exactly what the process output should be. Therefore, if work is first started on improving the internal process operations, then it's likely that much of it could be wasted when the real requirements are eventually discovered and likely to negate significant parts of the process redesign to that point. All process improvement work must start with clarification of the real output requirements. (Recall that in Chapter 4 on customer value, we discussed the importance of having deep understanding of the requirements for the 20% of customers who generate 80% of profits.)

The Customer-Supplier (C/S) Requirements Model shown in Exhibit 7.4 is a variation of the Kano Model for requirements (shown in Chapter 4 on customer value). Look at the three steps between the boxes: that's the natural sequence of development for a new C/S relationship, or for a current relationship that is beginning to develop requirements for a new product or service agreement. A couple of nuances need to be explained.

The first two arrows (Needs and Capabilities) are not simple one-time flows. The parties should repeat the first two steps several times (how many times depends on product/service complexity), until they have completely clarified the requirements necessary to satisfy both of them. And then the customer and supplier need to agree on the requirements.

Many leadership teams do not keep their customer requirements definitions up to date. They get by with tribal knowledge and assumptions about the must-be, primary satisfiers, and potential delighters (described in Chapter 4) of their customer requirements set. Only when something has gone wrong and immediate corrective action is needed will they step back and ask, "What is necessary to be sure we are *always* satisfying our customers' requirements?"

The key point is that infrequent, inaccurate agreement on requirements with either internal or external customers is not good. It's a prescription for

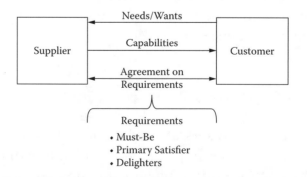

Exhibit 7.4 Customer–supplier requirements model.

eventual disappointment for both parties. This is especially important to do for internal customer-supplier requirements, where too many assumptions are made. Ideally, *internal* requirements should be filtered through a solid view of *external* customer requirements. The internal players (i.e., specific departments/functions) should periodically review their relationship to make certain no internal support systems (e.g., performance metrics) inhibit their ability to collaborate on maximizing overall process performance. Sharp, accurate requirements lead to faster and more effective elimination of waste/non-value-adding actions.

A senior GE executive shared this story about requirements:

> It's not good enough to only ask for customer requirements. Often, a customer's communication is not clear. About 20 years ago, I went on a best-practice tour to a number of world-class companies. I learned one of many lessons on that trip that has stayed with me. A major customer asked Company X to reduce the weight on one of their heat exchangers on a next-generation design. They built it into a design spec. It was proving very difficult to design. One of their salesmen had lunch with the customer. During the course of their discussion, the customer shared the reason they wanted the weight off, was they had to send two men to the site to do an install, and if they could get the target weight down to a specified level, they would only need one installer at the field site.
>
> Once the company understood this, their engineers added a hook for less than a dollar. The customer could hang the unit and make the connection with only one installer. The customer asked for a solution for a problem. Initially, Company X did not seek to understand the *real* nature of the problem. As a result, they spent time and money working on an inappropriate design; fortunately, they stumbled across an insight that saved considerable money for Company X, and resulted in a meaningful solution for their customer.*

You need to ask "Why?" and understand what your customer (whether internal or external) really wants to solve. The customer articulates a need, and the better job the supplier does of understanding the real need, the easier job the supplier will have of moving away from a customer purchase decision that is primarily based on costs.

---

* Personal communication.

In many ways, the GE example above is a fractal (i.e., a repeating pattern) of the value discussion and the "understanding why" conversation we have had repeatedly throughout this book. You need to ask,

■ Why are we doing this (value/purpose)?
■ What drives performance of the purpose we are trying to accomplish (how do I capture the essence)?

You need to do this for your overall business, for your key customers, and for the processes operating inside your company. In the initial conversation (as in the GE story above), at a surface level, you catch a *hint* of what the user requires. Only through probing further, however, does the supplier develop deeper understanding. In this particular GE story, the supplier really just lucked out and stumbled across the insight. However, if you wish to become a Level 5 organization, *you can't rely on luck*; instead, *you need to routinely develop that level of insight and understanding*. People working in a manufacturing cell do not need to know what the CEO knows, nor vice versa. But people do need to have a deep understanding of what they do and why they do it. That is a pretty basic foundation level for effective improvement.

After you have clarified your customer requirements, the next block to address is the Value Creation Process (see Block B in Exhibit 7.3). What capability do the processes have to meet the needs? Let's take a closer look at this next step.

Step B: Streamline Value Creation Processes

Designing processes in a complex world is a voyage of discovery that never ends. Processes look like the software example in Exhibit 7.2 because they have evolved to address new problems as they arose over time. As mentioned earlier, business processes are complicated, and we don't know enough about how to design them perfectly. No one can design a process that will handle every scenario, every contingency, or every problem.

And, because processes are complex, people are often not sure what to do when they run into a problem. So their natural reaction is to *work around* the problem, and try to do the right thing to the best of their ability—whether that work is treating a patient in an emergency room when a nurse has to run to another room to get an instrument needed, getting the software code written when the requirements are not clear, or getting a product on a truck for shipment when the loader is not sure if this is the right product.

Throughout the day in an average organization, there are hundreds and maybe thousands of workarounds that take place as associates try to do the right thing. Unfortunately, from a process thinking perspective, *every time someone does a workaround, a learning opportunity is lost, and the credibility of the process owners (management) is eroded.* For some reason, the process did not work the way the designers of the process and the owners of the process (management) thought it would. This happens one time, two times, three times, and more. As time goes by, of course, the process starts to look like the maps shown in Exhibits 7.2 and 7.5.

Make the invisible, visible is a key foundation of process improvement. It is not a new idea or unique to Lean. Statistical process control charts are intended to make process performance more visible. 5S (a Lean improvement tool) is sometimes confused as just a housekeeping tool, but it is

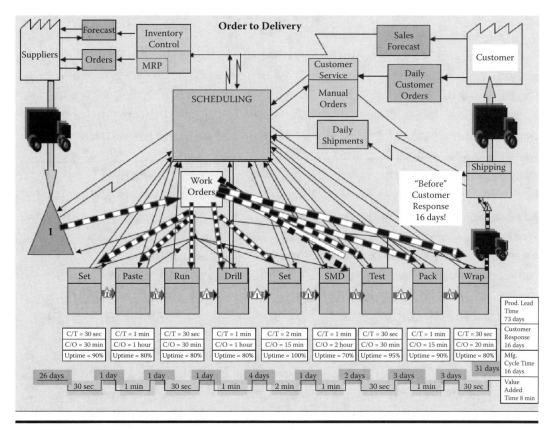

Exhibit 7.5   "Before" value-stream map smoke detectors.

really there to make sure that everything is in the proper place for efficient in-process use. If something is not where is should be, it can interrupt the process flow; 5S methods make routine process pieces visible and maintainable for efficient daily use.

One of the primary objectives of the Lean movement is to have customers pull work from their suppliers. How can processes be designed to flow in a continuous way, once an order is received from a customer? In the ideal world, pull minimizes the need for forecasting and inventories are kept at a minimum. In the real world, however, this is a challenge, and it's why lead time reduction is so important. The process improvement analytical tools help, but leaders need to decide if they are going to move from a functional-(departmental-)centric way of operating to instead have a more customer-driven model. This is a more radical change than you might think if you have largely been operating in a traditional way.

Value-stream maps help us to better see process performance. Exhibits 7.5 and 7.6 tell a story about an organization that moved from a push, batch-manufacturing process (shown in Exhibit 7.5) to a customer pull process (shown in Exhibit 7.6). The production process became much more visual without doing anything fancy by simply focusing on lead time reduction.

You don't need to know much about the actual process shown in Exhibit 7.5 to know that it is ugly. It is a process that evolved over a very long period of time. If you were to walk through that factory, it would be almost impossible to know if people were working on the right things for the customer because it looked like chaos. You can see from the arrows coming out of scheduling and work orders that there were a lot of push production controls and overhead expense. The print in Exhibit 7.5 is small, but there are two key numbers. This company manufactured commercial smoke detectors, and when it received a new customer order, it would take workers 16 days to produce the product to fulfill the order. The other interesting tidbit is that it took only 8 minutes of value-adding time to actually make one smoke detector. So if an average order was 100 to 300 smoke detectors, they had 800 to 2400 minutes of value-adding time (40 hours max.), yet it was going to require 16 days to do the work. Obviously, they had an improvement opportunity.

Exhibit 7.6 shows the new process. Again you don't have to know anything about the specifics, yet it is pretty clear from this second map that there is much less confusion. The visual clarity of this value-stream map provides effective communication—at a glance—so you can easily see how the redesigned process has taken advantage of improvement opportunities.

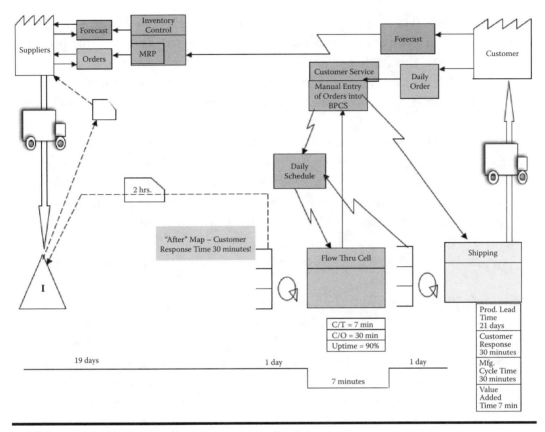

Exhibit 7.6   "After" value-stream map smoke detectors.

The physical process itself is also going to be much more visual, because the company quit making batches of parts and instead focused on making one smoke detector at a time. Work was now *pulled* by customers; workers did not make a smoke detector that did not have a customer order, so work-in-process inventories did not build up between production steps. Management and associates on the line could then focus on making certain that work flow is not interrupted. This makes problems very real and important to deal with on the spot. The metrics become visual, and you get rapid feedback to see if there is a problem. Problems don't get hidden amidst the clutter. That is a key component of Lean thinking and Lean action.

Notice the up-and-down stepped graphic at the bottom of the map in Exhibit 7.6. That is a key feature of value-stream maps, which differentiates them from other process map conventions. The stepped line is a graphic display of the lead time through the process, including both non-value time on the high-water steps, and value-adding time on the base-level steps. Think of that base level as the zero-base value stream of work that the customers are willing to pay money for. The rest of the time in process up to the high-water line is *waste time* caused by the current process configuration. That waste should be a prime target for elimination through process improvement efforts using Lean, Six Sigma, and other methodologies.

In the new process, the value-added time was 7 minutes, so not much changed. However, lead time to get through the complete production process dropped *from 16 days to 30 minutes!* The use of customer pull-type production controls reduced work in process (WIP) and overhead expenses. There was still some front-end lead time for purchased parts (circuit boards), which they needed to carry in inventory.

There are several key metrics to understand when looking at a process:

1. **Cycle Time:** The *actual* elapsed process time from the completion of one output unit to completion of the next unit. Cycle time for a process is the length of time for the longest step within the process. So if a 4-step process has 3 steps of 2 minutes each, and 1 step of 5 minutes, then the cycle time is 5 minutes, because the bottleneck determines how fast a process can go. Obviously, you can try different strategies to minimize the impact of bottlenecks (e.g., added stations or personnel).

2. **Lead Time:** This is the length of time from the beginning point of a process to the completion of a finished output (calculation varies depending on scope; it includes queue, wait, and move times).

3. **Takt Time:** This is the unit-to-unit pace of production *required* to meet customer demand. This is the ideal pace for doing work. At this rate, production and demand are in balance. If the cycle time achieved is longer than the takt time, then something will have to be done to scheduled hours, staffing level, available equipment, or other factors to meet the required demand.

4. **Value Added Time:** This is the time spent changing the form, fit, function, or information content of a product or service in a way the customer values and is willing to pay for.

Any Non-Value Time Is Waste. This seems too obvious to be worth mentioning, however, the complexity of business processes often makes it difficult to distinguish between the value-added and waste steps. This is also a good metric for senior leadership awareness, especially as a percentage of total lead time to value-added time, and as a percentage of total value-added time to total personnel time. It simply opens people's minds to the vast magnitude of improvement that is possible.

Lead Time Is the Common Thread. Everything that happens in a process shows up in the overall lead time. So there is considerable power in using lead time as a key process performance indicator (KPI) since it can be an effective continuous education tool as the entire workforce looks for ways to remove waste to improve customer service and operating efficiency. *Lead time* is a great metric for senior leaders to know for important business processes.

The lead time common thread is visible in the value-stream spreadsheet in Exhibit 7.7. Notice that the cumulative lead time line in the middle ties all the steps together as the process flows back and forth between inventory queue steps and processing steps.

Also notice in the right-hand column the time of items as percentages of lead time. The low process time and value-add time percentages are not unusual. Making those facts visible has a powerful effect on how business teams view their opportunities for business-process improvement.

We need to design processes so people can discover how to make them better quickly. First, we need to practice process thinking to increase our

◇	A	B	C	D	E	F	G	H	I	J	K	L	M	N	O	P
1	**Typical VSM Data Blocks**										* With Lead Time "Common Thread"					
2																
3	Step Name	Mail Room						WIP Queue						O. A. Process		
4	Inv or WIP Queue Qty	Qty	40					Qty	6					Qty	46	% of LT
5	Queue Time (= Qty * CT)	QT	120			Initial Review		QT	18		Sched. & Mail			QT	138	92.6%
6	Cumulative Lead Time *	LT	120			LT	123	LT	141		LT	149		LT	149	
7	Process Time / Unit					PT	3				PT	8		PT	11	7.4%
8	Non-Value Time / Unit					NVA	1				NVA	3		NVA	4	
9	Operational VA Time / Unit					OVA	1				OVA	2		OVA	3	
10	Change-Over Time Avg/Unit					CO					CO	1		CO	1	
11	Value Add Time / Unit					VA	1				VA	2		VA	3	2.0%
12	Cycle Time / Unit (= PT / SC)					CT	3				CT	2		CT	3	
13	Staff Time (= PT * SC)					ST	3				ST	32		ST	35	
14	Staff Count					SC	1				SC	4		SC	5	
15																
16	Step Type Templates		Queue			Process		Queue			Process			O. A. Process		
17																
18	Step Type Examples		WIP Queue			Analysis										
19			Inventory			Investigation										
20			"In Box"			Calculations					Time in Days / Hrs / Min / Sec as appropriate					
21			Setup Kit			Sceduling					Adjust time units to suit situation					

Exhibit 7.7   Value stream lead time.

understanding. Then we need to do something about it. And there are practical steps in the common improvement tool sets (Lean, Six Sigma, supply chain management, etc.) that leaders can use for more effective process analysis, design, and improvement execution.

With the process scrubbed and streamlined, now we need to turn our attention to how to sustain it at a high performance level. That leads us to the next step—support systems.

Step C: Align Support Systems

This is the Achilles' heel of most business process improvement methodologies. Most organizations do not manage these well inside their own walls, let alone across the walls of different players in the supply chain. However, Level 4 and 5 companies have very effective internal support system structures, and they are expanding them through their supply chain (forward and backward). The support systems block contains many activities that support the work of the core business processes—where value creation occurs. They are important—and dangerous—for two main reasons:

- If any of the support systems are inadequate for *current, newly installed, or newly improved* value creation processes, then performance will not be sustained at a high (competitive) level.
- Over time, support systems tend to become bloated relative to the value they provide to the value creation. If not periodically reevaluated, they can take on an artificial importance, organization structure, and costs rivaling the value creation processes.

Organizations fritter away a lot of time because there is so much variation in most business processes. Standard work is not clearly defined, operator friendly, or even up to date. So jobs get done in different ways. Managers spend way too much time managing what should be normal rather than the abnormalities. A key part of process improvement and support systems management is to stabilize the process so the person doing the work can manage normal activities. Managers are then freed to focus their energies to look for the abnormalities and solve those issues. The Gemba Walks (described in Chapter 8 on the executive mindset) help to move an organization in this direction.

Typical Support Systems

Let's take a look at typical examples of support systems shown in the bottom block of Exhibit 7.3, before we go on to discuss how to manage them for business performance improvement:

Planning. Management practices and systems have been aligned from the macro strategic level down to inside the micro business planning for practical workloads, crew assignments, schedules, and so on. The organization or department has thought through what it is trying to accomplish ahead of time, and people understand the plan. People have the necessary tools for success.

For example, if multiple departments need to cooperate, they are actively involved in improving the plan, which increases their buy-in to the concept. People are aware of the proven best methods to do work (standard work) and use them routinely.

Communications, Instructions, and Visual Signals. Simple, direct verbal communications and visual signals are used so people understand what is going on or what needs to be done. Standard methods, procedures, and process data are well documented and easy to use (e.g., one-page guides). The organization, department, or team has clearly stated what it is trying to accomplish. Leaders walk their talk; they don't say one thing and then do something else. Listening is a key part of communicating to make sure that people understand. Mechanisms exist for feedback to make certain the messages were understood. The organization acts in a manner consistent with its communication messages.

For example, marketing, sales, and operations communicate seamlessly from a customer perspective.

Organizational Structure, Alignment, and Staffing. The right people are in the right places and fully trained and equipped to succeed. Leadership effectively sets broad stretching aspirations that are meaningful to employees, they focus on real customer and business goals, and they drive alignment across functional areas of responsibility. Value streams or some other mechanisms are used to give as many people as possible a direct line of sight to customers. The organization structure is built around the horizontal, cross-function business processes—not vertical, functional silos or fiefdoms.

Essentially, people serve their downstream customers, not hierarchical functional authorities.

Accountabilities, Standard Work. Roles and responsibilities are clearly defined to promote cross-functional collaboration in order to maximize overall process performance. The best-known practice for doing work is clearly understood by the people responsible for doing the work. Observers can quickly see if work is being done that way.

For example, if people have a problem or variance in getting their work done, clearly defined pathways exist to reach a quick resolution. They don't simply work around a problem to keep things moving.

Measurements. Measures are few in number and meaningful. Individual, department, and high-level company metrics promote learning opportunities. Metric feedback is timely and provides useful information to improve performance. Metrics track progress versus the required process outputs, key process steps to be managed upstream, workplace orderliness (5S), and support systems' effectiveness.

For example, metrics exist that clearly show how well the organization is generating value for key customer groups. Cross-functional process metrics promote collaboration across functional lines of authority.

Recognition and Rewards. An appropriate rewards and recognition balance exists between department/functional performance and cross-functional process performance. And the same holds true for individual versus team performance. Employees trust their superiors and the overall organization to act in a fair and consistent fashion.

For example, purchasing is not simply rewarded for buying at a low purchase price; instead, purchasing's rewards and recognition take into account a broader perspective that might include ease of use, availability, quality, flexibility, and/or other value-added support actions beneficial to the organization.

Continuous Improvement (CI). Industry-leading continuous improvement business cultures routinely practice four CI subprocesses:

1. Education
2. Measurement
3. Search for Opportunities
4. Improvement Action

They are embedded in the management processes, the operating processes, and the CI cultural norms for "how we naturally do things here, every day."

For example, people openly contribute their ideas, point out barriers to success, and share best practices (i.e., what is working well and should be replicated).

What to Avoid with Support Systems

Support systems are instrumental in guiding the actions of departments and individuals in concert with the needs of the local process customers and the overall organization. Inadequacies in any of the support systems can lead process performance off in undesirable directions. Don't mess with the support systems until the process issues have been addressed (i.e., are lean, streamlined, and well controlled). Any premature support systems work is likely to be wasted if there is still significant work to be done in improving the core process.

Organizations often try to fix process problems by changing the support systems first, rather than fixing the value creation processes they support. Many dollars have been spent implementing expensive information/automation systems (enterprise resources planning [ERP], factory automation, customer relationship management [CRM], etc.), only to have that new investment fail to fix the situation. A similar problem happens when companies try to fix process problems by changing the performance metrics or incentive compensation. No doubt you have probably experienced support systems adjustments (reference the key words in the Support Systems Block in Exhibit 7.3) that failed to yield the expected benefits.

Managing Support Systems for Overall Business Performance

A nontraditional, higher leverage approach can include stepping back and using the management support systems categories as a tool to look at a value creation from a broader perspective.

A *support systems assessment* for a core business process would include asking several questions about each of them that might be summarized in something similar to Table 7.1.

Additional considerations may include implementation effort, issues, costs, and so forth. The adjustments required to support a core (value creation) process might be summarized on a worksheet similar to Exhibit 7.8.

Table 7.1 Questions to Ask When Assessing the Support Systems of a Core Business Process

1. What specific *support systems* in each category (e.g. accountabilities) are currently in place and operating?
2. What is the *current impact* of each support system? Or, to what extent does each support system facilitate (or impede) the supported process? This question requires some critical thinking to identify the cause-and-effect relationships between each support system and the practices it elicits from the core process team. In other words, how is the core team's performance different than if the support system did not exist?
3. For each support system, what *possible modifications* could be made to it to better guide performance of the supported process?
4. What *expected impacts* will be derived from each new or modified support system? How important would that be to the process team, customers and company?
5. What *annual benefits* might be expected? Note that the expected impacts may include powerful intangibles that can't be quantified in dollars.

A Support Systems Improvement Case Study: The JK Manufacturing Company

Some learning from a large, well-known consumer products manufacturer (alias JK Manufacturing Company, to protect the company's privacy) will illustrate the concept. JK Manufacturing launched a critical process redesign team, focused on the core manufacturing functions. It was all about finding ways to reduce the company's already low material waste levels, improve workload balances, increase fixed asset utilization rates, and postpone a plant expansion. The team's goals were pretty normal:

- To save a few pennies per unit
- To become more cost competitive in the marketplace
- To increase revenues
- To increase market share
- To increase profitability
- To increase returns on shareholder equity

Along the way, the project team members often found themselves pointing at improvement opportunities outside of the core process. Routine

Support Systems for Xxxxxx Xxxxxxx Process

Categories and Systems	Current Impacts	Possible Modifications	Expected Impacts	P&L Chgs $/Year +/(-)	$ Costs to Implement
Planning					
Customer demand forecast	Planned staff time is often much greater than or much less than the realized requirements	Add a current customer demand sampling survey to the historical data now in use	Reduce non-value staff time costs by 20%	$90,000	$175,000
Daily staff time plan	Planned staff time is often much greater than or much less than the realized requirements	Develop standard work times that better reflect the actual work content for particular types of repetitive jobs	Reduce non-value staff time costs by 30%	$135,000	$200,000
Organization, Training					
Xxxxx xx xxxxxxx	Xxxxxx xxxxx xx xxxxxxx	Xxxxxx xxx xxxxxx x xxxxxxx	Xxx xxxx xxxxxx xxxx	($xx,xxx)	$xx,xxx
Xxxxx xx xxxxxxx	Xxxxxx xxxxx xx xxxxxxx	Xxxxxx xxx xxxxxx x xxxxxxx	Xxx xxxx xxxxxx xxxx		$0
Xxxxx xx xxxxxxx	Xxxxxx xxxxx xx xxxxxxx	Xxxxxx xxx xxxxxx x xxxxxxx	Xxx xxxx xxxxxx xxxx	$xx,xxx	$0
Communications					
Xxxxx xx xxxxxxx	Xxxxxx xxxxx xx xxxxxxx	Xxxxxx xxx xxxxxx x xxxxxxx	Xxx xxxx xxxxxx xxxx	$xx,xxx	$xx,xxx
Accountabilities, Std Work					
Xxxxx xx xxxxxxx	Xxxxxx xxxxx xx xxxxxxx	Xxxxxx xxx xxxxxx x xxxxxxx	Xxx xxxx xxxxxx xxxx	($xx,xxx)	$0
Xxxxx xx xxxxxxx	Xxxxxx xxxxx xx xxxxxxx	Xxxxxx xxx xxxxxx x xxxxxxx	Xxx xxxx xxxxxx xxxx		$0
Measurement, Review					
Xxxxx xx xxxxxxx	Xxxxxx xxxxx xx xxxxxxx	Xxxxxx xxx xxxxxx x xxxxxxx	Xxx xxxx xxxxxx xxxx	$xx,xxx	$xx,xxx
Recognition, Reward					
Xxxxx xx xxxxxxx	Xxxxxx xxxxx xx xxxxxxx	Xxxxxx xxx xxxxxx x xxxxxxx	Xxx xxxx xxxxxx xxxx	$xx,xxx	$0
Continuous Improvement					
Xxxxx xx xxxxxxx	Xxxxxx xxxxx xx xxxxxxx	Xxxxxx xxx xxxxxx x xxxxxxx	Xxx xxxx xxxxxx xxxx		$xx,xxx
Overall Process Supports	Efforts are somewhat unfocused, less efficient than desired	All above	Balanced, productive workload better matched to realized demand	$xxx,xxx	$xxx,xxx

Exhibit 7.8 Support systems adjustments.

planning, scheduling, and communications functions came up many times in various forms. Each time, they had to remind themselves that these issues were not part of the immediate mission to improve the core process, so those emerging ideas were put aside in a "parking lot list" for later work. That was comfortable because, early on, they had considered the Business Process Model (shown in Exhibit 7.3) and noted that their initial focus had to be on the process output (customer) requirements (A) and the Value Creation Processes block (B). The support systems (C) had to wait for later, after the redesigned process was in hand. The opportunities in the parking lot list were mostly support systems issues for later work.

After the team members identified solutions to their value creation process, they went through an assessment exercise similar to the example in Exhibit 7.8. Some of the support systems had been misaligned with the company's needs for years, but momentum and the lack of a way to rationalize their functions had stalled previous efforts at improvement. The team members incorporated a number of modifications, for example:

- They simplified scheduling to move to a visual pull system, rather than computer reports
- They eliminated more than twenty different information reports no one really used.
- They redefined roles and responsibilities (for years, some people had entered information for various things, and they were reluctant to let go of that responsibility, even though they were no longer directly involved). There were many fractional head-count responsibilities where different people did part of a job. When the roles were clarified, accountability became more focused, with fewer inefficient handoffs.
- They changed performance metrics so they were process focused, even though several departments needed to work together within the process.
- They gave responsibility for the overall value stream to a single manager, which ended years of infighting about which group was causing the problem.

The team's goal was to optimize the company as a whole, not any of the individual functions, and to make certain the support systems were in alignment with value creation.

Perhaps the most valuable learning from such projects is the need to frequently review the alignment of support systems with the core processes they serve. Things change quickly in business today. Just like the increasingly rapid changes in external customers' requirements, the same happens with requirements for support systems services to the *internal* value creation processes. The supporting functional departments need to constantly ask "What do we need to do to serve those needs?" Then, they need to rapidly adapt to the changed requirements. It's about what the core value creation processes need from the support systems (highest quality at lowest cost) to operate at a performance level to compete with the top 20% in their industry.

Support Systems Conclusions

The Five Missing Ingredients are mostly under the support systems domain. Examples have been shared about metrics, recognition, and rewards that optimize a piece of the process rather than overall process performance. And we have covered the importance of a meaningful purpose and clear value definition to drive value creation. Let's touch on one other support system—accountability.

Most businesses are organized in silos. One set of specialists hands off to another group of specialists to get work done. For example, Sales is separate from Engineering, and customer service representatives operate apart from Distribution and Operations. Even though the importance of process under-standing, process responsibility, and value stream organization has been emphasized for more than 20 years, most businesses still have organizational structures very similar to the way General Motors operated in the 1950s. We have readily accepted cross-functional work cells to improve process perfor-mance in a factory, but we cannot seem to accept this concept in front-end office or organizational leadership environments.

An organization does not need to be completely restructured to have a process view. For example, one way Toyota gets a process view is from the chief engineer's perspective when they design new cars. That person has responsibility for end-to-end success when designing a new vehicle. The Cisco Systems and Total Cost stories in the last part of this chap-ter also provide examples of support systems elements that drive dra-matically different business performance than found in average Level 3 companies.

If someone does not have responsibility for a process view inside an organization, then no one has responsibility for managing trade-offs between the various functional specialists, other than the senior leadership team. And senior leaders usually do not have the time or knowledge to look at these issues at a detail level (Cisco is an exception from the norm in their approach). So, learning opportunities, very similar to the workaround learning opportunities discussed earlier, are missed.

In the Lean world, a key reason for having a value stream is to get cross-functional process understanding and to make process performance very visual. A group of people who are focused on a product or service family is brought together to work as a minibusiness within the larger organization. A value stream largely keeps this group of cross-functional people busy servicing a specific group of customers. Support systems alignment in this type of environment is much easier.

Maintaining a Focus

Now that you have considered the ABC development sequence, look at the Business Process Model from another angle. What do you need to maintain focus as you negotiate a process-improvement journey? A key component of effective process improvement is creating a learning environment. In a learning organization, people don't get punished for not *knowing*, but they are taken to task for not *learning*. Realize a few basics about learning:

■ Learning occurs in small doses
■ Learning requires practice and reinforcement for full assimilation
■ Learning new behaviors requires a change in awareness or motivation
■ Learning occurs best when the learner personally benefits
■ And depending on the magnitude of the change, people may need to emotionally let go of the old way of operating

The tools listed on the following menus are learning aides. A detailed version is in Exhibit 7.9. Notice in the following and in the Exhibit that there are three distinct dimensions of process improvement work:

1. **Tools for Process Improvement Work:** To organize and diagnose process information and data. Process tools are for analyzing a process; they help to find and eliminate waste. Tool subsets include:
   ■ Process definition and visualization
   ■ Quality
   ■ Time

- Cost
- Analysis to find waste, variation, and causes
- Value stream and process maps

2. **Desired Lean Sigma Process Practices:** Process practices describe ways to operate, and almost represent improvement targets. Use the analytical tools to move the current way of doing work to these new practices.
   - Prepare the workplace
   - Improve daily work
   - Address setup and maintenance
   - Make value flow faster (through operations to customers)

   Once the appropriate Lean concepts are chosen and applied in an improved process, the leadership needs a reasonable understanding of what these practices require in the way of new or modified support systems (per previous discussions about the Business Process Model) in order to sustain the new practice.

3. **Project Organization and Management Methods:** Project methods focus more on how to organize projects for speed, efficiency, and effectiveness (project management). Methods include problem-solving methodologies and good project management practices to collaborate with people impacted by process changes and engage their support and knowledge.
   - DMAIC (define, measure, analyze, improve, control)
   - PDCA (plan, do, check, act/adjust)
   - Project chartering
   - Others

It is useful to keep these three perspectives (improvement tools, process design concepts, project management methods) separate in order to make certain you are using the right improvement tool or method in the right way for project effectiveness and in order to sustain the changes you seek to accomplish.

The range of improvement tools, process practices, and project methods may seem somewhat complex as a whole. But none of the individual tools is particularly complicated. They mostly come from 100 years of industrial engineering study and application in business.

Using these tools may seem somewhat stressful at first, especially if your job has been mainly focused on managing existing processes and you have had limited support to take time to learn how to make a process work better. And there is often some confusion about when to use which particular tool.

People sometimes mix the tools, process design thinking, and project management techniques. It helps to separate these concepts. The menus are intended to help adopters get their bearings faster. It's not that mysterious, but it does take a while to become familiar with all the pieces and where they fit.

The Process Improvement Menu: Tools, Concepts, and Methods

Exhibits 7.9 and 7.10 contain the main items in a Process Improvement Tools, Concepts, and Methods menu. Whatever tool set you use (Lean, Six Sigma, etc.) for process improvement work, the menu will help organize your thoughts and actions.

Now, with the Business Process Model, the common thread of the value stream, and the Process Improvement Menu in mind, let's look at what others have done.

Process Thinking Stories

The following examples illustrate how process-improvement efforts have played out in various companies. Periodically, go back to the Business Process Model (described at the beginning of this chapter) to see where they fit. Notice that the stories often include elements from several of the ABC development sequence steps.

Get Grounded in Reality

In his book *Chasing the Rabbit* (2009), Steven Spear has a wonderful story* that makes this point. We paraphrase it here, because we have seen similar examples during the course of our careers.

A senior engineer named Mary Loeb had left General Motors and gone to work for Toyota in the United States. Her boss, Lynn Albright, told Mary that the president of Toyota's North American operations was coming to visit the plant. Mary found a car on the line that had a near-perfect paint job. She had it pulled off the line and put a rope around it, so that no one would touch it and no harm would come its way. When Lynn saw what was happening, she

---

* Steven Spear, *Chasing the Rabbit* pp. 283–284 (New York: McGraw-Hill, 2008).

asked, "What are you doing?" Mary said, "We want to show one of our best pieces of work!" Lynn said, "That is not the car he will want to see."

Mary asked, "Which one does he want to see?" Pointing at random, Lynn said, "That one! And he will want to see everything you found wrong with the car." So Mary and her team scoured the car and put sticky notes on every defect they could find. Lynn then said, "That is not all. He will want to know what you think caused those defects, and what you are doing to prevent them from happening again."

When the president came through the next day, Mary couldn't believe it. In her experiences with the Big 3, whenever an executive came in, it was all about showing the good news and the questions were about numbers (e.g., Did we hit our targets? What was our scrap?). But the Toyota executive wanted to know all about *the process* and what everyone knew about *the process*. If there was a bump or mark they could not explain, they walked the line with the executive trying to find the link.

This is a story about an organization trying to constantly get in touch with reality and stay grounded with just how far short it falls from perfection. This is so different from the typical happy talk that happens in most North American and European operations when a senior executive comes to visit. First of all, most North American senior executives would not spend that much time in operations, even though that is where value is being created. And most supervisors have been trained to show an example of their best work, so we can all feel good and pretend this is how work always gets done. The executive quickly tours the operation and then heads to a conference room where most time is spent talking about numbers. This is truly a sad state of affairs if one believes reality is a good thing to know.

Understanding Variation

Years ago, one of us had an opportunity to attend Dr. Deming's Four-Day Statistical Process Control training. It is an experience one never forgets. Deming used the Red Bead experiment to explain variation, and it is still a great way to explain the concept. He put a mixture of 800 red beads and 3200 white beads into a bin. He then "hired" six workers from the audience and a couple of inspectors to check quality. The workers' job was to use a paddle to scoop 50 beads out of the container. The customer would buy only white beads. Think of the red beads as typical process problems. They might be defects, wrong material received from a supplier, unclear requirements, last minute changes, waiting for a decision, and so on.

Tools, Process Concepts, and Project Methods for Business-Process Improvement					
	DMAIC Project Phases *3				
Tools for Process Documentation & Analysis *1	Define	Measure	Analyze	Improve	Control
Process Definition and Visualization					
SIPOC Diagram	A				
Voice of Customer Requirements; C/S Model *2	A				
Business Process Model *2	A				
Process Requirement Document	A				
Value-Stream Map	A				
Swim Lane (Process Deployment) Map	O				
Spaghetti Diagram	L				
Workplace Layout Drawing	L				
Operation Analysis Worksheet	O				
Quality Info on Process Outputs, Activities, and Inputs					
Control Chart		S			O
Data Collection Checksheet		O			O
Frequency Plot		O			O
Pareto Chart		O			O
Value Analysis Matrix		L			
Time and Physical Info On Process Steps and Overall					
Backlog Analysis		L			
Balance Chart		L			
Cycle Time Worksheet		L			
Combination Work Table		L			
Downtime Loss Worksheet		L			
Efficiency Calculations (OEE)		L			L
Process Characteristics Chart (spreadsheet) *2		L			
Rapid Change-over (SMED) Worksheet		L			
Sequence of Events Chart (SOE)		L			
Takt Time Calculation (vs. Process Pulse/Cycle Time)		L			L
Time Value Map		L			
Cost Info On Process Steps, Direct Resources, Overheads					
Spreadsheets		O	O		O
Cost Accounting Charts		O	O		O
P & L and Balance Sheet		O	O		O
Analysis Tools To Find Wastes, Variation, and Causes					
Ask "Why?" Five Times			A		
Collaborative Brainstorming			A		

Exhibit 7.9 Tools for process improvement work.

Cause-and-Effect (Fishbone) Diagram			O		
Five Whys Tree Diagram			O		
Failure Modes and Effects Analysis (FMEA)			O		
"5S" Work Area Audit Checksheet			L		
Interviews and Direct Observation			O		
Multi-voting			O		
Opportunity Flowchart			O		
Pugh Matrix			O		
Statistical Correlation Analysis			S		
Selection Matrix			O		
Sort Matrix			O		
Tree Diagram			O		
Value Analysis Matrix			O		
Video Recording and Photographing			O		
Wastes Assessment Worksheet			L		
Wastes Checklist			L		

Project Types Legend: A = Always use; L = Lean (waste elimination); S = Six Sigma (variation control);
O = Optional, Either L or S (Where typically first used in projects)

*1 Partial lists of common items

*2 From Process Management (PM)

*3 Or, DMADV for a new process design project

Exhibit 7.9 (Continued) Tools for process improvement work.

On each pass, a different number of red beads would be on the paddle. If it was a low number, Deming told the worker "good job"; if it was a high number, he told the worker to do a better job. A great count of red to white beads was 5 red and 45 white. He told the workers they were all using the same paddle, and there was no variation in the procedures, so why couldn't they keep hitting good numbers? If someone had a high count of red beads, Deming talked about how one of their coworkers had even better performance, and again, since they were all using the same tools, why couldn't they perform like the best operator?

He then asked the audience if the average result would settle to some certain number over time. Inevitably, someone would say 20%, because there were 800 read beads and 3200 white in the total population. One young engineer argued with Deming, stating, "That has to be the answer." Deming told the engineer, "You are wrong!" Having hooked a fish, Deming then reeled him in. He asked, "Why would you predict the average would be 20%? And I did not ask you what number. I asked if it would settle down to some number. And why did you say yes it would? On what basis are you making this decision?"

Tools, Process Concepts, and Project Methods for Business-Process Improvement

			DMAIC Project Phases *3		
Lean Sigma Process Design Concepts *1	Define	Measure	Analyze	Improve	Control
Prepare the Workplace					
Organization, Safety, Ergonomics			L		
O&S 5S Tracking Sheet		L			
O&S Worksheet (5S Action Plan		L			
Physical Arrangement and Layout			L		
Improve the Daily Work					
Standardization			O	O	
Standard Work Sheet		A	A		
Standard Practices and Procedures		A	A		
Support Systems		A	A		
Data Tools: Checksheet, Control Chart, etc.			O	O	
Error-Proofing, Auto-Stop, Autonomation			O	O	
Address Setup and Maintenance					
Rapid Set-Ups and Change-Overs			L		
Integrated Maintenance; Data-Bases, etc.			L		
Make Value Flow Faster					
One-Piece Flow and "Pull"			L		
Process Pulse/Cycle Time vs. Demand "Takt"			L		
Signalling Pull, Kanban			L		
Visual Management			L		
Andon Sign		L			
Workload Leveling			L		
Demand Sequencing and Leveling			L		
Leveling Tool (ABBABB)		L			

Project Organization and Management Methods *1	Define	Measure	Analyze	Improve	Control
DMAIC or DMADV project framework	A				
Charter for Process Improvement Project	A				
Critical Process Improvement Project	O				
Kaizen ImpAct Project	L				
Commitment Scale	O				
Communication Board	O				

Exhibit 7.10 Lean Sigma process practices design concepts.

Communication Planning Matrix	O				
Documentation Planning Worksheet	A				
Gantt Chart (Project Timeline)	O				
Involvement Matrix				O	
Kaizen / Lean Event Results Worksheet				O	
Kaizen / Lean To-Do List				O	
Lean Event Storyboard				O	
PDCA (Plan, Do, Check, Adjust)	O				
Planning Grid	O				
Targeted Lean Event Prework Checklist	L				

Project Types Legend: A = Always use; L = Lean (waste elimination);
S = Six Sigma (variation control); O = Optional, Either L or S

*1 Partial lists of common items   (Where typically first used in projects)

*2 From Process Management (PM)

*3 Or, DMADV for a new process design project

Exhibit 7.10   (Continued) Lean Sigma process practices design concepts.

Table 7.2   The Number of Red Beads Gathered by 6 Workers Working for 4 Days

Red Beads All Team Members	73	50	49	47	219
Average $\bar{X}$	12.1	8.3	8.2	7.8	9.1

Deming constantly challenged the lack of critical thinking and process understanding. Although one of his 14 points was to eliminate fear from the workplace, he was rather abrupt and short on patience in these conversations. He eventually asked, "What are some reasons why the x-bar (average) might not settle down to 20%?" After a pause, someone asked, "Are the red and white beads different sizes?" He responded, "Of course they are different sizes; no two are the same! What else?" Ultimately, through much cajoling and good humor, Deming got people to realize that the red beads were larger and heavier than the white and that the paddles introduced additional variation. He used several paddles; each one approached a different average result.

At the end of the exercise, a team of 6 people after 4 rounds might have results similar to Table 7.2. $\bar{X}$, the daily average, is calculated by dividing the total number of red beads drawn in that round by the number of team members, and the same for the overall 4-day total [219/(6 workers × 4 days)]. Deming then did a simple statistical calculation on process capability. The average proportion of red beads drawn each day, p-bar represents the ratio of red beads in the count to the total number of beads drawn.

$$\bar{p} = \frac{219}{6x4x50} = .18$$

You could use these figures to calculate statistical process upper and lower control limits.

$$\begin{array}{c} UCL \\ \\ LCL \end{array} = \bar{x} \pm 3\sqrt{x(1 - \bar{p})} \ \text{ or } = 9.1 \pm 3\sqrt{9.1x(1 - .18)}$$

A typical set of results might look like the graphic shown in Exhibit 7.11.

Deming challenged the thought process. "Why would the ratio not be what people thought it should be?" He tried to get people to understand that multiple variables exist. The prediction of 20% is important. When the actual results do not conform to the prediction, an investigation is necessary. Although describing this in a book is not the same as seeing it live, we hope you can still appreciate a few of the lessons:

■ All processes have variation.
■ People work within a system that is beyond their control; the system largely determines how they perform.
■ Management owns the system and is responsible for understanding the system's capability.
■ If you want to improve performance, you need to improve the capability of the system.

When you look at the graphic shown in Exhibit 7.11, you begin to understand the process capability and the variation that is taking place. It is important for leaders to be well grounded in this type of thinking. All processes have variation. The above process is stable. None of the data points went past the upper or lower control limits, which are calculated as three standard deviations away from the mean. In our simple sample, the output ranged from 5 red beads to 17 red beads. You will not improve performance by focusing on individual workers. There is too much variation in the process that is outside of the workers' control.

To gain better understanding of process variability at the leadership level, pick two or three key business processes to measure. It is a valuable investment of time and will create more profound knowledge about your business.

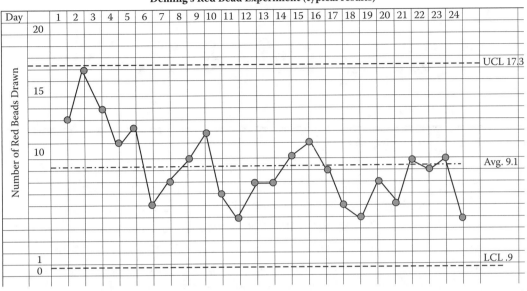

Exhibit 7.11   Red bead results.

Cisco's Evolving Approach to Process Understanding

Cisco has been trying to increase the engagement levels of its employees in understanding key business processes. The company has moved in a direction different from W. L. Gore; Cisco has been experimenting with new business structures. For a period of time, Cisco was reorganizing to a process focus, so one manager might have had responsibility for order-to-cash for a large customer group. Over time, Cisco found this a cumbersome way to operate.

Functional disciplines at Cisco are very important because they are the primary source of developing technical expertise within a specific discipline. But at the same time, it is critical for the organization to have a cross-functional perspective because that is how customers are served. So people need to have an easy-to-see view across functional lines of authority. For example, see Exhibit 7.12.

A senior leader at Cisco shared this description:

> John Chambers and senior leadership at Cisco determine which business segments require more focus; they create a council to address key issues; for example, enterprise customers or small businesses. A council might focus on how to more effectively sell (refine their value engine; scope might span from making the sale

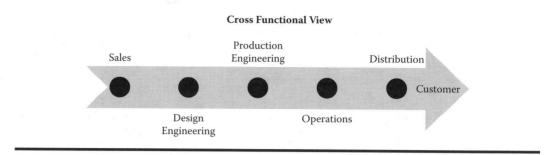

Exhibit 7.12   Cross-functional view.

to delivering the products or services) to enterprise customers. The councils then create boards composed of people with significant knowledge about those markets. The boards work with the functional groups to find innovation opportunities to improve Cisco's performance. The issues tend to be large multiyear issues. The boards and councils help create a shared view of the market.

This executive formerly worked for another large technical company. She said,

> This is a very different environment than my experience at my old telecommunications company. Here at Cisco, people are very strong on providing immediate feedback. They maintain openness for dialogue. If someone thinks you are doing something wrong or there was a better way to go about it, you hear about it. It's not issued as a command; it's a great opportunity for learning as things are happening. It's so refreshing to have a culture that allows people to talk about issues; how "that was not good, and let me tell you why."

Total Costs and Process Thinking (Cost of Outsourcing)

Total cost is not a simple concept. Total costs are important to understand from a process perspective. Decisions made by sales can have a direct impact on other costs: operations, maintenance, logistics, warehousing, engineering, and so on. Salespeople may make their short-term numbers by selling to the Ugly 50, but there is a ripple impact on cost for the rest of the business. Or salespeople may try to meet their revenue goals at the end of the month or the end of a quarter. But the uneven order flow significantly increases costs in other functional departments. Most business systems do not provide total costs information from a cross-functional perspective. When you dig deeper, you learn more.

For example, Linux software is advertised as freeware. But is it cost free? *Not from a total cost of ownership perspective.* Let's just assume for a moment that you are a school system, and you believe that getting free software is great! But the cost to use Linux will include:

- Training to use it
- Hardware to run it
- Development of standards or protocols for using it
- Perhaps upgrade costs
- Administration
- Other costs

This is not a good or bad thing; the point is to make sure you understand what the total costs are for something before you commit to a particular pathway.

The same issues exist when people look at part of a cost, but don't take total cost into account for key decisions. For example, a supplier can sell a part that may cost purchasing *more*, but the part or product *decreases* engineering or maintenance costs. If the customer is completely driven with functional performance metrics, that customer may miss on a significant opportunity to reduce its total costs. A supplier can try to address issues like this in its sales process, but it makes for a more complicated selling process.

George Koenigsaecker, retired CEO of Jake Brake (Danaher Division), spoke at the Lean Accounting Summit* and said this about customer–supplier partnerships:

> Very little competitive advantage is likely to come from supply chain relationships, unless you have a captive relationship with your suppliers. Money spent today on innovation in partnership with a supplier is very likely to improve your competitor's business tomorrow, as your suppliers look to grow their business.

Imagine how hard it is to achieve alignment when you own the resources. If key parts of the organization are outsourced, is this likely to get

---

* George Koenigsaecker, Keynote at Lean Accounting Summit, September 22, 2009.

easier? Like most things in life, there are two sides in this argument. There is something to be said for core competencies, but it seems like too many organizations have an extremely narrow definition of that term.

Outsourcing for lower labor costs may look great when you put labor rates together side by side. But from a total cost perspective, there are other considerations, including these:

- **Quality:** Will it be the same? For example, many companies importing food items have found quality is not the same; food processors in China have not adhered to manufacturing polices, practices, and procedures used in other parts of the world. So the cost is cheaper, but at what price? Thinking longer term, do suppliers follow environmental guidelines that customers might care about?

- **Employee treatment:** A few years ago, Nike and other shoe manufacturers were in trouble with their customers over the practices their outsourced suppliers used involving unsafe employee working conditions and child labor.

- **Delivery and delivery flexibility:** Someone making an outsourcing decision would certainly take into account the costs of shipping product from the new location to the company's markets. However, volatile energy prices make even estimating those costs a challenge. But would they also give consideration to, for example, buying boatloads versus buying component parts on a just-in-time basis as the company has orders? Rarely does expedited premium transportation service seem to be part of the equation; no matter how good the process, there will typically be some form of premium transport from time to time. There is less flexibility in the outsourced long-distance shipping model. Companies in North America often struggle to make sure trucks leave a plant with a fully loaded shipment. In the outsourced model, you are now dealing with fully loaded containers from halfway around the globe. These costs are typically significantly understated.

- **Inventory:** If an organization has a just-in-time relationship with its suppliers, inventory can be kept at minimal levels within an acceptable level of risk. If it is procured over long distances, more must be carried. Although there is an inventory cost differential, the more important risk cost is quality related. If a quality problem happens in a just-in-time environment, it can be corrected quickly with minimal inventory impact. For longer supply chain relationships, however, the cost of quality in fixing those issues can be significant. People often do not take this cost into account because there is a tendency to believe that no interruptions will take place. Yet the reality is that they do!

■ **Future new products:** In traditional manufacturing companies, design engineers (on the second floor) bicker with operations managers (on the first floor) to find time to test new product designs on the factory floor. If facilities are moved halfway around the globe, isn't it likely this would become even more of a problem? Is this ever part of the total cost consideration in an outsourcing decision?

■ **Oversight:** In order to make certain quality standards are followed, companies typically need to periodically send highly paid professionals (quality, engineering, training, etc.) to the supplier's location.

■ **Ethics:** Companies that outsource products to other countries often find new competitors cropping up very quickly in the host country. Often, there has been a compromise of design drawings, where the engineering drawings were shared or sold locally. Even the ethical views of standard manufacturing practices may differ significantly from country to country.

■ **Customer impact:** Call center dissatisfaction has caused some outsourced centers to fail.

■ **Other issues:** And there are language and cultural issues, loss of intellectual property, counterfeiting, flexibility, additional stocking requirements due to long supply chains, loss of flexibility, and more.

And now the important considerations:

■ **Loss of application knowledge or intellectual capital:** Company leaders often do not take into consideration "why they know, what they know now." Current levels of knowledge inside an organization are attributable to a legacy of years of experience. It is relatively easy for the current staff members, with their current level of knowledge, to manage distant operations. But how will that knowledge be obtained by future generations of professionals and managers, and what is the cost? How will new future value be created?

■ **Lack of understanding the organization's true value-creation engine:** This is going to be a bigger and bigger problem for North American industries over the next 20 years because the value engines have been given away.

- ■ **Cyber crime:** Here is something you probably did not expect to see on this list, but it is going to rise in importance over the next decade. As information becomes more and more digital, it also becomes more and more portable and vulnerable. A company such as Lockheed, Boeing, or another large manufacturer may have reasonable cyber security, but many of the digital leaks have taken place in smaller supplier operations where the electronic information infrastructure is not quite so secure. (In fairness, this issue applies to all suppliers, not just those that are outsourced.)

- ■ **Complexity of managing a more dispersed infrastructure:** They may get it straightened out at some point, but Boeing tried to do an end run around union problems by outsourcing large segments of its new 787 Dreamliner. As of this writing, it is currently 1.5+ years behind schedule. When Boeing outsourced component parts to third parties, the third parties turned around and outsourced segments to other organizations. Problems have ranged from lack of skills, to language translation problems, to something as simple as keeping change orders up to date. There have been many issues that were never taken into account from a total cost perspective. This is not to say that the Union of Aerospace Workers is not a problem. There are major union-related issues, but both sides seem to be playing a game of chicken rather than working together to create long-term customer value. Union leaders also need an understanding of total cost; they cannot simply lobby for their piece of the pie and not worry about the whole.

If you look only at sales per employee, outsourcing will improve that metric, even though total costs might have gone up due to materials, distribution, and other related costs. A better metric to measure employee value added is:

$$(\text{Sales} - \text{Purchased Cost of Materials}) \div \text{number of Employees} = \text{Value Added per Employee.}$$

This formula is different from traditional sales per employee because it removes a misleading benefit of outsourcing and measures only what is done inside the company. Is your value-added percentage increasing or decreasing? How is that likely to impact your ability to add new value moving forward?

Total cost requires deep understanding and facilitates total process knowledge. The above is not intended to be an anti-outsourcing diatribe.

Commodity-type items should be produced wherever they can, at the lowest possible costs. Tom Friedman's book *The World Is Flat* (2007) states a compelling case for global markets and infrastructure. But for long-term prosperity, it is important that an organization has a clear understanding of its value proposition and its value engine. We personally believe that many leadership teams and boards of directors have lacked this insight, and that over the long term, value creation inside many North American companies will suffer.

It's very obvious when total cost issues arise inside an organization—one department begins to vigorously complain about the work done by another department. The truth is usually somewhere in the middle. When these fights arise, rather than ignoring them, do a total costs analysis from a cross-functional business perspective, taking a process view into account. This can have a very significant favorable impact on profitability if it is done in the right way.

Refer back to the Mity-Lite chair story told near the end of Chapter 6 for a reinforcement of this total cost discussion. In that story, a group of employees were given an opportunity to save jobs that were important to the local community. They demonstrated that a hot new product could be manufactured locally using existing employees. The employee team clearly defined standard work practices using Lean manufacturing methods, which resulted in lower cost. They did take total cost into consideration in their analysis and were able to effectively demonstrate why outsourcing was not the appropriate course of action. Leadership needed to invest a few capital expenditure dollars for a solution that provided considerably more flexibility to the company.

DEVELOPING PROCESS THINKING AT INDEPENDENCE ENTERPRISE

New division president Margaret Allavoine had commissioned a team to look at the custom design process and the manufacturing process in the Maintenance Controller Division (MCD). There were really three segments to the MCD business.

A. One segment represented 50% and was devoted to minor custom-designed new controller products. These products needed some engineering, but it was for simple changes. They won approximately 12% of the proposals bid to this customer group.
B. The second segment represented 25% and involved sales to less-sophisticated customers who pretty much wanted a simple controller purchased off the shelf.
C. The third segment also represented 25% and was for controllers at the leading edge of technology working with very knowledgeable customers. These products had major customization. This part of the business had a better track record, winning 40% of their proposals.

The production process at MCD was actually very similar to the "before" value stream map shown in Exhibit 7.5. The lead time for the highly custom-designed product was several months. And even the off-the-shelf products took more than a month to manufacture. Products for all three of those markets were manufactured on one production line. For the basic controllers (B), there were approximately 5 hours of value-added time on the production line, yet it was taking almost 5 weeks to get those products through production. Even for the simple products, engineering was reviewing the customer's request.

Operations redesigned their production layout to something similar to the value stream map shown in Exhibit 7.6; it was much cleaner. One cell manufactured the minor customized and off-the-shelf (A and B) products and the other cell manufactured the highly customized C products. Lead time for the A and B products dropped from 5 weeks to an average of 4 days. The ability to quickly respond to a customer order, especially the off-the-shelf B products with no customization, resulted in a 25% increase in orders for those products. Engineering had one day to review a B-type product request and 3 days for A items that had minor customization.

Manufacturing lead times for the highly customized C products also dropped, but the primary changes to that product line were made in sales and engineering. The sales people argued strongly that they were developing relationships with customers, so a failed proposal was not a complete failure. But when the data was looked at over a 5-year period, less than 10% of customers who did not buy from Independence after two proposals actually became future customers. So the conversion rates were very slow. For customers who did buy the customized products from Independence, there was actually considerable future business available. Margaret guided the sales force to begin looking at sales of multiple products over a 3-year time horizon, rather than just focusing on the single sale. These changes allowed Engineering to spend less time working on proposals the company would not win.

Margaret's MCD leadership team members decided they actually had two value streams focused around the A, B, and C products. So they started to measure performance as two separate mini-businesses. Sales designed a new front-end process to qualify customers. Customized sales had several different buyers in a customer's organization. Purchasing and Engineering were almost always part of the decision. A customer sale might also involve a project manager, a regulatory affairs specialist, and a business manager or executive. Each of those parties played a different role in the buying process, and typically one of them was the real buyer. Independence needed to know the real power buyer. In the past, Independence's Sales Group did not have a key responsibility to specifically identify the power buyer, so proposals were often created to the wrong set of specifications. In the new process, sales tried to identify this key person or group. If they could not identify this person, it was noted in the working file.

The customized controllers were usually purchased as part of a larger customer project. So the sales force needed to learn how far along in a development project the customer was. Was this an early stage opportunity, where MCD could propose some new ideas that would reduce the customer's total costs? Or was this a later stage, where the customer was simply looking for a customized controller that met a very specific set of requirements? In the latter instance, customers had little patience for new ideas, even if they might save overall costs.

Knowing the economic buyer and knowing how far along the customer was in the development cycle were defined as key sales responsibilities. They developed a sales worksheet similar to the one shown in Exhibit 7.13.*

The team studied successful sales practices and discovered that two important activities differentiated salespeople (people who sold >150%+ more than their target numbers vs. those who failed to meet targets (<80%):

1. Successful sales associates captured knowledge about the customer (similar to the worksheet in Exhibit 7.13).
2. Successful sales associates spent 50% more time with customers gathering knowledge about customer needs.

Successful sales associates had a success rate 200% higher than salespeople in the bottom third of the group. These changes were incorporated into the sales management and sales training processes. Successful salespeople mentored people who were having problems operating in this fashion.

Engineering also had some process changes to make. It divided engineering into two value stream groups: one to support the highly customized C product line and the second group to support minor customized and off-the-shelf (A and B) products. The engineers were very proud of their highly customized controllers, and their ability to educate customers on why a more expensive product was better for the customer's business. They felt no one made a higher-quality product than Independence. But many of the proposals MCD was losing for the customized C products were to potential customers who were already far down the road in their development cycle.

The proposal quoting process for late-stage development prospects needed improvement. Engineering essentially adopted a hybrid of the process that it already used for A-type products, which were only slightly customized. There was more customization to the C products, but engineering needed to focus more tightly on the specifications received from sales and less on the more advanced features of the products that the customer had not requested. Also, early-stage development projects, which had higher margins and more opportunities for MCD to add value, were given a priority over late-stage project bids.

Margaret had further opportunities on her plate: she realized there was a major opportunity to sell maintenance services to the company's customer base, but it would not be an easy sale. Several people also made this buying decision. MCD

---

* Our sales story and Exhibit 7.13 was partially drawn on our research and client discussions regarding complex sales. We drew on insights and knowledge we gained from three publications: Thomas Bonoma, "Major Sales: Who Really Does the Buying?" *Harvard Business Review*, 2006; Rick Page, *Hope Is Not a Strategy* (New York: McGraw-Hill, 2002); and Neil Rackham, *SPIN Selling* (New York: McGraw-Hill, 1988).

	A	B	C	D	E	F
1	**L. Sales Strategy Plan (SSP)**			Job Description:	Nucor Timbuktu Mill	
2	(Used in step L in the Development Plan and process diagram)				Gantry crane for xxxxx xxxxxx xx xxxxxxxxxxx	
3						
4	**Buying Stakeholders**	[L4]	John Doe	Bob Smith	Jim Anderson	Ed Johnson
5	**Title / Position**		Mfg Engineer	Production Manager	CFO	Chair of Customer Team
6	**Buying Role** *1	[L5]	Influencer	Initiator, User	Influencer	Decider
7						
8	**Power Type** *2 and Clues		Attraction, Expert	Reward, Coercive	Coercive	Status
9	Formal authority					
10	Deferred to by others		Persuasive communicator			
11	Disliked by others			"dictator"		
12	Copied on most correspondence					
13	Sends others to negotiations			usually sends assistant		
14	**Champion, or Veto Threat?**		Is an ally	TBD Important!!!		
15						
16	**Priorities / Benefits Classes** *3		Political / Personal	Product functionality		
17						
18	**Decision-Making Process, Basis, Wants or Benefits Goals**		Analytical; fact-based; protects professional credibility; most interested in maintainability	Only interested in performance and ease of use; unhappy with xxxxxxx competitor's xxxxxx xxxx feature	costs to switch from a competitor's units	process, but not disciplined use of it
19						
20	**Preference for Our Solutions?**		#2 technical preference	P&H fan		??
21	**Preference for Our People?**			Good relationship w/ Sales		??
22						
23	**Weight (Optional)**		30	40	20	10
24						
25	**Sales Strategy for Each Important Buyer** *4	[L6]	Collaborate on matching features to needs	Ask him to walk us through the operating cycle so we're clear on his requirements. Get his opinion on a couple alternate solution features.	Buy out the RMO change-over costs; bank on future orders	Do it, but better than the competitors
26						
27	**Sales Strategy for O.A. Project**		Concentrate on consultative relationships with Smith and Doe.			[L7]
28			Consider financial values for Anderson and the overall buying team. Don't over-build the solution.			

> **Process Development Test Questions:**
> * The Arrow running down the page implies a visible logic flow in this one-page summary. The sales person is probably in the best position to prioritize the key points from a customer perspective.
>
> Those key issues become input to other Front-End Team members who might contribute useful additions to the sales strategy plan (i.e., increase the chances of a Win).

Exhibit 7.13   Sales strategy planning worksheet.

would continue to develop its more sophisticated sales process selling A and C customized products and would use the knowledge gained to enter the services market next year. Margaret also felt the changes they were making now would address some of the new product development issues. There simply was not enough time or resources to run further, so the new product development process also had to wait until next year to become a priority.

CHAPTER WRAP-UP: DEPLOYMENT ACTIONS FOR BETTER PROCESS THINKING/UNDERSTANDING

Once again, we reference the first missing ingredient: It is critically important that the entire leadership team have a deep understanding of the value-generation process inside their business. Alignment is completely driven from that key insight. Value will differ by company and by industry. Reread the Procter & Gamble quotes from then-CEO Alan Lafley in the section "Principles to Consider Regarding How Your Organization Improves Value to Your Customers" in Chapter 4 on customer value. Leaders need to accurately know what value the company provides. As we said earlier, leaders learn this only by talking to customers face-to-face; you cannot gain this knowledge from third parties or reports, so start here!

Subsequently, it's important to gain more insights about process capabilities to generate that value. Back in the 1980s, there was an explosion of companies doing SPC (statistical process control) charts, but they were not done for the right reasons. The charts were used for too many operations, and people did not act on the information. So eventually the movement died a quiet, peaceful death (although smart operators have retained it in appropriate applications). Leaders need to reorient their thinking to develop more in-depth understanding of cross-functional process performance. You will do a much better job of allocating improvement resources with this perspective.

Look back at Exhibit 6.4 in Chapter 6 on key metrics, and focus on shifting your processes capabilities to the right, as shown in that example. If you make this shift, your processes will more reliably produce the desirable results. It will be done across a very narrow bandwidth (you bring the tails of the normal distribution curve much closer to the mean), so the end result is much more predictable—you can count on it! This is a significant shift in traditional thinking perspectives and leadership knowledge. Gaining insights about process capabilities helps leaders better understand what is happening with their business. You move away from people telling you stories about why things happened, to knowing why they happen. Deming talked about this as developing more profound knowledge.

There is an infinite list of things that can be improved inside any organization. But fixing everything that is broken is not necessarily important. From a leadership perspective, where resource allocation decisions are being made, it is critical to deploy those resources effectively. Level 3 organizations almost seem to practice a push method of improvement, where people find things that are broken and need to be fixed, and then based on their functional responsibilities, lobby for those precious few resources to get their problems fixed. Everyone hopes that by fixing these problems, the organization will improve its competitive position, but as we have stated earlier, this does not happen. The functional *department* may get better, but the *business* overall does not.

It is critical to move to more of a pull method of improvement, where business leaders have a responsibility and a vested interest in reporting on their critical process levels of performance. The latter view is much more real. When people report from an end-to-end process perspective, it eliminates all discussion about the improvements people claim to have implemented from a functional perspective in the middle of the process. If the overall process performance does not improve, it does not matter what you do in the middle. If you ignored all the other ingredients, and simply began to report from a cross-functional process-effectiveness perspective on how well your organization serves key groups of customers, you will increase the effectiveness of your improvement activities.

After you have taken the above actions, consider the questions/actions outlined below:

1. *Remember that a process is an experiment in the best-known way to do work at this point in time.* Constantly have people looking for learning opportunities to improve process capabilities.
2. *Do* not *automate a process that has not first been simplified* and where the value creation process steps have not been aligned to meet the needs of key customers (for the process).
3. *Spend some time doing a Gemba Walk* (explained more in Chapter 8 on the executive mindset) to become more familiar with process interconnection points. What happens when process 1 hands-off to process 2? You will often find improvement opportunities at the handoff points where different processes interconnect.
4. *Use process customer value and process performance metrics to identify where improvements are needed.* But don't go fishing for projects—that is a push method of improvement. Let important improvement issues surface in leadership meetings where process performance is reviewed and business leaders are accountable for cross-functional process performance.
5. *Once you decide to launch an improvement team, recognize that the differences in approaches between average organizations and the high-performing ones is not that significant,* with the exception of a couple of steps:

a. Initially target one to three critical cross-functional processes that should operate more effectively.

b. Select a few metrics (consider the section "True North Performance Metrics" in Chapter 6 on key metrics) that span across functional responsibilities and focus on customers.

c. Identify a few key goals for process improvement that would be meaningful for the customers, company, and employees involved. Consider all dimensions: quality (better), time (faster), and productivity (cheaper).

d. Remember that an average organization will look to identify a manager who has enough span of control over it to pretend, for purposes of the project, to own the process, but in fact, they don't. And that is a significant difference. They will probably report on some amount of dollars that were saved, but savings are typically an estimated, abstract number. Savings generally do not equate to specific business performance results. In contrast, in a top 20% company, someone does own the process, and that person will report on the business results of the process after the project team does its work. That person will not report how much money was saved. Either cost went down or revenues went up. It is very simple. So this step is quite different.

e. Identify a project team of respected cross-functional process members (four to eight members, depending on project scope).

f. Use whatever appropriate improvement tool sets are on hand (Lean, Six Sigma, etc.) to organize the team's project work.

g. Maintain a quick project pace by allocating and protecting team members' time for it.

h. Encourage active participation and process learning by recognizing the importance of the project journey (not just the destination).

i. Remember that an average organization will plan to hold functional managers responsible for overall process performance, not just their piece of the process. (*Right! Like you have never tried that before.*) If someone or some group doesn't own the process, then no one owns the process.

6. ***Keep in mind that it is much easier to sustain the gains and spread best practices when one person or a specific group has clear responsibility/accountability (real ownership) for the performance of key cross-functional business processes***—and when that one person or group routinely reports on it. Remember the Cisco example; you do not need to restructure your business to do this.

A process view (the Business Process Model, Exhibit 7.3):

■ Broadens our perspective beyond one functional department, starting with the real customer requirements, so the big picture is always in view as we look for ways to improve our local processes to contribute to more competitive performance of the whole business.
■ Helps us avoid overoptimizing subcomponents of a local process that might suboptimize or even cause failure of the larger processes to which it is connected.
■ Reminds us to develop and manage the support systems necessary to sustain the improvements made to a process, so they operate at the higher performance level.

You will need to study and eliminate waste in a major process at least five times from end to end to begin to approach world-class levels of performance. Seek to eliminate 50% of the waste on each pass.

This process thinking chapter completes our review of four critical ingredients missing in most improvement recipes. The fifth ingredient, the executive mindset, is required to pull everything together, and we cover it in the next chapter.

Chapter 8

Ingredient 5: The Executive Mindset

Focus on Customer Value, People Development, Process Performance, and Business Improvement Outcomes, Not Solely on Savings

INDEPENDENCE ENTERPRISE ASSESSES ITS OWN EXECUTIVE MINDSET

Andy Fletcher announced a meeting and invited the entire senior leadership team, Will Rasmussen from the board, the team members from the several cross-functional teams working to strengthen the improvement process at Independence, and Basem Hafey, the external consultant. He wanted to know the status and progress of each team and to determine what actions the senior leaders needed to take moving forward.

He had a conversation with COO Jack Morel the night before. They regretted not doing a full assessment of the Independence improvement process. They knew they were doing a better job of improving today, but they were not certain about their baseline starting point. So it was difficult to quantify how far they had come. They might have shifted a few of the priority actions if they had a more holistic picture at the start. But things seemed to be progressing well, and they planned to do an overall assessment before the end of the year.

Basem Hafey met earlier with Andy and Jack to discuss leadership behaviors most appropriate to accelerating improvement activities. Both were perceived by their subordinates as bright, take-charge individuals, with high standards of accountability for their work and their expectations of others. They were seen as fair in their decision making; they did not play favorites or like political posturing. Jack was known to be abrupt if he felt someone was not getting to the point quickly enough. Andy was seen as keeping his cards close to his vest, so sometimes in their work, people were not clear about Andy's expectations.

When they spoke with Basem, it became quite clear to Andy and Jack that when they became impatient, they tended to tell people what they wanted them to do. Jack said, "That is a great way to get something done quickly." As soon as the words left his mouth, he realized this type of behavior was not conducive to the critical thinking skills they were trying to develop. He chuckled and told Basem, "Oops! Guess I'm going to need to do some critical thinking myself. And not act quite so abruptly, as we strive to instill more critical thinking skills throughout the organization."

Basem reiterated a discussion they had now had many times. "The executive mindset is the glue that holds these ingredients together and provides focus. If leadership is loose on any of the above items (and most leaders are), the company will not rise to the top of its industry in a sustainable fashion. Anyone can have a brief moment of fame and luck. But staying there takes discipline."

Andy chuckled and said, "I have always perceived Jack and myself to be the teachers. We were supposed to know and convince the rest that they should follow our lead. We are still responsible for knowing enough to ask good questions, but we now learn as much as we teach. It's actually pretty exciting and an amazing transformation in the way we were both trying to do our jobs."

Jack nodded in agreement and added, "You know Basem, I was not at all happy when we started down this pathway. But that expression you used from Satchel Paige—"It ain't what you know that gets you in trouble, it's what you think you know, that just ain't so"—that expression has an entirely new meaning to me. I'm still working hard to do this, but I have become a better listener during the last 24 months. I'm also not quite so grouchy when I go home at night, a change in personality that has very much charmed my wife Kathleen."

Clearly, the Independence leadership team was working hard to continue to learn and to apply the principles and ideas discussed in this chapter.

Principles to Consider Regarding *Your* Organization's Executive Mindset

This is where it all comes together. As stated several times earlier, the executive mindset is the glue in the white space that holds the other missing ingredients together. This does not mean executives do it. Referring back to an earlier quote from Peter Drucker, "Leadership's primary responsibility is to create an environment where people can do their best work."* This absolutely does not mean a hands-off policy of letting

---

* Peter Drucker, *The Essential Drucker*, HarperCollins, 2001.

people do what they want. It's the opposite—leadership has a responsibility to create a management system that will deliver superior business results in an environment where:

1. Direction of the business is clearly focused to provide value to targeted set(s) of customers, where the business can provide meaningful solutions faster and better than its competitors. (This is the essence of Ingredient 1, covered in Chapter 4.)
2. People are encouraged and expected to find and eliminate distractions and waste that inhibits their ability to get meaningful (value-adding) work done to serve key customers and potential key future customers. (This is the essence of Ingredient 2, covered in Chapter 5.)
3. Metrics provide rapid, meaningful feedback at all levels to people inside the organization, so they constantly learn how to do a better job of adding value. (This is the essence of Ingredient 3, covered in Chapter 6.)
4. Process management maximizes cross-functional process performance and fosters deeper process understanding. Process capability is constantly improved to reliably deliver value without waste. (This is the essence of Ingredient 4, covered in Chapter 7.)
5. The executive mindset focuses on the business and having the above four ingredients seamlessly aligned to guide/drive improvement. (This is the essence of Ingredient 5, covered in this chapter.)

Alternative pathways certainly exist to become a Level 4 or 5 company in terms of improvement maturity. We are not saying this is the only pathway. But leaders who have tapped into the hearts and minds of people, who become passionately and creatively engaged to increase value for their customers, and to eliminate all forms of waste—that seems pretty hard to beat.

Still, many leadership teams seem reluctant to relinquish command-and-control behaviors! Perhaps it's a trust issue, or a lack of patience with the front-end investment of time necessary to develop more critical thinking. There is no question that the fastest way to get something done on a one-time basis is to tell someone how to do it. Unfortunately, this robs the person doing the work from developing a deeper understanding of how things work and why they work that way. It even removes some of the responsibility from the person doing the work. If things don't turn out exactly right, the excuse is, "my boss told me to do it this way." The end result is that it is much easier to be average than great.

Leaders must actively engage and do the hard work to develop more critical thinking skills in their peers and subordinates, if they seek to have their associates become more passionately engaged in the work they do. It is easy to let this slip away. One supervisor can quickly undo a year's worth of progress by reverting back to command-and-control behaviors. This type of transformation to Level 4 and 5 status requires diligence, openness, and hard work.

Here is another simple test of this truth:

■ Based on your personal experience, are the employees who work for other companies you deal with on a day-to-day basis passionately engaged in what they do?
■ Or for the most part, do people you see in other organizations simply try to do just an OK job?
■ Is there any reason to believe that the average employee in your organization behaves in a significantly different way from what you see in the sea of mediocrity that surrounds us?

Few managers have been exposed to or are experienced with a holistic view of the organizational performance necessary to create high-performance business teams. Individual manager views are fragmented, seeing pieces of the puzzle (strategies, tactical plans, IT systems, etc.), but not fully understanding how they fit together and drive each other as a whole. Once understood, the choice is clear. It starts with a more complete understanding of organizational infrastructure and drivers. This chapter is about gaining that understanding.

Using Strategy Deployment to Find True North

True North is about a shared vision across the enterprise, which must be based on timeless principles. There is a deeper element to True North than simply metrics (which is where we last discussed this topic, in Chapter 6). Leadership should be guided by timeless but very important ethical behaviors, including *honesty* (to customers, employees, stock holders, citizens, family, etc.) and *integrity*. These are the kinds of elements that define True North. Companies should define a lasting definition of customer value as part of this exercise, and then stick with the definition and ensure that their actions support the definition. These principles will determine how customers and employees ultimately judge the company. Then choose the right metrics to define your shared vision.

One tool that some companies use to drive alignment is Strategy Deployment. This particular tool is often referenced by several different names; *policy deployment* and *Hoshin planning* are two other common labels.

The primary power of Strategy Deployment is its ability to force decisions throughout an enterprise to allocate scarce resources on the targets most important to success. Strategy Deployment is about surfacing and prioritizing what must go right in order for a business to succeed. It needs to focus on the handful of critical issues (i.e., three to five such issues) that are most important to success. Obviously, every issue listed at the top level of an organization expands as it goes down the organization, very much like a rock thrown into the water makes a splash followed by many ripples; see Exhibit 8.1.

It doesn't matter what you call these top priorities; for example, they might be referred to as *critical success factors (CSFs), breakthrough strategies,* or simply *key strategies.* Identify the three to five CSFs that matter most for any one business. Remember, one CSF has a ripple impact inside the organization. Improvement resources should cover the CSFs first; then, to the extent resources are available, other teams can address other improvement opportunities, which are priorities for lower organizational levels.

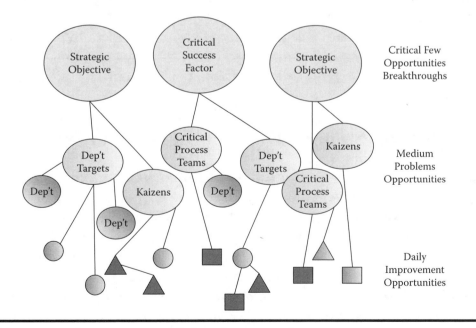

Exhibit 8.1   Deployment (Dep't) links to key strategies.

Daily improvement actions will be a blend of eliminating hassles that inhibit doing value-adding work and focusing on key priorities. When people ask for more resources, remind them that reducing waste activities in business processes frees up resources for additional work.

When you have more CSFs than you have fingers on your right hand, you begin to lose focus. By definition, a CSF should offer broad benefit; if it does not, then it is not a critical success factor. So you do not need very many of them. Organizations that have several businesses should still seek to identify the handful of CSFs for the overall organization. But senior leaders for a multiple-business-unit enterprise need to avoid the temptation to overly control what is happening beneath them. Focus on the most important, and build an environment of trust where sub-business unit leaders can manage their affairs and openly share with higher levels the key issues they face.

The basic steps for doing strategic policy deployment are not complex. The concept (under this label) has been around for more than 20 years. And the idea of focusing on what is important is not a new concept. If you are looking to move your organization to a more mature level of improvement, begin with an open dialogue about strategic intent. Imagine the dialogue and debate that happened at Toyota when it discussed launching their new Lexus division, or Apple with iTunes, or Chrysler with the minivan. Do your strategies stimulate a debate inside your business? If they don't, is it really a meaningful strategy? If it is so obvious that something in particular should be done—just do it. But your competition will also be making a similar move. Remember a strategy is or should be an improvement hypothesis for your organization. Once you have agreed on a strategy (and it might be only one), then use the following logic to deploy it inside your organization.

Basic Steps for Strategic Deployment (Refer to Exhibit 8.2)

Step 1: Determine key strategies, as outlined in Chapter 1 on value proposition and strategy. Typically, these focus on a several-year time horizon. The example shown in Exhibit 8.2 shows that this organization's key strategy is to "Double Revenues with Key Customers in the next 4 years." Clearly, that is not a strategy statement; instead, it is the metric that will monitor success of the key strategies over that time frame.

Step 2: After you've identified your key strategies and break-through objectives, determine your annual objectives. This must be done with a discussion, not by management decree. And the same

Policy Deployment - X Matrix

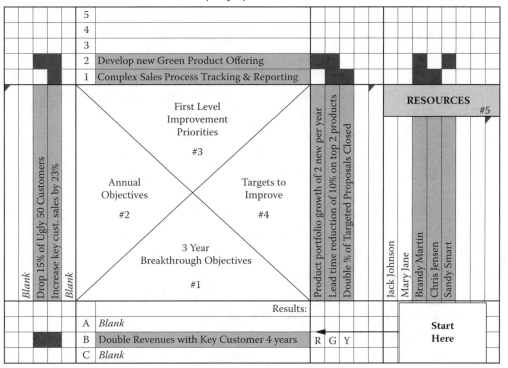

Exhibit 8.2 Policy deployment—X matrix.

thing should happen as you move down each level. Ask "What do *you* think? Does this make sense as an important CSF or breakthrough objective?" The time horizon for implementing a breakthrough objective might be three years, but it should definitely have a longer time horizon than 12 months.

Step 3: Once you've set your annual objectives (targets), identify your first level of improvement priorities. Again, ask if these targets make sense. Involve other people in the organization to set the improvement targets. The dialogue helps everyone get more in touch with reality. You don't want leadership to impose a fictitious sense of reality on lower levels, and you want lower levels of the organization to clearly understand why significant improvements in performance are necessary and to develop local *ownership* of them.

Step 4: Indicate your specific metric targets to improve. In Strategy Deployment language, people use the expression *catch ball*, meaning if the higher level wants to toss it, a lower level needs to catch it and own it. A dialogue takes place for each step of the matrix, where the next level down agrees the handoff took place, and they now own it.

Step 5: Decide exactly who will do the work. People are often looked at as an infinite resource, and some leaders just keep piling on work that good people will get done somehow. Adding people resources to this matrix forces a discussion of who is going to do this work. If some people are already overburdened, this matrix helps highlight the issue, thus forcing a dialogue about which opportunity is the most important priority.

This is a great reality check. Once the organization begins to discuss who is going to do this work, it forces a priority discussion. When senior leaders toss out key things to do without considering the resources needed to make it happen, they lose insight to a very valuable reality checkpoint, they lose credibility in the eyes of the workforce, they lose the opportunity to engage the workforce for truly inspired business team performance, and they risk driving the organization into a going-through-the-motion mode of underperformance that fails to keep pace with the industry leaders.

Step 6: Track your progress. Most of the time people use a second worksheet to track the actual progress on the "Targets to Improve" shown in Exhibit 8.2. Don't get carried away with spreadsheet mania and track too many levels down. Look one level below your direct reports and have that model cascade inside the organization, so you don't try pulling too much detail together on one spreadsheet. Refer to the Nissan Case Study later in this chapter for how to hold people accountable.

Case Example of Strategy Deployment

A number of years ago, a famous Chicago institution, the Old Town School of Folk Music (OTSFM), was having a near-death experience. On revenues of $200,000 per year (perhaps $1 million in today's equivalent dollars), the school was losing $40,000 per year and had no money in the bank. The school had ceased to be relevant to its markets, and new customers were not being attracted to the school's programming. In order to survive, the school needed to develop a new strategy. So it developed three:

1. The school could not pay its bills, so one strategy was to reduce costs and raise cash. Goal: Return to net profitability within 12 months.
2. Develop relevant new products to attract new customers. Goal: Increase revenues by 40% per year through new product offerings.

3. Raise money to renovate the school's main building and conference hall. Goal: Raise $600,000 over the next 24 months.

A new executive director, Jim Hirsch, was hired at the beginning of the turnaround. One member of the board and Jim reviewed all of the financial numbers and decided what they could control, and where cuts were necessary. Reducing costs involved laying off guitar instructors, who were struggling to make a living as artists. The little that the OTSFM paid them was still a meaningful amount in their lives, but an expense the school had to reduce in order to survive. The layoffs were painful, but amazingly, half of the staff agreed to work for free during the transition. They understood the situation faced by the school. Each creditor to whom the school owed money (and there were many) was met face to face. A plan was offered to pay them, if they could extend a little more credit to the school.

Growth takes time to build, but cost reductions can happen (no matter how painful) immediately. The school faced several tough choices. The school owned two buildings. It was a painful choice, but the school needed to sell one of its buildings, so that bills could be paid and agreements kept.

The school also needed to look at its programs and concert offerings to the public. The school's programs were pretty much geared to a middle-class, middle-aged, white-faced public. If the school wanted to survive over the long term, it needed to offer more exciting products (concerts, lessons, etc.) and draw in a broader, more ethnically diversified customer base. The OTSFM expanded its concert offerings and guitar instruction lessons. A new Wiggleworm program was put together to teach music to little children (under 5 years old), and Jim put together a Latin Music Festival that was the first such offering in Chicago by a non-Latino institution. Both of those programs resulted in significant revenue increases for the school.

Execution of the above changes was primarily done by the school's staff. The board (a group of volunteers) took responsibility for raising $600,000 to do the renovation. Just like a good song needs a "hook" to resonate with a listener, the school needed a hook to interest funding organizations and individual contributors. The school's success with its new products for a diversified audience was a primary reason funding organizations agreed to provide support to the school's capital campaign.

A number of other changes were also made, but cost reductions came first. Key metrics were directly related to the above goals and were monitored on a weekly or monthly basis. They focused on reducing excess teaching capacity, freeing up cash, pulling down all nonvital costs, making and keeping agreements, fulfilling all commitments made, and raising new revenues.

Fifteen years later, the school has had a renaissance. Its annual revenues are in excess of several million dollars. It successfully renovated its old building, and a new one was later purchased and renovated with money from an even larger capital campaign. The new venue has a larger concert stage and teaching capacity. That new building helped to lead the way for revitalizing a Chicago neighborhood. Currently, the school's concerts and teaching programs are full, and there is a very healthy involvement of volunteers, customers and staff. It impacts more people's lives today than at any time in its past.

Don't Go Nuts with It: Too Much of a Good Thing Is Not a Good Thing

Organizations that use Strategy Deployment can run off the deep end. This happens when too many breakthrough objectives are set. For example, one electronics company had more than thirty-five breakthrough objectives for a single business unit. That's not exactly a fine-tuned focus! Less is actually better.

Also, resist the temptation to overcontrol people. Another senior leader shared a conversation with one of his subordinates, when she commented about micromanagers. She said, "I can see that you are interested in this project. If your intention was to work on the project, maybe you should not have assigned it to me and just did it yourself; otherwise let me get it done."

Exhibit 8.3 shows a modified view of how one company perceives Strategy Deployment to be the foundation for their improvement management system.

Leadership Must Balance Time between the Business and People Development.

Effective leaders split time between making certain the organization is creating value for customers and making certain the organization is a learning environment, where knowledge is rapidly spread across the enterprise. Refer to the comments from W. L. Gore's CEO, Terri Kelly, on how she allocates her time (see Chapter 5).

Level 4 and 5 organizations do a wonderful job of helping people at all levels of the business to more readily see and to act on eliminating

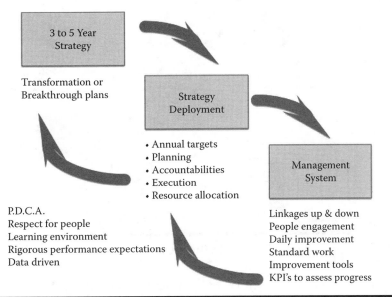

Linked Performance System

3 to 5 Year Strategy

Transformation or Breakthrough plans

Strategy Deployment

• Annual targets
• Planning
• Accountabilities
• Execution
• Resource allocation

Management System

P.D.C.A.
Respect for people
Learning environment
Rigorous performance expectations
Data driven

Linkages up & down
People engagement
Daily improvement
Standard work
Improvement tools
KPI's to assess progress

Exhibit 8.3   Linked performance system.

waste. People can't eliminate waste they cannot see, so a key leadership responsibility is to educate your eyes to better see waste. The Gemba Walk described later in this chapter is one way to open your eyes and see more clearly. As we described earlier (in Chapters 6 and 7), you can probably improve your productivity by 400%—four times better than the way you operate today. If that level of improvement is possible, you are irresponsible as a leader if you simply try to outsource your problems without first exploring opportunities to improve.

Once you begin to see waste, it is almost overwhelming. It is everywhere! Leadership has a responsibility at all levels to coach and guide people to focus on value to customers and to eliminate activities that do not add value. If leadership has not begun to engage people throughout the enterprise, the waste is so overwhelming it will quickly burn out a small group of people trying to attack it. There is too much waste for 10 to 15% of the minds in an organization to eliminate it all.

That is why it is so crucial to show real respect for people. In order to implement the magnitude of improvements suggested above, you must passionately engage people at all levels of an enterprise. Being treated with respect and given the opportunity to better use your mind to do meaningful work goes a long way toward passionately engaging people in a business.

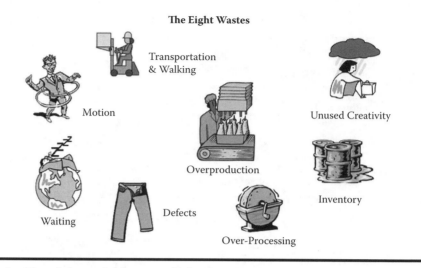

Exhibit 8.4   The eight typical wastes in business processes.

People who work on the floor can more easily see waste because they operate in a physical world on a day-to-day basis, but they will not necessarily know how to fix it using a scientific thought process. That's why it is important for leadership to coach people in critical thinking skills. Get more people using the scientific method to better solve problems: gather the facts, do rapid experimentation, and document the results.

Learning to See Improvement Possibilities by Finding Process Wastes

The classic 8 Wastes, shown in Exhibit 8.4, which are commonly addressed in most Lean improvement initiatives comprise a reasonable way to approach looking for process improvement opportunities. Sometimes people use the Japanese word *muda* to refer to these wastes.

1. ***Overproduction:*** People produce too much or too soon. Typically, this is a hidden waste because people are very busy operating in a batch mode: processing lab tests, writing software code, producing products. The takt time (i.e., the customer's pull rate) isn't visual, so people and their managers don't know if they are ahead or behind schedule for work that should be done that day. Schedules focus on utilization (keeping people busy or keeping equipment busy) rather than letting customers pull work on an as-needed basis.

2. ***Waiting:*** This is one of the easiest wastes to see, but people get used to their situation and no longer see this type of waste. For example, people

wait for machine cycles to finish. The process bottleneck is not clearly managed, so workstations after that point starve for work, patients wait for test results, software developers wait for decisions, and so forth.

3. ***Transportation/Conveyance:*** Examples of this type of waste are when we move stuff out of the way into some other space, or when extra parts are made (which internal or external customers do not need on that day) and they are moved into or out of storage. To combat this type of waste, allow one move to bring work in and one move to send work out to the next step, because any moves beyond that are wasteful.

4. ***Motion/Walking:*** Walking could be considered as transportation if carrying something, and as motion if you're looking for something. If you have ever done a spaghetti diagram of real work being done on a shop floor, in an office, in a hospital, in a warehouse, or in just about any working endeavor, you have likely been amazed at the wasted amount of motion while people are working hard, trying to get the right things done. Watch work being done, draw an imaginary square box on the floor, and simply observe how much people move into, out of, and inside the square. Looking for supplies, tools, information, and so on all fit in this category.

5. ***Inventory:*** In the manufacturing world, this is any product or parts in storage or being worked on that the customer does not need—in other words, any overstocks. In the world of software development, projects represent work-in-progress inventory. In financial service industries, service requests sit in queues (online "In" boxes) waiting to be processed. The problem with inventory is that the older it gets, the less likely it is to be the right thing because it becomes out of date, requirements change, it gets damaged, it takes up space and time, and it requires people to keep track of it Worst of all, work-in-process in queues between work steps exponentially extend the overall lead time to turnaround orders for service or product deliveries. Customers are often perplexed by "how long it takes some suppliers to process their orders." WIP queues are often the main culprit.

6. ***Defects/Errors:*** These are a pretty obvious type of waste. Unfortunately, the timeliness of when an error is found is usually inconsistent, and the source of errors is often not obvious. In fact, it can be very difficult to see, due to some of the other wastes around it. For example, overproduction hides errors inside queues of excess inventory. Compounding the problem, when the requirements, standard work practices, and/or procedures are unclear or overly difficult, or when there is a lack of visual control, then errors are much more difficult to detect at the source.

7. ***Overprocessing:*** This includes rework and redundant work (e.g., when doctors and nurses in the emergency room each do a patient assessment independently and don't share the information, or when a software product is edited extra times, multiple people giving approval, etc.).

8. ***Human Talent/Capability/Creativity:*** This is one of the worst wastes because it destroys morale, robs people of their dignity, and wastes the essential resources a company needs to find and capture improvement opportunities to compete and win—maybe even just survive—in the marketplace.

We could not prove that most work includes a substantial amount of this list, but we can state that we have never observed a job that did not include a substantial amount of the above wastes. They all do, based on our experience. It isn't at all unusual for 50 to 80% of a work activity to be waste. Unfortunately, people become very accepting of the status quo, and they lose their ability to see the waste without a fair amount of effort.

In addition to the classic wastes listed above, there are a few drivers of waste—things that cause waste to happen—shown in Exhibit 8.5 and described here:

■ ***Overburden*** (Japanese word: *muri*): This occurs when there is more work assigned than a person, a group, or equipment can reasonably do. Work is added layer by layer until the person, process, or equipment can't handle anymore. Material requirements planning (MRP) scheduling systems are famous for doing this. It is also common to overburden your best people because they get things done. But over the long term,

Waste Drivers

– Work that is difficult to do (overburden)

– Running or operating at an uneven pace (unevenness)

– Unclear requirements or standard work practices

Exhibit 8.5 Waste drivers.

you risk burning them out. The bottleneck point inside a process is overburdened when its demand rate (from customers or management) is greater than its operating cycle time. The bottleneck point in a process is one place where you definitely want visual controls to make sure it is performing appropriately.

■ ***Unevenness*** (Japanese word: *mura*): There are also natural causes of uneven workflows and self-induced causes. If your customers' workflow systems are out of balance, that will bounce back to the supplier's world. It is an outside cause, initially, as uncoordinated customer demands result in peaks and valleys in the short term. However, self-induced uneven flows may come from performance metrics incentive systems or other sources. For example, for the salespeople to make their periodic performance numbers, or for the company to hit some quarterly target, a major influx in orders happens at the end of a period. The ripple impact of that action is significantly higher costs (usually unseen) inside an enterprise in terms of errors, overtime, returns, and so on. Companies actually train customers to wait for end-of-the-period discounts, resulting in excessive incentive payments when they repeatedly accelerate sales at the end of a month or the end of a quarter. What is robbed from the beginning of one period needs to be repaid later. This results in escalating problems for subsequent monthly and quarterly period results.

■ ***Unclear Requirements:*** This often comes from a lack of standard work practices and sometimes results from the way we do work. Consider the long lead time it takes to do work in the software development world: it often takes so long to develop a new system that the requirements truly do change. Problems also happen with work instructions that are difficult to understand (they are confusing or lend themselves to interpretation). Often, the work instruction system is so difficult to keep up to date that people let it slide due to other priorities.

These waste drivers fit with the ineffective process practices that were described in Chapter 7 on process thinking. These drivers are actually negative practices inside a company that cause waste. They are challenging to see because we are used to operating this way.

Effective leaders need some familiarity with the above wastes and causes of waste. Line managers must be held accountable to maintain a customer-first perspective and to fix quality and delivery issues. They need to do this without adding additional resources. Plenty of resources are wasted, trapped by the above issues. When the waste is eliminated, more time is available.

- How are you progressing against the customer's takt time?
- What is your capacity utilization?
- What is your most significant source of scrap?
- What was your last customer complaint?
- What frustrates your key customers the most?
- When people quote a performance statistic, do you test it for realness? If someone claims 98% on-time delivery, ask about the specific shipments made that day—e.g., what is on the trucks? Is it exactly and completely what the customer wanted? How does what you see compare with what you hear?
- Where is the bottleneck in this operation, and how do you manage it?
- What was your last injury in the workplace? What caused it?
- How are you organized to solve problems?

Exhibit 8.6   Questions leaders should ask when reviewing work activities.

Leaders help line managers by addressing cross-functional issues. When leaders do a Gemba Walk (described later in this chapter), they should have *question filters* in mind to coach people to be more critical thinkers. When a leader from outside a department or plant reviews work activities, he or she might ask questions such as those shown in Exhibit 8.6.

There's nothing particularly magic about the questions listed in Exhibit 8.6. Make up your own that are relevant to your area of responsibility and your industry, but have a set of questions you ask to increase your understanding of process performance reality and to coach your associates in more critical thinking skills. The goal isn't to catch people. Instead, the questions are to help everyone see problems more realistically. You need to develop your own set of questions, and they will vary by situation.

Problems must be exposed! And it must be safe to do so, because hiding problems undermines the system. Also, people must be held accountable for deeper thinking. Authority is generated by taking responsibility for problems, building consensus on their causes, and developing strategies to solve them. At Toyota, the burden of proof is clearly on the subordinate to justify why a proposed action is necessary. Managers in Toyota rarely say "Yes" easily; instead, they simply ask "Why?" multiple times. For example:

- "Why did things go wrong; what is the root cause?"
- "Why do you propose that?"

Exposing problems in an open way is a huge difference from traditional operating practices and philosophies. Traditional companies think of a plan as a *prediction* of what will happen. In contrast, Lean leaders think of a plan as an experiment to be tested; they are constantly looking to learn what they did not know. Leaders need to constantly ensure true organizational learning throughout the organization, if they seek to move to Level 4 and 5 improvement maturity.

Conducting Gemba Walks—A Reality Check

A great way to practice learning to see waste is to do a Gemba Walk. The word Japanese *Gemba* is popular in organizations implementing Lean improvement initiatives, but whether you actually use this word or not isn't important. However, the concept of a Gemba Walk is very important! Leaders need to regularly get out of their offices or conference rooms and go and see for themselves to gain a real understanding of what is happening where the value-adding work is being done. Leaders use Gemba Walks to ferret out the truth and better understand what is real. If a leader talks too much, the learning opportunity is lost. Leaders should ask questions and then listen, listen, listen. The questions asked by the observer help people in an organization better understand why their work is important; it is a magnificent teaching opportunity, truly a gift to both parties (observer and observed) for learning.

It helps to determine a purpose for doing the walk before you do it. Some walks may focus on flow, asking the question, "What things happen in an organization that interrupt the ability to get value-added work accomplished?" A walk is typically done in production operations, but engineering and sales (as described in the previous section) also create value, and are good Gemba Walk subjects. Or, a walk might focus on information boards, where the questions might include those in Exhibit 8.7.

Gemba Walks can also help to gain more understanding of how customers pull work from the organization. A Gemba Walk is a valuable way to enlighten the observer and the only way to understand the current reality. You will not learn reality by sitting in a conference room, or even by

■ How often do people look at your information boards?
■ Do employees value the information?
■ Are the information boards up to date?
■ What decisions have been made as a result of information on the board?
■ What improvements have been implemented as a result of insights learned?

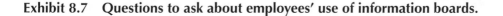

Exhibit 8.7   Questions to ask about employees' use of information boards.

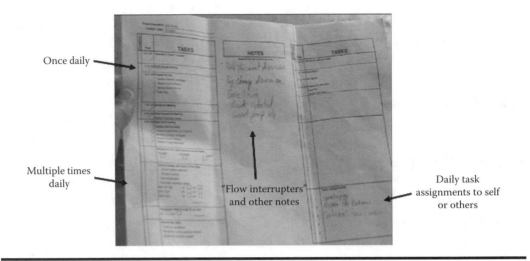

Once daily

Multiple times daily

"Flow interrupters" and other notes

Daily task assignments to self or others

Exhibit 8.8   Cell leader's Gemba checksheet.

- Is the line meeting its Takt Time commitments?
- Are standard work practices being followed?
- Are cell information/performance boards being kept up to date?
- What actions are taken on issues from the floor?
- What are the operators' concerns of the day?
- Are there opportunities to coach people on better work practices?
- Are safe working practices followed?
- Are people working, or are they waiting for work?
- To what extent do people on the floor take responsibility for 5S practices?

Exhibit 8.9   What supervisors should look for when assessing the work line.

reviewing numbers. The numbers are important, but numbers are *not* reality; they are only one dimension of it!

Some companies use a review document to instill a sense of standard work for managers in doing a Gemba Walk. Exhibit 8.8 shows a cell leader's Gemba checksheet.

A first-line supervisor might be walking the line several times a day. Observations could include taking note of the considerations listed in Exhibit 8.9.

Each walk could have a separate theme. One might focus only on safety. During a one-week period, the entire list could be covered.

A senior leader doing a Gemba Walk would not be at the same level of granularity as a cell manager. Instead, he or she might focus on flow interruptions or simply do a good job of listening to people on the floor as they explain the work they do and the issues they face. Then in an open way, the senior leader should try to gain more understanding, from a process perspective, why some of these issues exist. Get a feel for reality; don't try to prematurely develop a solution. For example, one senior operations leader from GE described his Gemba Walks in this fashion:

> I walk twice a week with the Site Operating Manager at our main operation, because I happen to be here. We touch each major line during these walks. Typically the Plant Manager, Value Stream Leaders, Flow Leaders, and Lean Leaders meet us at the Gemba board. We typically look at performance over the last week on Takt attainment, hours/unit, manning, and safety, as well as any nagging large quality issues. We also review the PDCA [plan, do, check, act/adjust] process, the status of open PDCAs and often choose a couple to drill into for deeper understanding.
>
> At this point, we have not standardized everywhere. Most of our Plant Managers do their own standard work, taking Gemba Walks once to twice a day. Typically, it consists of walking from line to line and reviewing key metrics at the visual boards, which are at the line. If there are problems, they may choose to drill in and under-stand what is driving it and how they are recovering from it. They also typically review PDCA status on problem solving and improve-ment. Their main focus on these is Takt attainment (production pace). If there are issues, we expect the team to focus on solving the issue right then and there. The expectation on these walks is that the line is balanced and moving at the right pace all the way through. These are the most important Gemba Walks we do! We have other Gemba Walks that are more treasure-hunt related (look-ing for waste and opportunity), or problem-solving oriented (going out to see a problem firsthand), or status checking (project progress or results). Most managers have stopped all conference production meetings, and do their meetings out on the floor.*

David Mann recently wrote a book entitled *Creating a Lean Culture* (2010). He provides quite a few examples of how supervisors and mid-level managers should incorporate a Gemba Walk into their daily standard work practices. Gemba Walks, at this level, often focus on schedule attainment and problem discovery.

---

* Private communication

---

1. What are the business issues with this product?
2. Who is responsible for the value stream for this product?
3. How are orders from the customer received?
4. Where is the pacemaker (bottleneck) process, triggered by customer orders?
5. How capable, available, adequate, and waste-free are assembly activities?
6. How capable, available, adequate, and waste-free are the fabrication activities feeding assembly?
7. How are orders transmitted up the value stream from the pacemaker process?
8. How are materials supplied to the assembly and fabrication processes?
9. How are materials obtained from upstream suppliers?
10. How are employees trained in Lean procedures and motivated to apply them?

Exhibit 8.10   Jim Womack's 10 questions that assess an organization's progress toward a Lean production system.

Jim Womack, cofounder of the Lean Enterprise Institute, wrote about taking a walk through operations to get a quick assessment of how well an organization practices Lean thinking. Jim picks one product family at a site visit and asks to follow its value stream from the customer back to materials in receiving. "Once we had selected a sample product family and started walking, I ask 10 very simple questions* [shown in Exhibit 8.10]. After a 30-minute walk to answer the 10 questions, I knew everything that I needed to be able to tell the senior managers just where they stood regarding their progress toward a truly lean production system."

Strength of Character Is a Litmus Test for Leadership Credibility

We discussed the importance of fairness in compensation practices in Chapter 5 on engaging people. Another important attribute of Level 4 and 5 organizations is the strength of character in their leadership teams.

"Character building is the most important work ever entrusted to human beings; and never before was its diligent study so important as now. Never was any previous generation called to meet issues so momentous; never before were young men and young women confronted by perils so great; as confront them today." Those words are as true today as they were when Ellen G. White wrote them in "Education" in 1903.† Strength of character

---

* Jim Womack's letters, "Taking a Walk at Firm A," March 12, 2003. In the letter he gives answers to the questions; this is worth reading. Available at http://www.aug.edu/~sbajmg/quan6610/Lean%20 Concepts/taking%20a%20value%20stream%20walk%20(text%20version).pdf

† Ellen G. White Estate, http://www.whiteestate.org/books/Ed/ed.asp

seems to have lost some focus with the "what's-in-it-for-me?" attitudes that currently seem so prevalent. If North America and the European economies are going to successfully compete against low-cost new entrants into the global marketplace, strength of character will be very important, once again.

Strength of character is still important with employees. People value leaders who demonstrate ethics, integrity, and a willingness to do the right thing, regardless of the consequences to themselves. If associates see leaders making sacrifices and exercising some degree of humility, they are encouraged to act in a similar fashion.

This is very similar to our discussions about process performance. You cannot independently maximize component parts of the process. Pieces of the process need to work in harmony in order for smooth overall flow. Leaders in Level 4 and 5 companies show a high degree of improvement maturity when they move beyond their narrow self-interest and serve a greater good in order for the community as a whole to prosper.

This requires real strength of character; it is one of the key attributes in Jim Collins's definition of Level Five Leadership. To some degree, every individual is a leader. We are all responsible and accountable for our own actions. Parents certainly have responsibilities to the next generation that go beyond simply meeting their own personal needs. Business leaders and employees also have a responsibility beyond simply meeting this year's numbers. Whether they are your boss's numbers or Wall Street's does not matter.

A powerful insight guided leaders in the Iroquois Confederacy. Leaders had a responsibility to consider the impact of their decisions on the seven generations around them. One man, one leader, could only hope to know the seven generations around him: the three that preceded him (back to his great grandparents, and the three that will follow, to his great grandchildren). The leader was bound by a moral duty to care for the Seven Generations.*

Because we are all leaders responsible for our own actions, what might we do differently if we take into account how our behaviors and our decisions impact seven generations of people? Might we think a little bit longer term than what needs to happen this week, this month, or even this year? Accomplishing something this week or month or year can be important, but it needs to be looked at on a broader scale.

Seventh-generation leadership principles certainly fit with the idea of actively engaging people to identify and implement better ways to operate

---

* From the Great Law of the Haudenosaunee (Six Nations Iroquois Confederacy). http://www.indigenouspeople.net/iroqcon.htm

and to act in an environmentally sustainable fashion. Principle-based leaders create organizations that enable people to live in accordance with their core values and beliefs, beneficial over the long term. People development, enlightenment, and capability become the True North in times of great complexity rather than trying to fix ethical issues via corporate directives. Thinking of this magnitude truly moves leadership toward creating a place where people can do their best work. And it begins with you. If you are not responsible for acting this way, who is?

Being Part of a Larger Purpose

Being part of a larger purpose is a challenge in today's world and it relates to the value discussion we have had throughout this book. Young people in China, in India, Latin America, and the Eastern-bloc countries in Europe have new opportunities that were not available to their parents. The traditionally established economies in the United States, Canada, Europe, and Japan in many ways need to redefine their core purpose in order to successfully compete moving forward.

Why do companies exist? The classic responses might include:

■ To create shareholder value
■ To make profits
■ To reward the founders of the business

And those are certainly part of the reason that companies exist. But are they the primary reasons? Other organizations with reputations of excellence, for the most part, over a long period of time, say they exist for these reasons:

■ To alleviate pain and disease (Johnson & Johnson)
■ To change the way people live, work and play (Apple Computer)
■ To bring happiness to the millions (Walt Disney)

Would seventh-generation leadership thinking fit with the latter purpose statements? *Probably.* Does a more noble purpose all by itself automatically engage employees? *No!* Terri Kelly, W. L. Gore's CEO, in her MIT presentation (referenced in Chapter 5), clearly states several times that there is no single action you can take to passionately and positively engage employees. It is part of a larger system. Meeting employees' emotional requirements is a step in this direction. Treating employees and leaders in a fair and honorable fashion is part of this equation. It also includes a more holistic approach to improvement that is clearly focused on customer value and looks at more than just project savings in terms of improvement.

How does this translate into the real world? Fetzer Vineyard has a reputation for high-quality products and low costs. They experienced 15% earnings growth for more than a ten-year period. Fetzer's CEO, Paul Dolan, wrote a book titled *True to Our Roots* (2003). He describes how his company used the challenges of environmental sustainability to catalyze a business revolution at Fetzer for the benefit of customers, shareholders, employees, communities, and the planet. The company has made quite a few changes under the environmental sustainability banner. Since 1990, it has reduced its trash by 95%, even though wine production doubled during that time frame.

True to Our Roots sets forth the management principles that enabled Fetzer Vineyard to become a model for environmentally sustainable businesses. Fetzer strives to preserve its environment, strengthen its communities, and enrich the lives of its employees, while adding to the bottom line. The principles Dolan developed at Fetzer to create a larger sense of purpose include:

- Your business is part of a much larger system.
- Your company's culture is determined by the context you create for it.
- The soul of your company is found in the hearts of its people.
- True power is living what you know.
- You can't predict the future, but you can create it.
- There is a way to make an idea's time come.

These principles at Fetzer, and the same at W. L. Gore & Associates, are very different from an average organization's "we're gonna be the best _____ *(fill in the blank)*" purpose statement.

A Radical Whack at Who Adds Value

Part of the problem with traditional industrial engineering as practiced during the twentieth century was its focus on value-added time rather than non-value-added time. Value-added time is typically 10% or less of the overall lead time. Did it make sense for industrial engineers to focus on the 10%, rather than reducing the 90%? *Obviously not!* The classic Lean wastes put much more focus on the 90%. In many ways, leaders seem to follow the same myopic view of traditional industrial engineering when they reorganize and outsource with a too-simplistic view of cost.

Who adds value inside a business? In a manufacturing company, value is added by:

- The *design engineers* who create the new product.
- The people in *operations* who change the form, fit, and function of raw materials and transform them into a product.
- The *people who sell the products or services* as solutions for customers.

Everyone else in the organization should be supporting those three groups:

- *Marketing* is intended to help Sales sell.
- *Supervision* in a factory is intended to remove barriers that constrain the conversion of raw materials into finished product.
- *Financial and management reporting* should organize business process information to help Design Engineering, Operations, and Sales create more value.
- And *leadership* should create an environment where all of these players can do the best possible job.

The further leaders move an organization away from creating the actual real value for the key 20% of customers, the more those leaders jeopardize that organization's future, and the organization begins to live in the moment, off of its legacy investments in knowledge, skills, and capabilities. Very much like third-generation grandchildren taking over a family business and running it into the ground, they lose sight of the basic value proposition and focus too much on making money for their personal use. You can milk the legacy investments for a period of time, but if the value proposition is not kept current in rapidly shifting markets, companies lose their competitive edge.

The electronic information age has exacerbated the problem. Real value creation still happens at human speed, but speculative capital gains can be manipulated at electronic speed. Ambitious, self-centered players naturally take advantage of the opportunity to skim short-term gains rather than doing difficult, time-consuming, real value creation. Morale-killing examples of unjustified executive largesse are chronicled regularly in the press. Examples of altruistic executives who care about the long-term common good seem to be an increasing rarity, but they are whom this book was written for; we wish them well.

China is already looking to move to higher-value-adding products, as it should. In a frightening way, this is a repeat of what happened in the automotive industry, where leaders in that industry conceded small cars years ago to the Japanese. And they further believed that the Japanese would never make a luxury car, whereas time has proven that prediction to be short-sighted and a major fallacy.

North American leadership (management and union) in the automotive industry has lost a lot of manufacturing jobs to Japanese and Korean manufacturers. That loss has a ripple impact beyond just manufacturing. Just consider software. The intellectual capital of the world for automotive software development used to be in North America. When the Society of Automotive Engineers held its annual conference in Detroit, the vast majority of leading-edge application knowledge was by North American companies. People went to Detroit to learn. Yet today where do they go? They go to Germany. Germany has become the center of automotive software excellence. Why has this shift taken place? The best people don't go into developing automotive software applications. They go into other fields. People like to work for winners. And the North American automotive industry leadership has been anything but a winner for a long period of time. A decline in one industry has ripple impacts that drive further value out of the supply chain.

Transformation at Nissan Motor Company: A Case Study

When Carlos Ghosn came to Nissan as the chief operating officer, he could have taken control and began dictating orders. In fact, that was what most people expected him to do. Instead, he spent much time listening, and with minimal personnel changes had the employees at Nissan develop solutions to the major business challenges faced by the company. In October of 1999, Nissan announced a recovery plan* designed to return the company to profitability, which is summarized in Table 8.1. Nissan's actions align very closely to most of the points made in this book, as shown in the following sections.

Customer Value (Ingredient 1). Regarding customer value, Ghosn said:

Investing in new products is vital to restore Nissan's brand power and increase worldwide market share and profitability. While cost cutting will be the most dramatic and visible part of our plan, ***we***

---

* Nissan Motor Company Press Release, October 18, 1999. http://www.nissan-global.com/GCC/
Japan/NEWS/19991018_0e.html

Table 8.1 Summary of Nissan Revival Plan (NRP)

Key Goal Themes	Return to Profitability in Three Years			People Development	Revenue Growth
Key Goals	Reduce operating cost by ¥1 trillion; purchasing, manufacturing, and SG&A	Reduce purchasing cost 20% (60% of overall costs)	Reduce net debt 50%	Transparency (openness) in all communications	Create exciting new products; introduce 4 new models
Initiatives	Operating profitability (target 4.5%)	Centralize global purchasing	Sell off non-core assets	Cross-functional teams to deploy NRP	Faster rollout of new models from Japan to U.S.
	Reduce the number of manufacturing platforms from 24 to 12	Give more buys to cooperating suppliers	30% inventory reduction target	Create a system of accountability for goal execution	Share research with Renault
Metrics	Reduce headcount (excess capacity) by 21,000 employees	Cut the number of suppliers by 50%	Debt level from ¥1.4 trillion to ¥700 million	Performance-oriented compensation	New product sales as % of total sales

Source: Mostly the Nissan Press Release, October 18, 1999.

Note: This was originally a 3-year plan, but was accomplished in 24 months.

cannot save our way to success. Our primary objective is to free resources from non-strategic, non-core assets *(80/20 thinking*)* and invest more in our core business—cars—while at the same time significantly reduce our debt. The aim is to grow the company, not shrink it.

Ghosn also revealed that he was in touch with the reality of Nissan's business situation when he said:

> The plant closures, however painful, will guarantee the future of the remaining plants by allowing them to be industry leaders, both in terms of productivity and cost effectiveness. Nissan will take advantage of the reduction in the number of platforms to further simplify the manufacturing scheme. This will better align Nissan's production resources with its core customers' demands.

At the time, Nissan was producing 24 platforms at 7 assembly plants. It has since reduced capacity to 12 platforms divided between 4 plants. It has put plans in place to further reduce costs by rationalizing logistics. Sales, general, and administrative costs were to be reduced 20% by cutting incentives, rationalizing worldwide advertising, and reducing support staff that inhibited effective decision making. The company had become burdened by excess production capacity and high fixed costs.

From a value perspective, Ghosn realized a great product covers many other problems. The one senior leader change he made was to bring in a new head of design. The key charge for this group was to create designs people would want to buy. That seems obvious, but that was not how the company had been operating.

Engage People (Ingredient 2). Decisions at Nissan were not solely made by a senior executive team. An international team of 200 Nissan managers developed the Revival Plan. "What this global team has done is fully understand the root causes of our current problems and develop solutions that allow Nissan to act decisively," said Ghosn.

Nissan launched 9 Cross-Functional Teams to look at all aspects of the enterprise. Over the course of 3 months, those teams assessed more than 2,000 improvement ideas. They ultimately presented ideas dealing with new model launch, reduction in the number of suppliers, a realignment of Keiretsu relationships, cost reductions, capacity reductions, and so on. The

---

* authors added.

final recommendations accepted by the Executive Committee became the foundation for the Nissan Revival Plan (NRP).*

Changes were also made to adjust traditional practices of Japanese companies awarding compensation based on seniority. Ghosn and the leadership team decided to more directly engage young people in the organization and focus compensation on execution effectiveness.

Most international companies in Japan were reluctant to reduce staffing. Nissan broke from traditional practices to deal with real-world issues. But it did this in a fair way. Employees at the facilities to be closed were given the business case on why it was a necessary action in order for the company to survive. In most instances, the employees stayed until the end and supported the company's transition.

Goals/Metrics (Ingredient #3). The first goal of the Revival Plan was to return Nissan to profitability for FY2000. The combination of growth and cost reduction would allow Nissan to achieve a consolidated operating profit of 4.5% of sales by FY2002 (i.e., within 3 years). Nissan shuttered 5 plants (an unprecedented action in Japan).

The company planned a ¥1 trillion cost reduction in threw major areas: global purchasing; manufacturing; and sales, genera, and administrative costs. Other goals included a 30% reduction in inventory, and a plan to reduce the gap between a model's debut in Japan and its launch in the United States. The company actually accomplished its goals in a 2-year period.

Process Thinking (Ingredient #4). Nissan's Keiretsu relationships needed restructuring. Many of the company's traditional partners were taking advantage of Nissan rather than giving the company favorable pricing. Agreements were made with Nissan's suppliers, and those who eliminated waste from the process to reduce costs were rewarded with more business. Purchasing was centralized and executed globally, in contrast to the previous practice of purchasing on a regional/country-by-country basis. Purchasing costs, which represented 60% of the company's total costs, were reduced more than 20% over 3 years, and the number of parts and materials suppliers was reduced from 1,145 to 600.

Financial operations worldwide were centralized to develop global financial controls and risk management. Research and Development (R&D) was reorganized to give regions more responsibility for their entire product line, while creating a globally integrated organization. More power was given to the R&D unit in the United States, which was doing a better job of designing

* David McGee, *Turnaround: How Charles Ghosn Rescued Nissan* (New York: HarperCollins, 2003)

cars people wanted to buy. Nissan also planned to rely on suppliers to reduce development time and costs and to closely integrate suppliers into the design and development process.

Leadership (or the Executive Mindset, Ingredient 5). With regard to leadership, Ghosn said: "This plan shows not only can Nissan recover and become a strong company again, but, walk tall with Renault as the world's 4th-largest car maker. We must be bold to be strong again."*

The fact is that leadership acted; it did not just study. In this instance, employees did not need training on a new methodology. They needed to execute the plan. And that is what happened. Over the course of two years, Nissan:

- Returned to profitability
- Achieved an operating profit greater than 7.9%
- Reduced its debt
- Rolled out several new products

Implementation was accomplished because of:

- A steady stream of communications
- A clear direction that did not change
- Accountability enforced throughout the enterprise
- The breaking down of barriers between functions, departments, and regions
- Building on a steady stream of successes

Ghosn frequently uses the word *commitment*. Once you commit, you are expected to deliver. If a problem arises, people were expected to bring it forth immediately. Otherwise, the commitment was expected to be on track. The executive committee reviewed critical commitments every month and worked immediately to find solutions if promises were not met. Ghosn's rules for leadership included:

- Start with an open mind. Don't prejudge and feel you (as one leader) have all the answers.
- Set a clear direction.
- Hold people accountable for their commitments.
- Use metrics to track progress and maintain objectivity.
- Focus on the facts; don't trash people.

---

* Nissan Revival Plan Press Release October 18, 1999 http://www.nissan-global.com/GCC/Japan/NEWS/19991018_0e.html

- Be relentless in demanding execution, not perfection; get something done, learn and grow from there.
- Take responsibility for your actions; avoid placing blame.

Ghosn fostered the idea that "95% of time should focus on execution and delivery" and "5% on planning."* He says too much time within a company is spent planning and not enough doing. When the leadership is not clear in its directives and if it does not insist the job gets done now, that is when organizations get into trouble and people act with uncertainty.

Governance Should Focus on the Big Picture, Not a Narrow Slice of the Business (Savings)

The approach outlined in the Nissan transformation story does a good job of describing leadership's governance responsibilities in guiding improvement activities. Nissan certainly had savings targets, and that was the primary objective for some projects (e.g., cost reduction in Nissan's Keiretsu relationships). But the primary purpose of the transformation was driven to better enable the organization to deliver more customer value and thereby sell more cars.

Level 2 and 3 companies use words like "World Class" in their discussions, and the term may even sit as a line item on some type of policy deployment worksheet. But when leaders are challenged on what that term means, they cannot give you specifics. You get more generalities, such as "Be a low-cost producer." If you try to find the big cross-functional problems that stand in the way or to learn what countermeasures are being pursued to resolve the big problems, no specifics exist and no one person has a clear responsibility for implementing this plan by a specific date. Given the lack of specific objectives for major change, it is not at all surprising that the organization's competitive position does not meaningfully change.

Yet if you ask the leaders of a Level 3 company how much they saved, they will tell you they saved millions of dollars! But if you can't see it in the P&L, in the cash flow, and in growing market share, these savings are a figment. They are largely made up based on savings reports from functional departments talking about how much they saved somewhere in the middle of a process. If you measure the effectiveness of your improvement initiatives by looking at savings reports largely administered by a staff group of dedicated employees

---

* McGee, 2003, p. 103.

pushing improvement projects, then you too live in a figment world. Motorola reports on its Web site that the company saved more than $17 billion from its improvement activities. Yet if you look at the organization's financial performance and market share, it is dismal. A focus on savings looks totally in the wrong direction. The continuous improvement people (at Motorola, in this instance, the Six Sigma Black Belt organization) report on their accomplishments, while the businesses flounder. Although we pick on Motorola in this paragraph, we could list many companies here (since most are indeed average) that follow this same misguided approach to improvement governance.

In contrast, Nissan took a much different approach. And so do other organizations like Toyota, Autoliv (which manufactures the explosive device in airbags), Theda Care (which is leading a revolution in health care via open reporting and improvements in patient care), and other organizations doing this in a highly effective fashion.

Level 4 and 5 organizations are process maniacs, and they focus on the outputs from those processes. Leadership reviews don't focus on savings, although these companies do seek lower costs. The primary emphasis is to look at improving process performance, generating better customer value, and continuously increasing the skills and capabilities of the people who work in an organization to do their best possible work. If your governance process does not look at those items, you are looking at the wrong list. The more you can break your business down into bite-sized pieces that serve specific customer groups, the easier this is to see.

Developing a One-Page Plan

The Nissan Revival Plan described earlier in this chapter is a great example of a one-page plan. That type of document provides focus to all parties. It is a guide regarding what should be entered into a Hoshin or Strategy Deployment Worksheet, and it guides where leaders should focus their improvement energy. Nissan had several key strategic targets:

■ Develop more exciting products that will excite customers.
■ Reduce cost, including the traditional Keiretsu supplier relationships.
■ Reduce overcapacity.
■ Generate cash to reduce debt loads.
■ Actively engage employees in making the above happen.

Those five strategic targets drove the Nissan Revival Plan, which was summarized in the one-page plan shown in Table 8.1.

A one-page plan can serve as a powerful focusing tool for any organization. Let's take the Independence Enterprise story we have shared in most of the chapters, and look at what might comprise its one-page plan, as a working example. As you read, consider how the ingredients all link into the concluding executive mindset.

INDEPENDENCE ENTERPRISE DEVELOPS ITS ONE-PAGE PLAN

Ingredient 1: Customer Value. Background: Independence Enterprise discovered that some customers were not profitable on a recurring basis. Sales, Engineering, and Operations fought over "the right" customer requirements without clear customer guidance. The results were that operations did not meet target costs, largely because of Sales and Engineering changing the design. Lead times were overly long as a result of the infighting and lack of clarity. Growth opportunities existed in all of Independence's businesses, but they were not pursued in the most effective fashion. So on their one-page plan, they cited two key drivers to align the above issues:

- Seek to double sales with key customers over the next 4 years.
- Reduce the Ugly 50 by 25% and double profitability for the remaining customers.

Ingredient 2: Engaging People. Background: Less than one third of the workforce (of bright, energetic people) rated themselves as highly engaged. People were frustrated when the work on improvement gains was not sustained. People also felt that much of what they spent their time on was not important, that the organization did not make it easy to serve customers well, that there was too much direction from above, and that people were not held accountable for their performance. These items were part of the one-page plan:

- Launch fewer cross-functional teams with more focus on strategically important actions.
- Learn which managers had the most engaged employees and determine which best practices could be learned and spread across the company.
- Make much greater use of peer-to-peer and subordinate-to-boss performance reviews, especially in the case of project team performance (which is a major way much of the work inside Independence gets done) to foster better accountability for results.

Ingredient 3: Key Metrics. Background: In the measurement survey, people pretty much felt their internal metrics were good in terms of fostering cooperation, and other department's metrics were poor in terms of fostering cooperation.

Metrics were not very visual or timely. People wanted their metrics to look good so they did not get into trouble. Metrics did not emphasize learning about process performance and process capabilities.

The one-page plan is not going to correct the above metrics issue, but leadership at Independence did plan to use metrics in a different way. They planned to look to discover problems early and take into account that 95% of all performance problems are process problems, not people problems.

Ingredient 4: Process Thinking. Background: Process thinking was very internally focused. People tended to think from a silo-oriented functional performance perspective, not a cross-functional customer-oriented view. Execution was largely based on functional performance, not process performance. So the one-page plan incorporated the following:

- Allocation of resources for major business-process improvements was focused on four cross-functional teams aligned with implementation of the Independence Revitalization Plan.
- One of these cross-functional teams focused on aligning processes to increase sales with the Mojo 20 and to change the way the Ugly 50 customers are serviced.
- A second team focused on better alignment of the new product development process with execution effectiveness and true customer needs.

Ingredient 5: The Executive Mindset. Background: Like many companies, the ambitious leaders of Independence Enterprise had been overly focused on their individual areas of responsibility, and not enough on overall enterprise effectiveness. People at most levels of the business focused too much on how good they were and not enough on the improvements potential that existed in all aspects of the business. To begin shifting the executive mindset, and to send a signal to the rest of the organization, the executive team included several objectives for leadership roles in the one-page plan:

- Commit to gaining more in-depth understanding of our business processes and value from the customers' perspectives.
- Engage more people in a passionate pursuit to revitalize the business.
- Create an environment that is more open and receptive to making the reality of the situation more visible.

Some might argue that Ingredient 5 should not be a direct part of the one-page plan because it's mostly dependent on leadership behavior changes. However, the same can also be said of the other four ingredients. They are all mechanisms used by the leadership team to provide more openness and clarity about what is important. If leadership fails to walk the talk on any of them, then the whole plan is jeopardized. The weakest link in a chain, one missing or weak ingredient, can

Table 8.2   Independence Enterprise's Revitalization Plan

Strategic Themes	Improve Profitability		Customer Management	People Development	Revenue Growth
Key Goals	100% hit rate on target costs for all new products	Double sales to Mojo 20 over next 4 years	Reduce Ugly 50 customers by 25%	Engagement score of 50% (highly engaged), and transparency (openness) in all communications	Create meaningful new products
Key Initiatives	Improve capability of the new product development (NPD) Process	Focus Sales on selling to Mojo 20	Double profitability of remaining Ugly 50	Cross-functional teams to deploy IRP	Launch new Maintenance Controller Services Bus. Unit
	50% Lead time reduction for A&B product proposals	Free production capacity to service Mojo 20, with no major capital investments	Increase proposal win rate for complex sales	Create a system of accountability for goal execution	Focus on Mojo 20 customer business issues
Metrics	Improve hit rate for NPD launch & cost targets 50%/year for next 3 years	Increase Gross Margin $$ by 50% over next 3 years	Improve Net Promoter Score to 50% level	Performance-oriented compensation	New product sales 85% of total sales

Note: Plans and initiatives can be further detailed in the strategy development process.

spoil the stew; the Executive Team needs to show and walk a complete commitment to it.

Table 8.2 shows Independence Enterprise's Revitalization as a one-page plan.

HOW INDEPENDENCE ENTERPRISE HAS CHANGED

Human Resources Vice President Kate Beck had the lead responsibility to implement a 360° feedback reporting process for the Leadership Team. Leaders had their performance rated by their peers and subordinates. Independence evaluated leaders in a fashion similar to the W. L. Gore questions (described in Chapter 5). The results of this assessment, along with customer problems, were one of the key reasons the business unit manager of the Maintenance Controller Division had been replaced with Margaret Allavoine.

Earlier in the year, Andy and Jack had decided to also have Kate apply this same concept to measuring team member performance. Kate gave a summary report of what was happening with Team Member 360° Feedback. Twice a year, or at the end of a project, team members would rate all other members on their team (if they felt they had enough interaction to do a meaningful evaluation). These ratings were available in summary for everyone to see.

Not surprisingly, the top third of team members tended to be in the top third for most of the teams in which they participated. The average level of performance for the middle third improved, so their average scores were higher. People consistently in the bottom third were being counseled and given assistance in creating a development plan. If the issues were not addressed or a better home could not be found, people in the bottom third were ultimately separated from the organization. Quite a few people in this group had left the company on their own during the last year. In addition, departmental managers and their leaders were being counseled if their subordinates were not developing better skills for execution and cross-functional cooperation. This was deemed as a critical skill for successful leaders.

Ralph Voigt, director of Continuous Improvement, gave a report on his actions. Ralph said, "At first, I was very nervous about my new role and responsibilities, I always imagined that I had control over project savings. It took me a while to see how savings was somewhat of a mythical number and that it was more important to focus on business performance. Now, I would never want to go back to the old way of operating."

He went on to describe the new approach: "We still look at savings, but we no longer do a monthly savings update in our leadership meetings. We look at savings in a totally different way now":

1. ***Hard dollar*** savings are directly traceable to the bottom line and should primarily be attributable to one of the following:
   a. ***Revenue growth:*** This is growth in volume or margins from specific sources—existing customers and existing products or new products and new customers. Projects indicate which groups are targeted and how much revenue is expected. For example, Medical Products freed sales time from

working on the Ugly 50 customers. We tracked how that time was used for more face-to-face customer time with the Specialty Plastics customer, and we were able to grow revenues and margins with that group over the last 12 months. In the past, we rarely focused on revenue growth.

b. **Cost savings:** This used to be our primary metric, but usually the P&L for the business did not show much savings. Now we look at cost savings by value stream. Cost savings come primarily from a net reduction in resources used, such as materials, outside contractors, transportation cost, and so forth. We have done a great job of reducing logistics costs and the use of outside contractors over the last year; we also totally eliminated the use of one outside warehouse since we moved to a pull system with customers for the electronic controllers unit. We have also had some hard savings over the last year from scrap reduction and lower warranty costs.

2. **Soft dollar savings:** This used to comprise the bulk of our savings report. We waited for them to turn into hard dollars, but it rarely seemed to happen. We still track soft dollar savings, which mostly come from increasing productivity and eliminating wasted or non-value-adding time. Now the leadership team in each business unit is responsible for soft savings, but we focus much more on the time aspect, because that is freed capacity. If more time is made available, leadership needs to figure out how to use it. When Sales quit spending so much time with the Ugly 50, leadership made sure that time was effectively applied with customers in the Specialty Plastics segment. The soft dollars quickly converted to something real! We still have some soft time savings, but now we use that time and energy to do even more improvement work.

Ralph said, "I used to think those savings reports were real numbers. It is so much better to have each of the business unit leaders report on their business. Services from my group are requested more than they ever were in the past. I used to go look for projects my team could work. Now the business unit leads invite me to talk about their business and improvement possibilities focused on real customers. This is so much better."

Dana Herring then gave a brief report on the Electronic Controllers Group. He said, "Kate Beck and I went to visit Sheila Carroll, who is a VP at our largest customer and who had planned to move her purchases to China. When we reviewed the new designs with her team members, they were very enthusiastic. They liked the simplicity of the new electronic controllers. And they were one of our first customers for the new service where Independence provides technical support staff to operate the diagnostic equipment. She felt this was a very beneficial relationship for her company."

Jack Morel asked Dana if he and Mark Ekberg had done any work on the value of an incremental sale? Dana looked over at Mark, who jumped up and said, "Well, I feel a little bit like Ralph Voigt. My view on sales has changed—somewhat. I used to think incremental sales were totally free beyond material cost. You can probably always make that argument for a single sale, and there is some truth to this belief. The labor is already there as long as overtime is not being paid, and it does not really add any overhead costs, unless engineering time is required; so in fact, your only extra cost for that one sale is the material.

"But when we started to look at costs to expand the product line, increased possibility of errors for small modifications, and the fact that many of our incremental sale requests were from the Ugly 50, not our Mojo Group, my view started to change. It's not quite so simple, and there isn't one simple answer, at least not that we have discovered so far. We also need to look at opportunity costs. Could we be doing something else with that time? In the case of Specialty Plastics, an incremental sale to the commodity plastics customers took time away from our new focus on high-end specialty plastics. So any incremental sales to the commodity group represents time lost from where we should focus.

"So what we are doing now is using a few rules. We will validate over the next year if these rules make sense":

1. If a Mojo (key) customer makes the request and we have available capacity, we will try to meet the demand.
2. If the request is from an Ugly 50, and we have the capacity, we will sell it at full price or no deal. If engineering time is required, we increase the price to cover that cost.

Mark continued: "The third piece we are looking at isn't really a rule. When we get an incremental sale request for something we do not currently do, we want to assess whether there is a potential market for this product. If we feel the incremental sale gives us an opportunity to begin testing an interesting concept, we will talk to other potential customers about the product. If there is some interest from multiple companies, we will try it. The current rules are a temporary solution. The rules are not natural. People need to stop and think about which rule applies, so the current method can definitely be improved further. We will continue to work on it this year."

Andy Fletcher thanked everyone for their reports and the hard work they had done over the last year. All three of Independence's business units were showing improved performance with their customers. Many problems with the new product development process seemed to be getting better, largely due to more effective interactions with the customers early in the process.

CHAPTER WRAP-UP: DEPLOYMENT ACTIONS
TO APPLY THE PRINCIPLES

Traditional leadership operates under the belief that leaders can control what is happening. You might question if this was ever a truth, but it certainly is not true in today's complex, chaotic environment. It is much more realistic to operate based on a few core principles. Principles are easy to write, but they only develop deep and real meaning when times are tough. J&J stuck to its core principles when the Tylenol disaster occurred. Seventh-generation thinking also promotes that type of behavior. Does your organization repeatedly and daily live according to the principles professed? Do your leaders walk the talk, or is the talk cheap?

If you believe the old Soviet-style central planning was a good thing, then by all means, *go for it*. But for the most part, that model has not seemed to work very effectively. In many ways, too much control translates to no control because the people doing the work cease to take ownership or responsibility for their actions. They do what they were told to do. This is a very different model from the high engagement, active learning, and rapid execution we have been discussing throughout this book.

Leadership actions to realize more benefit from your improvement activities include:

1. *Make a major effort to get in touch with reality.* End the game of pretending that your best work is your normal work.

2. *Make certain your entire leadership team has a clear understanding of value from the customers' perspectives.* A business is about more than simply making a profit, although that is a very important end result.

3. *Focus your resources on your three to five most important critical issues.* Don't subdivide your resources across too many fronts.

4. *Get your leadership team out talking to customers face to face.* Every single person on the leadership team should individually know at least five things your company can do better to serve customers. Validate and prioritize the joint list before you allocate resources to fix those perceptions.

5. ***Don't hide in an office or conference room.*** Instead, get every individual member of the leadership team to routinely meet face to face with the people who create value in your business and listen to what those people have to say.

6. ***Become more aware of things inside your business that interrupt value creation.*** The major problem with batched work of any kind is that a company keeps busy by making things customers do not want at that point in time. Look for ways to let customers pull the work you do, just in time, as needed. Many processes need better alignment and elimination of waste to accomplish this transformation.

7. ***Hire and develop the best talent you can get, and then let them do their work.*** Mold your enterprise to focus on customers and to treat people fairly, including your compensation practices. Hold people accountable for their commitments and accountable for coming forward quickly when a barrier gets in the way of meeting a commitment. Make certain you understand the impact of your business processes on performance issues before placing blame on an individual.

8. ***Work for the common good, not personal gain.*** In today's world, especially in the winner-take-all U.S. culture, if you are at the top of the organization, you can maximize your compensation. Is that your primary purpose, or do you seek to build something bigger than yourself? If it is the latter, you should operate with a degree of humility. We love the Mark Twain quote that fits this way of operating: "There are basically two types of people. People who accomplish things, and people who claim to have accomplished things. The first group is less crowded."

9. ***Keep in mind that you will need to study and eliminate waste in a major process at least five times*** from end to end to begin to approach world-class levels of performance. Eliminate 50% of the waste on each pass. (We mentioned this in Chapter 7 on process thinking, but it's worth repeating here as well.)

10. ***From a governance perspective, move away from savings reports.*** Instead, have business leaders describe what is happening with their business. Ideally, a process perspective is a key part of this dialogue. If your business is not getting better, then

the improvement process is not effective; it really is that simple. Admittedly, when you first get started there is a transition period. Ghosn's team turned around Nissan, a large, slow-moving global enterprise, in 24 months; shouldn't you be able to do something similar? Are you on track to double your business with your most important customers over a 3- to 5-year time horizon? If you are not moving at this *velocity*—you are falling behind!

11. ***Finally, incorporate the five missing ingredients into your improvement recipe, and you will be ahead of the game from a competitive standpoint.*** They are important ingredients to move to a Level 4 and 5 of organizational performance improvement maturity. To give you a practical way to approach that challenge, Chapter 9 gives some guidance on how to assess your current level of improvement maturity using an assessment instrument that will help you identify ingredients that are currently weak or missing, and therefore should get near-term priority.

Chapter 9

Assessing Your Organization's Improvement Maturity Level

A moment's insight is sometimes worth a life's experience.

—Oliver Wendell Holmes

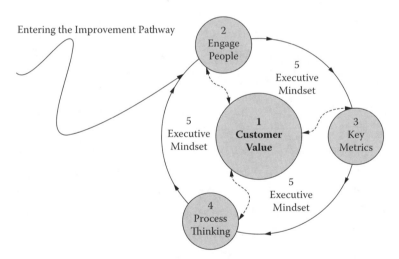

Assessing Business Progress within an Industry

Most industry groups perform at levels much higher than 20, or even 10, years ago. Competition and customer demands have dictated overall industry improvements. But, interestingly, there are only a few companies that have been able to break out of the pack and achieve a *significantly* better competitive position. Most of those who tout their progress using the

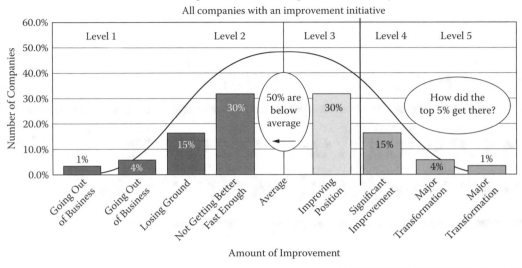

Exhibit 9.1   Competitive results of improvement maturity.

popular improvement tool sets (Lean, Six Sigma, etc.) have fared little better than the rest of the pack—typically they are clustered around the mean, as shown in Exhibit 9.1.

This book is for the organizations that are serious about breaking out of the pack by taking a more holistic approach to business performance improvement initiatives. If that's you, and you're looking for a way to move to the right in the bell curve, then consider starting with an assessment. We have tried to broaden your thinking about the business of improvement and the way you improve every year. No doubt you already have some type of improvement activities underway, but if your competitive position is not getting better, they are not highly effective. Start with the simple assessments discussed earlier in this book, and then use the more formal assessment outlined in this chapter. This assessment does not focus on traditional improvement tools. Rather, it looks at your effectiveness relative to the five ingredients missing (or underutilized) in most improvement initiatives.

Take the Quick Test Again to Assess Your Organization's Improvement Maturity

We will look at the broader assessment tool for your level of improvement maturity shortly. First, let's redo the simple assessment we introduced in

Question	Rating
Have you been able to dependably sustain, and replicate elsewhere, the gains from improvement projects?	
Have key overall business performance metrics (e.g., financials, new revenues, customer loyalty, strategic results) shown meaningful change as a result of improvement initiatives?	
Are your employee engagement survey scores more than 2x above your industry average?	

Ratings:

(–) Failing to do a good job of this; more negative than positive.

(+) Inconsistent; sometimes we do it well.

(*) We consistently do this very well.

Exhibit 9.2   Quick Test: Assess your organization's improvement level.

Chapter 1, to get us in the ballpark; we've repeated it here as Exhibit 9.2, so you don't have to turn back to Chapter 1. If your rating has less than two stars (*), then at best you are a Level 3. A Level 5 company does all three consistently, including the very difficult third one.

It's quite simple to determine if an organization is a Level 3 or lower versus Level 4 or higher. Your first reaction may be to ignore the survey because it looks too simple to be meaningful. But the questions are serious, and it is a starting point for a reality check. It's a struggle in most organizations to consistently do these three things well. Think about your organization, and try to realistically (without the rose-colored glasses for in-house cheerleading meetings) answer the three key questions in Exhibit 9.2. Ask several people with different perspectives about the business to do this assessment, so you can have a thoughtful discussion. Ask them to have some evidence to support their rating; don't just do it based on gut feel.

Assessing Improvement Maturity

We have tried to emphasize in this book that your level of improvement maturity is a matter of both breadth and depth.

Breadth indicates completeness of the ingredients in the improvement process recipe. If any one ingredient is weak or missing, then the results of the whole are jeopardized. In this book, we chose to focus on five commonly problematic ingredients that we see most often dooming otherwise good efforts to failure or mediocrity.

Depth indicates the level to which the ingredients are performed, relative to a "world-class" standard. You will see in the rating legend in the "Rating Standards for the Improvement Maturity (IM) Assessment" section later in this chapter that a world-class Level 5 is significantly beyond the performance of "tool masters" (Level 3) who might otherwise believe they have achieved world-class status. That misguided belief can be a heavy weight holding them back. In contrast, very few organizations manage to achieve performance of an overall improvement maturity reaching Level 5: this is only 5% of an industry.

It's a challenging target. As more organizations begin to exhibit what used to be a Level 4 or 5 improvement maturity, the leaders have moved on. They are not standing still. This is one of the reasons Toyota has been so hard to catch. Every year the company focuses on how it can do a better job of getting better. It will keep you humble, if you can maintain that mindset—something Toyota is currently trying to regain.

Five Missing Ingredients Are Not a Magic Pill

We focused on the five missing ingredients highlighted in this book because they are frequently causes of business improvement stagnation and failure. Also, they are rarely covered in context with the popular tool sets (Lean, Six Sigma, etc.) that companies so earnestly use to get maximum leverage for their journey to competitive advantage. If these five problematic ingredients are not in place, most business performance improvement efforts will fail to significantly change an organization's competitive position.

However, once you grasp and do these five well, your journey will not end. The five are only meaningful because most (average) organizations do not do them well. If more companies begin to address these ingredients, that ups the ante. Then, you'll need to push the frontier working these ingredients at a more sophisticated level in order to further improve your competitive position.

Calibrating the Scoring

The next section of this chapter outlines an improvement maturity assessment instrument. Before we get there, let's give some consideration to how people rate their performance. There is a bias toward a higher self-rating than the actual reality. Most of us believe we work hard, we believe we do the right thing, and mostly we are simply not capable (at the beginning) of seeing how much opportunity for improvement exists, all around us. So when you look at the instrument, focus mostly on the descriptions, rather than the numeric scores. Which description most fairly describes your reality? And how can you do a reality check? One of the best reality checks we ever saw happened in General Electric.

Lloyd Trotter was the senior vice president of the Electrical Distribution & Controls Division of GE. At GE, there is always a push to be at world class. Lloyd's team developed an assessment instrument. He sent the survey to his 10 plant managers and asked them to fill it out. Being GE managers, and being competitive to some degree with other facilities, each general manager filled out the form based on his or her view of reality. Most of them rated their operations world class in multiple categories. Then a "magical" calibration exercise took place.

Lloyd took the highest-scoring plant and required the other nine plant managers to attend a meeting there so they could learn about world class. Upon arrival, the nine managers were asked to conduct their own assessment of the enterprise. Needless to say, their view of reality for the host company was slightly different than the internal perspective. Then the fun began. In the debriefing, the other nine managers ripped into their host leader. They had a long list of things that could be done better. This is pretty normal behavior at GE. After the roasting session was over, Lloyd took out his list of assessment scores and looked at the second-highest plant. He suggested that next month, they could visit that facility.

The manager of that facility responded, "Wait a minute. I think we need to go back and redo our assessment." The other eight plant managers agreed this was a very good idea. The end result was scores that were much more aligned with reality. Each of the plants indeed had great practices they could share with the other facilities. But more important, they had an assessment score with a much higher level of integrity. And they were able to set improvement targets based on a reasonable understanding of reality.

Perhaps you will not need to act in such a dramatic way as the above story, but you do want to start out with a realistic score. First of all, look at the competitive position for your business. If you are not in the top 5% or top 20% of your industry, it is reasonable to conclude that your net scores should be below 80%. And if you're truthful, it's probably considerably below that number. It is much better to be humble rather than boasting with these scores. You are looking to *get better*, not to brag about how great you are.

Rating Standards for the Improvement Maturity (IM) Assessment

Understanding the difference between a Level 3, 4, or 5 company needs some explanation.

- ■ *1 = Poor.* Not doing well on this question; perhaps tried and got off to several false starts; little results to show for efforts.
- ■ **2 = Some Capability.** For example, you may have adopted some of the popular tool sets (Lean, Six Sigma, etc.), but only a small percentage of your employees are involved in using these tools for business process improvement. The organization has improved, but the gains are difficult to sustain due to sometimes competing functional department performance targets and the fact that variances exist in the way people go about performing standard work practices. The business is losing ground to competitors.
- ■ *3 = Tools Master.* After several years of effort, you have trained many employees in the popular tools, and a significant percentage of them are involved in at least periodic bursts of improvement work. Much of the improvement is done using project teams. In terms of effectiveness, the organization has improved considerably, but gains are still difficult to fully sustain, and they are not replicated across the enterprise. Level 3 companies have accomplished significant improvements, but they are isolated and have not resulted in business transformation. The organization is still largely managed with a focus on performance by functional departments. The organization's competitive position has not substantively changed.
- ■ *4 = Systemic Capabilities.* This is the tools master Level 3, plus some management systems that actively cause repetitive use of the tools for significant business performance improvements. It's not yet a fully self-sustaining part of the business culture, but much improvement happens from interactions between people without the need for a formal improvement team. The support systems (Business Process Model) are in alignment to

drive value creation for customers. From a competitive perspective, you should be able to factually demonstrate that you are in the top 20% of your industry and growing your share to score at Level 4 performance.

■ *5 = Holistic Improvement Maturity (IM).* This is systemic capabilities Level 4 plus complete cultural integration of the IM ingredients. All of the ingredients are seamlessly linked in the overall enterprise operations, and most importantly, the entire workforce is steeped in the culture of Improvement Maturity. It's how they think every day about continuous improvement of their work and the overall business. A Level 5 company is a model site for best practices (people come here to learn how to do this). At this level, you have things to teach Toyota (for example) and other companies that are the best in the world at what they do. If that is not the case, you are not at a Level 5.

Assessing Your Organization's Improvement Maturity (IM) Level

The assessment questions for each ingredient are not intended to be all-inclusive for that particular topic. They are intended to be reasonable questions to do three things:

1. Help you better integrate that ingredient with improvement activities
2. Push thinking about improvement beyond a single project, to consider improvement from a business perspective
3. Provide focus on what is important, managing trade-offs across functional lines of authority, to yield "ideal" outcomes from the overall process

There is nothing magical about these questions. They were not handed to us from a cloud at the top of a mountain. If you feel a question is highly irrelevant to your industry, change the question. Try to keep the spirit of pushing thinking in the organization to deeper, more holistic levels in your revised version.

Use the rating standards above to score your organization's performance on the following Improvement Maturity ingredients. Circle the appropriate numbers, then total at the bottom. As we cautioned earlier, try to be realistic about your ratings (i.e., without the rose-colored glasses often used for in-house cheerleading meetings).

Assessing Your Organization's Improvement Maturity Level

1. Customer Value					
The direction of the business is clearly focused to provide value to a targeted set of customers, where the business can provide meaningful solutions faster and better than competitors.					
1.1 Business Strategy and Goals	*1*	*2*	*3*	*4*	*5*
The overall business strategy and goals are more than just growth objectives or motherhood-and-apple-pie statements; they result in actions that truly would differentiate the organization, if done well. And the organization has a clear focus on the 3 to 5 factors most critical to overall business success.					
1.2 Target Customers	*1*	*2*	*3*	*4*	*5*
The organization uses the 80/20 Rule or some other mechanism to differentiate its Mojo high-value customer group and the Ugly 50 who represent a small portion of profits and excessive utilization of resources.					
1.3 Customer Value	*1*	*2*	*3*	*4*	*5*
There are clearly defined, measurable requirements for what each major customer or group values from our organization, so everyone in the company is aware of how their own functions might improve their contributions to the defined customer values (versus unverified opinions or assumptions).					
1.4 Strategies and the Ugly 50	*1*	*2*	*3*	*4*	*5*
Specific strategies have helped the organization effectively deal with low-value customers; e.g., the Rule of 16 and avoiding sources of value destruction. We have clearly defined what we do not want to do or should not be doing. And that is well known to everyone involved.					
1.5 Improvement Opportunity Selection	*1*	*2*	*3*	*4*	*5*
Process improvement opportunities are selected based on their relative business value potentials (for contributions to business strategy and goals) and available resources to develop them.					

Assessing Your Organization's Improvement Maturity Level (Continued)

1.6 Strategy Implementation/Execution (Results)	1	2	3	4	5
Implementation of key strategies over the last 3 years has made a meaningful difference in the organization's competitive position. Over a 3- to 5-year period, the organization is showing a significant (e.g., doubling) increase in revenues with the Mojo (key) customer groups.					
2. Engage People					
Leaders create an engaging environment where people can do their best work, and the environment fosters and facilitates collaborative innovation. People are encouraged and expected to find and eliminate distractions and waste that inhibits their ability to get meaningful (value-adding) work done to serve key customers and potential future key customers.					
2.1 Communications about Strategic Requirements	1	2	3	4	5
The strategic business goals are communicated well enough for project teams, functional departments, and individuals to align their efforts for substantive collaboration across functional lines of responsibility.					
2.2 Scientific Thought Process Developed & Used	1	2	3	4	5
Leadership mentors employees in becoming more critical thinkers. They routinely consider issues beyond just their functional responsibilities and strive to identify root causes of issues/problems.					
2.3 Employee Engagement	1	2	3	4	5
Employees are passionately engaged in what the organization is trying to accomplish versus simply showing up and trying to do a decent day's work. Employee engagement (which differs from employee satisfaction) scores are rated at least twice as high as the industry norm (which is typically less than 30%).					
2.4 Employee Trust	1	2	3	4	5
Employees are comfortable pointing out reality to organizational leaders. The organization uses employee feedback to challenge assumptions and misunderstandings, and as a result, the organization has better alignment on value creation and innovation.					

(continued)

Assessing Your Organization's Improvement Maturity Level (Continued)

2.5 Employee Involvement in Improvement	1	2	3	4	5
Employees are actively involved in identifying and implementing improvement opportunities, ranging from strategic issues to major cross-functional process improvements, and daily improvements in their local work areas.					
2.6 Fairness in Compensation and Rewards	1	2	3	4	5
The ratio of total compensation for the top five executives is less than 100:1 when compared to average compensation for the rest of the organization. World-class organizations around the globe actually have a ratio of 60:1.					
3. Key Metrics					
The organization is focused on the vital few meaningful metrics for the current environment, and avoids drowning in irrelevant details. Metrics provide rapid, meaningful feedback at all levels and in all functional groups, to people inside the organization, so they constantly learn how to do a better job of adding value.					
3.1 Clear Linkages to Key Strategies	1	2	3	4	5
People clearly understand the top-level business strategies and goals. They have a reasonable line of sight to them as they maintain linkages of the work they do to one or more key organizational strategies or business goals or objectives.					
3.2 Relevant Process Results (Wins) Metrics	1	2	3	4	5
Process performance metrics provide visual, timely, meaningful information for controlling business process results and implementing sustainable gains. A reasonable definition of a win (successful performance) for each process, department, or function exists, and has a mathematically proven correlation to the overall business wins. The metrics are routinely used for fast feedback and improvement-action decisions.					
3.3 Relevant Process Management Metrics	1	2	3	4	5
Business process metrics are used for routine upstream operations management and process improvement work, and they are frequently reviewed, validated, and/or updated to ensure that they are appropriately aligned with the key process results goals (cascaded from the overall business goals).					

Assessing Your Organization's Improvement Maturity Level (Continued)

3.4 Metrics Foster Collaboration	1	2	3	4	5
Performance metrics and definitions of wins help business units, departments, work groups, and individuals to fully cooperate with one another. They do not accidentally trigger self-centered win–lose behaviors to the detriment of the overall process.					
3.5 Visual Metrics for Rapid Feedback	1	2	3	4	5
Visual tools make the process metrics and other operational health indicators readily accessible to jog corrective or improvement actions. Departmental/functional metrics provide visual feedback (information used for decision making) on a frequent basis (as close to real time as possible).					
4. Process Thinking/Understanding					
Process management practices maximize cross-functional process performance and foster deeper process understanding and knowledge. Process capability is constantly improved to reliably deliver value and minimize waste.					
4.1 Process Standardization and Documentation	1	2	3	4	5
The best practice methods for doing work are clearly understood, documented, and used on a daily basis for standard work practices (e.g., work instruction documents, displays, checklists, etc.). And process-design information (e.g., flowcharts, process maps, procedures, etc.) is well documented, up to date, and frequently used for reference during improvement activities.					
4.2 Process Purpose	1	2	3	4	5
The process purpose is clearly defined and in alignment with the requirements for the customers of the process (internal and external). The requirements are regularly tested with updated customer/supplier agreements to ensure validity.					
4.3 Process Ownership	1	2	3	4	5
Process owners (sponsors) are aware of their role and responsibilities, and they provide effective guidance to cross-functional departments to manage trade-offs and to maximize overall process effectiveness.					

(continued)

Assessing Your Organization's Improvement Maturity Level (Continued)

	1	2	3	4	5
4.4 Process Support Systems	1	2	3	4	5
Support systems (e.g., planning, communications, organization structure, training, accountability, metrics, recognition and rewards) are in alignment with the core purpose of each process, and they foster cooperation across functional lines of authority. The organization routinely simplifies and improves the process *before* implementing major support system changes (e.g., automated solutions); that is, it avoids accidentally "putting the cart before the horse."					
4.5 Process Capability	1	2	3	4	5
The organization continually tries to improve (closer to the mean) process capabilities, especially for strategically important and value-generation processes. There is good understanding of process capability and variation at a leadership level.					
4.6 Process Total Costs	1	2	3	4	5
Total costs are well understood and taken into account when making major cross-functional process improvement decisions. Time is not wasted debating or manipulating arbitrary overhead allocations or fragmented cost variances.					
5. Executive Mindset					
The executive mindset focuses on the whole business, and is not unduly distracted by fragmentary cost savings from improvement activities. The focus is on the overall business and having the above four ingredients seamlessly aligned to guide/drive business performance improvement.					
5.1 Clear Purpose Driving Alignment	1	2	3	4	5
The organization's vision, values, and key success factors are routinely communicated and drive alignment of all business performance improvement activities, typically looking at a 3- to 5-year time horizon.					
5.2 Clear Understanding of Value Generation	1	2	3	4	5
Leadership has and routinely communicates a clear understanding of the organization's value engine. Innovation efforts keep the value engine fresh and relevant to customers.					

Assessing Your Organization's Improvement Maturity Level (Continued)

5.3 Gemba Walks (in touch with reality)	1	2	3	4	5
Leaders use Gemba Walks to ferret out truth and to stay in touch with the reality of routine business operations. Senior leaders' walks are more about listening and learning, rather than teaching. Walks by first-level supervisors and their managers focus more on finding improvement opportunities.					
5.4 Shared Knowledge & Learning	1	2	3	4	5
The executive team facilitates new learning and process knowledge sharing throughout the organization, especially between related functional departments. Processes are considered experiments: when a process fails to perform, people immediately seek to learn why the process failed.					
5.5 Execution Effectiveness	1	2	3	4	5
The organization is sustaining the gains from improvement activities, gaining ground on competitors, approaching (or already in) a market leadership position (top 20% or higher), and growing and improving overall business financial performance.					
5.6 Process Leadership Behaviors	1	2	3	4	5
Most people in leadership positions have experience with process management practices and routinely demonstrate them in dealings with other process owners, operating teams, and process improvement teams.					
5.7 Improvement Maturity Governance Processes	1	2	3	4	5
Leaders focus more on the five Improvement Maturity ingredients, business processes performance, and overall business results rather than dollars saved when looking at improvement projects. There is a constant effort to improve value added to the Mojo 20 and to eliminate waste that inhibits value creation.					
Total Score = _____					

Ratings may be done by one person or with several people. You can print copies of the Improvement Maturity Assessment Scoring Worksheet (Table 9.1) to capture ratings by individual scorers. Remember, this is an improvement tool. It is not a race to see who has the highest score.

Table 9.1   Improvement Maturity Ratings—Assessment Scoring Worksheet

Customer Value	Score				
1.1 Business Strategy and Goals					
1.2 Target Customers					
1.3 Customer Value					
1.4 Strategies and the Ugly 50					
1.5 Improvement Opportunity Selection					
1.6 Strategy Implementation/Execution (Results)					
Customer Value Score					
Engage People					
2.1 Communications about Strategic Requirements					
2.2 Scientific Thought Process Developed and Used Routinely					
2.3 Employee Engagement					
2.4 Employee Trust					
2.5 Employee Involvement in Improvement					
2.6 Fairness in Compensation and Rewards					
Engage People Score					
Key Metrics					
3.1 Clear Linkages to Key Strategies					
3.2 Relevant Process Results (Wins) Metrics					
3.3 Relevant Process Management Metrics					
3.4 Metrics Foster Collaboration					
3.5 Visual Metrics for Rapid Feedback					
Key Metric Score					
Process Thinking					
4.1 Process Standardization and Documentation					
4.2 Process Purpose					
4.3 Process Ownership					
4.4 Process Support Systems					

4.5 Process Capability			
4.6 Process Total Costs			
Process Thinking Score			
Executive Mindset			
5.1 Clear Purpose Driving Alignment			
5.2 Clear Understanding Value Generation			
5.3 Gemba Walks (in touch with reality)			
5.4 Shared Knowledge & Learning			
5.5 Execution Effectiveness			
5.6 Process Leadership Behaviors			
5.7 Improvement Maturity Governance Processes			
Executive Mindset Score			
Total Assessment Score			

Improvement trends over time are much more important than your overall score.

Keep in mind that if you rate your effectiveness at a Level 4 or 5, you are claiming there are things your company could teach to the best companies in the world—organizations as sophisticated as Toyota—about how to more effectively improve for that particular trait.

Summarizing the Assessment of Your Organization's Improvement Level

Take the ratings from the individual Improvement Maturity Rating Scores and put each rater's score in one column (see Table 9.2). Our example limits this to nine, though you could certainly have more people than that doing the rating. Create an electronic spreadsheet to summarize the information. Divide the total individual scores by the number of raters to get a company average. It may be worthwhile to capture the high and low scores and to have a dialogue about why some people scored it from that perspective. Insights can be gained during those conversations.

Table 9.2   Improvement Maturity Diagnostic Score Summary

Raters	1	2	3	4	5	6	7	8	9	Total	No. of Raters	Average
Customer Value												
Engage People												
Key Metrics												
Process Thinking												
Executive Mindset												
Total Score												

Table 9.3   Your Improvement Maturity Score Compared to Level 1 to 5 Companies

	Your Score	Level 1 Co.	Level 2 Co.	Level 3 Co.	Level 4 Co.	Level 5 Co.
Customer Value		6	12	18	24	30
Engage People		6	12	18	24	30
Key Metrics		5	10	15	20	25
Process Thinking		6	12	18	24	30
Executive Mindset		7	14	21	28	35
Total Score		30	60	90	120	150

Compare your company average to the Improvement Maturity Scores for Level 1 to 5 companies in Table 9.3. After you enter your average company score, look for the corresponding value in one of the boxes to the right. Color in that matching box for a very simple visual of your improvement effectiveness levels.

Interpreting the Results of Your Assessment

The overall score and individual ingredient ratings are qualitative indicators of your improvement level, in the opinions of the respondents.

Average organizations (Levels 2 and 3) will score in the 48 to 112 point range. Although that may strike some as being short of "hard data" findings, many front-runner companies rely on such information as primary evidence of the current state (i.e., current health) of their overall business performance improvement processes. For example, FedEx uses a quarterly survey to uncover opportunities for improvement in both operating processes and organization (people). The survey, along with other inputs, feeds their continuous improvement process.

To complete the assessment:

1. Test some of the rated ingredients for reasonableness. Look for any bias that might be caused by an insular internal view, not in tune with the real world outside. If necessary, repeat the survey with a partial cross section of the original group, and ask them to be critical in their ratings and consider benchmark companies outside.

2. From the raw survey data, identify the low-score ingredients. In line with our "weak or missing improvement recipe ingredients" thesis (the weakest link concept), it will be fairly obvious to the people involved why they rated those items lowly.

3. Collect some hard data about the low-rated ingredients. Actual process metrics, performance reports, audits, and so on would be useful. If possible, take information from the current operations.

4. Validate or discount the survey ratings by comparing them to the hard data. Review with the operations team and internal customers involved to see if they have other views that might adjust the findings.

5. Document the assessment findings and conclusions for use by process owners and improvement project teams. For each low-rated ingredient, include:
   a. Description
   b. Score from the survey
   c. List of findings from the reviews (item 4 above)
   d. List of conclusions drawn from the findings and review discussions

Using the Assessment Results

Don't work the whole list! The instrument is intended to stimulate a dialogue at the leadership level. Select a few areas to get started; it may be possible to work on the few worst ones during the near term. Working these issues

will help your organization "improve the way you improve," to increase your improvement maturity. The management team must decide which of the issues get resource allocations for near-term improvement work, and at the same time, make sure to stay focused on real customer issues. Ultimately, working the issues surfaced from this assessment should help better align your company with meeting key customer needs and improving financial performance.

Remember that the Improvement Maturity Assessment is focused on the problematic people-side ingredients in the business performance improvement recipe. You may also want to look at the technical tools side with another assessment instrument you can download for free on the Association of Manufacturing's Web site at www.ame.org. That assessment focuses on Lean tool effectiveness. Its location changes from year to year. Go to the AME site and click the Events link, and then click the Annual Conference link. The free assessment is typically referenced on the right-hand side of that page.

As mentioned earlier, *the purpose of these assessments is not to see how high of a number you can score. The assessments are intended to assist your organization in having an open dialogue about what is important to improve. Improvement projects are driven by customer value and major operating problems, constraints, or opportunities.

The other important part of the Improvement Maturity Assessment is in aligning the support systems. The Five Missing Ingredients largely belong to the world of support systems. Our experience has shown that most organizations do not address them very well. If you do embrace them, you have a chance to improve your competitive position and make your organization a better place to work.

A Few Closing Thoughts

Because so many people refer to Toyota as the benchmark in terms of organizational effectiveness, let's visit a few key principles from their world. We mentioned (in Chapter 3) Three Perspectives at Toyota (refer back to Exhibit 3.3):

1. Respect for People
2. Management Control (the Toyota Production System)
3. Executive Mindset

Throughout this book, we have tried to emphasize the need to respect people. We did not talk very much about the actual improvement tools used in the management control systems at Toyota because people know the tools. Rather, we focused on process thinking and understanding, which is a primary foundation block for that perspective. Even though process under-standing has been talked about for more than 30 years, it does not get the depth of thoughtful attention it deserves.

People like to talk about the Toyota Production System and the many tools used to implement improvement activities. They are powerful! But what is leadership doing to *use* all of that capacity that has been created from those improvements? What about Toyota and the executive mindset? Toyota leaders are certainly masters at working the five ingredients high-lighted on these pages. Consider the first ingredient—customer value. Does Toyota have a strategy that is focused on customer value? Toyota started in the small car market, and it became so good at execution (i.e., building small cars) that the traditional automotive manufacturers in the United States conceded that market in the 1970s.

What did Toyota do next? It looked around for growth opportunities. What did it see? It saw the small truck market, which was new at the time. It saw opportunities to expand its small-car production lines and move up to the family sedan market. And it saw the fun-to-drive sport sedan markets. As the company entered each market, Toyota leaders made certain they had a clear understanding of the requirements for consumers who purchased in that market—no untested assumptions.

Then Toyota used its capability from the Toyota Production System to execute its process delivery of products to that market in a near-flawless fashion. Once it began to have success in these realms, Toyota pulled off a phenomenal strategy (mentioned in Chapter 3), where it redefined the luxury car market with the launch of the Lexus division. More recently, the company launched a foray into the large-truck and SUV markets as those markets expanded.

A key element in all those Toyota successes—respect for developing people's talents and capabilities—is quite legendary, but the principles are not magic. They tightly couple respect for people with process understand-ing and for leaders at all levels to be better in touch with reality. They do a very rigorous job of hiring talented and open-minded people, so they have a solid foundation there as well. People's performance is held to a high stan-dard of accountability, but always filtered through process-tinted glasses, so that the organization first of all takes responsibility for all performance

problems, Toyota leaders do not blame the person. This creates a much more open environment for problem visibility.

At Toyota, leaders do not believe that any manager can run anything. Executives for the most part have a deep, experienced understanding of the parts of the business they manage. They use that knowledge to stay focused on process capabilities and to mentor people in deeper thinking, holistic process understanding, and faster execution of improvement.

We certainly believe this level of transformation is possible. There are companies throughout North America and Europe that are doing it. But most organizations do not transform. Most get better, but they remain average relative to their industry.

Significant improvement can happen at all levels of an organization, but transformation must be driven from an executive mindset to do it. Therefore, we urge you to:

■ Look more deeply at your enterprise.
■ Gain more insights about value for your customers.
■ With that customer focus, engage as many people as possible in passionately moving forward to create an organization where people can indeed do their best work.

We wish you good fortune, new knowledge, and opportunities to make a more meaningful difference in your employee relationships, supplier relationships, customer relationships, and most important, in your life.

The Authors

Michael Bremer has worked in the world of business process improvement since 1980. He led the creation of a company-wide improvement initiative for Beatrice Companies, a Fortune 30 Company at the time, where he had the opportunity to study under the tutelage of Dr. W. Edwards Deming and Dr. Joseph Juran. The Beatrice Improvement initiative was one of the models studied in creating the Malcolm Baldrige Quality Award. Michael is currently the president of the Cumberland Group. In recent years he has served as a Senior Engagement Manager for Motorola University, is a past Chief Financial Officer for the Association of Manufacturing Excellence and has held a variety of other positions in industrial and service businesses.

Michael currently teaches a class on innovation and process improvement for the University of Chicago's Graham School. He co-authored *Six Sigma Black Belt Handbook* (McGraw-Hill, 2004) and *Six Sigma Financial Tracking and Reporting* (McGraw-Hill, 2005), aka: I had a million dollars in savings, but my P&L did not change.

Michael earned a BS in accounting, from the University of Missouri – St. Louis. He is a CPA, certified MBB, certified Lean Bronze expert and a CMC. He was worked with organizations in many countries to improve the way they go about the business of improvement.

Brian McKibben is a founding partner of The Cumberland Group—Chicago. He has thirty years' experience in operations planning and management, helping business teams reduce waste, improve quality, smooth production flows, shorten order cycle times, and reduce inventories.

His approach to business performance improvement includes four elements:

- Clear definition of customer requirements, especially their loyalty factors
- Lean business processes; add only value to products and services; no waste

- Team-based methods for broad workforce involvement in improvement efforts
- Measurement = the springboard to Continuous Improvement

Before joining Cumberland in 1991, Brian held management roles in several manufacturing companies. That experience and the insights he gained from them contribute to his effectiveness in a consulting role. Managing the manufacturing planning functions for 140 Beatrice U.S. Food plants and warehouses provided perspective on optimization of a large-scale enterprise while providing for autonomy and job satisfaction of local operating teams. Directing product design, manufacturing engineering, industrial engineering and manufacturing services for The HON Company, Wesco Manufacturing, and All-Steel proved that even complex processes like product and manufacturing process development can be streamlined (made Lean) to achieve results in a fraction of "expected" times. His experience in a turnaround situation confirmed the saying that "the impossible is often the untried," and that the technical issues in business are less important than the people issues. Business successes are the result of carefully nurtured teamwork; not the rah-rah fluff type, but rather the practical nuts-and-bolts approach that is focused on the team's common goals and the mechanics of how they work together effectively to achieve those goals quickly.

Brian holds a BS in business and economics/industrial management from the Stuart School of Management and Finance at the Illinois Institute of Technology, Chicago. He is past president of the Chicago chapter of the Institute of Industrial Engineers, a speaker on operations planning and performance improvement to other professional organizations, and co-author of *Six Sigma Financial Tracking and Reporting* (McGraw-Hill, 2005).

Index